THE
BANKER
AND THE
BLACKFOOT

ALSO BY J. EDWARD CHAMBERLIN

The Harrowing of Eden: White Attitudes Towards Native Americans

Ripe Was the Drowsy Hour: The Age of Oscar Wilde

Come Back to Me My Language: Poetry and the West Indies

If This Is Your Land, Where Are Your Stories?: Finding Common Ground

Horse: How the Horse Has Shaped Civilizations

Island: How Islands Transform the World

J. EDWARD CHAMBERLIN

THE
BANKER
AND THE
BLACKFOOT

❖ A MEMOIR OF ❖

MY GRANDFATHER
IN CHINOOK COUNTRY

Alfred A. Knopf Canada

PUBLISHED BY ALFRED A. KNOPF CANADA

Copyright © 2016 J. Edward Chamberlin

www.penguinrandomhouse.ca

"Epic" by Patrick Kavanagh is quoted from *Collected Poems*, edited by Antoinette Quinn (Allen Lane, 2004), by kind permission of the Trustees of the Estate of the late Katherine B. Kavanagh, through the Jonathan Williams Literary Agency

LIBRARY AND ARCHIVES CANADA CATALOGUING IN PUBLICATION

Chamberlin, J. Edward, 1943– , author
The banker and the Blackfoot : a memoir of my grandfather in chinook country / J. Edward Chamberlin.

Includes bibliographical references and index.
Issued in print and electronic formats.

ISBN 978-0-345-81001-4
eBook ISBN 978-0-345-81003-8

1. Canada, Western—History—19th century. 2. Canada, Western—History—20th century. 3. Canada—History—1867–1914. I. Title.

FC3217.C53 2016   971.2'02   C2016-901164-X

Book design by Jennifer Griffiths
Cover images Courtesy of the Glenbow Archives
Map designed by Erin Cooper

Printed and bound in the United States of America

2 4 6 8 9 7 5 3 1

Penguin
Random House
KNOPF CANADA

for the Cowdry family
and friends

and in memory of
George Laforme
(1942–2016)

THE FOOTHILLS, 1885–1905

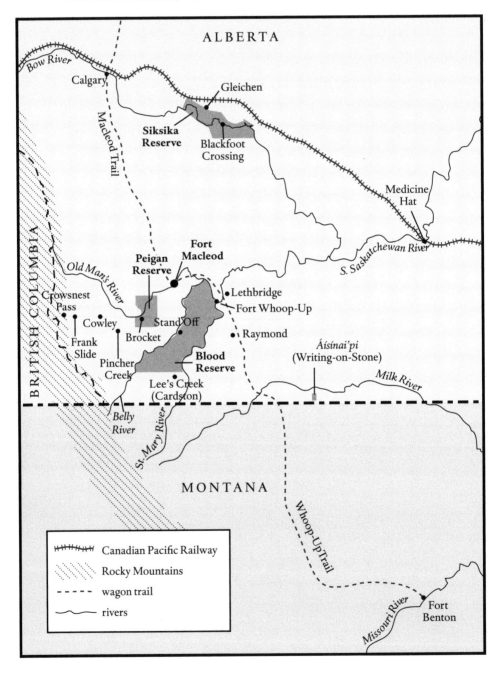

ALBERTA

Bow River

Calgary

Gleichen

Siksika
Reserve
Blackfoot
Crossing

Medicine
Hat

Macleod Trail

S. Saskatchewan River

BRITISH COLUMBIA

Old Man's River

Peigan
Reserve
Fort
Macleod

Crowsnest
Pass
Cowley

Stand Off

Lethbridge
Fort Whoop-Up

Frank
Slide
Brocket

Raymond

Pincher
Creek

Blood
Reserve

Áísínai'pi
(Writing-on-Stone)

Milk River

Lee's Creek
(Cardston)

Belly
River

St. Mary River

MONTANA

Whoop-Up Trail

┠┼┼┼┼┼┼┼┨ Canadian Pacific Railway

Rocky Mountains

╌ ╌ ╌ wagon trail

﹏ rivers

Missouri River

Fort
Benton

TABLE OF CONTENTS

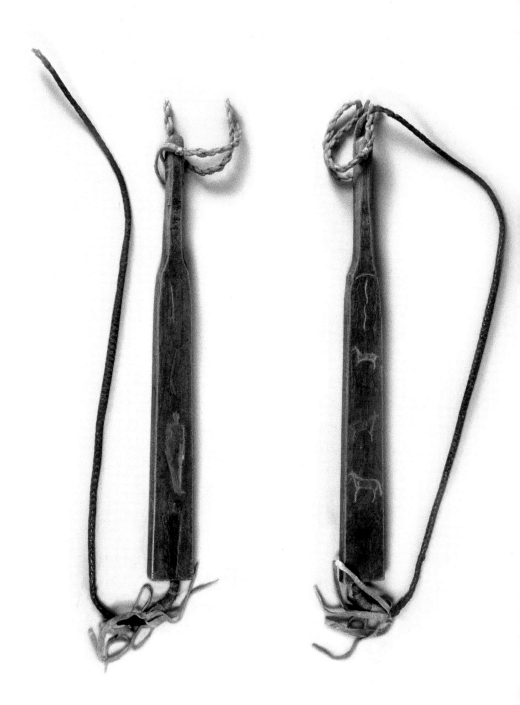

Preamble

SORRELTOP JACK AND CROP EARED WOLF

We had found most of the chocolate eggs so it must have been just after Easter, and I was sitting on my grandfather's knee in the backyard of our house in Vancouver. He was smoking a meerschaum pipe carved into the shape of a prancing horse, and I said I was going to be a cowboy and ride a horse just like that. He said he knew some cowboys and some Indians too; and they both believed in Jawbone. I asked, "What's that?" and he said it meant being as good as your word. Then he said, "I believe it's time to tell you a story."

. . .

IT WAS A LOVELY SPRING DAY in the foothills of southern Alberta. The snow-covered peaks of Chief Mountain and the Rockies—the Blackfoot "backbone of the world"—were shimmering on the western horizon, the colours of the grasses heightened by shadows when clouds crossed over, and the abiding wind whispering its promises of permanence and change. Riding down the main street of Fort Macleod in the spring of 1885, my grandfather saw a Blackfoot man riding towards him leading a string of horses ambling along at a lazy pacing trot, looking like country dancers on the way to a performance. He noticed from a distance that the Indian rider sat his saddle at an unusual slant, so the shoulder of his coat blanket was what my grandfather first saw of him; but when they came closer he turned to greet my grandfather in a sign-language gesture of welcome, and they exchanged names.

Makoyi-Opistoki, said the Blackfoot horseman. *Crop Eared Wolf. John Cowdry*, said my grandfather. *Jack.*

Crop Eared Wolf signalled his interest in my grandfather's horse, so Jack took the cue and made a wavy motion as he put his hand on the high withers in front of his saddle to indicate how comfortable his horse was on a long ride, and clenched his fist on the long, flat croup from his horse's hindquarters to the dock of his tail to signal lots of strength there. Crop Eared Wolf nodded courteously as though he was learning something for the first time; but my grandfather recognized from the easy way he sat his horse, even with the slight awkwardness he had noticed, that he was an experienced horseman and would have known all that at a glance. Then Crop Eared Wolf asked, in English, about its colour. "Chestnut sorrel," said my grandfather, knowing that the Blackfoot had over a hundred words for the colours of horses, none of which he had yet learned. To make up for his ignorance he told Crop Eared Wolf an Arab story he had heard, about how the creator went to the everlasting wind and said, "I want to make a creature out of you," and the dutiful wind became dust, and the creator took a handful of it and made a horse the colour of the desert ant—sorrel—and hung happiness from the fore-lock between the horse's eyes. Crop Eared Wolf took in the story, chuckled and pointed to my grandfather's hair—which was the same colour as his horse, burnt chestnut—and dubbed him *Sorreltop Jack*. My grandfather knew that the Blackfoot often named their horses for their colour, and that Crop Eared Wolf might be making fun of him, but he took to the name anyway because he admired his horse and was proud of his hair. Before he had time to reply, Crop Eared Wolf said he was sometimes called Many Horses—and that he did in fact have many horses— but he preferred the name Crop Eared Wolf because wolves had taught the Blackfoot how to hunt in packs, and how to work together. You can still see them in the night sky, he said. *Makoyi-yohsokoyi* was the Wolf Trail. The Milky Way.

He pointed to my grandfather's knees, which were bent as he sat in the saddle, signalling surprise that he rode with short stirrups—like the Blackfoot, in fact, but unlike most newcomers to Blackfoot territory, such as the North-West Mounted Police officers who had come ten years earlier and almost all the ranchers and cowboys who had followed them. My grandfather said he liked being able to shift his weight from side to side or forward when he needed to, showing how he did so—then stood in his stirrups smiling, and said it was also because he was short. He had noticed Crop Eared Wolf seemed to be too. He didn't say so, of course, but he did ask him why he rode with long stirrups, and Crop Eared Wolf indicated that he had been shot in the leg during a fight with the Cree twenty years earlier. Jack could tell he was proud of his time as a warrior.

They talked away for a long while, not always understanding each other but coming comfortably back to horses in a conversation that seemed to work just fine across the languages. Until Crop Eared Wolf asked my grandfather, in English phrasing that was fairly blunt, why he had come to Fort Macleod and Blackfoot territory.

And now my grandfather did feel uneasy and paused. The fact is, he wasn't sure, and had been wondering the same thing a few weeks earlier as he rode some four hundred miles across the prairies to the foothills from his homestead in a place called Pile of Bones in Saskatchewan. To break the silence, the newly crowned Sorreltop Jack said it was for the adventure of it, just like it was for Crop Eared Wolf, he suggested, when he went on raids—a comparison he immediately realized was silly enough to probably be insulting. Quickly, he said it was because he was bored. Which sounded pretentious. So he added that people had been going to new places, and meeting new people, forever. Isn't that how the Blackfoot got here? he asked. Crop Eared Wolf looked a little surprised at the idea, and said he himself was here because he was adopted when his parents got sick and died, and Red Crow, the chief of the Blood tribe—the *Káínai* in the Blackfoot language, he added, for my grandfather's improvement—chose him to come into his tipi and be his son.

That got Jack talking about his own family, and how his father, Thomas Cowdry, had travelled thousands of miles from England, where he was born, because times were hard there, sailing for days across a large and treacherous body of water to give his family a chance for a better life. As he said this he thought about the challenges now facing the Blackfoot with the buffalo gone. And because he didn't want to suggest that moving somewhere else when times got tough was what the Blackfoot should do, he said, quickly again, that travelling to other places was simply what his people had done for hundreds of years. Rambling around the world was like following the roaming buffalo and the ripening berries over the prairies and into the foothills from season to season. Sometimes his people had made friends, and sometimes not, he said, but he hoped he would make friends here. As he spoke he could tell from the way Crop Eared Wolf looked at his sorrel's big ears that he was asking the horse, "Did *you* hear *that*?" . . . and he knew he was really talking nonsense now. After all, the Blackfoot were the real settlers in a territory they had occupied for as long as anyone could remember—deliberately moving from place to place in their own homeland, rather than "wandering" about. The wanderers were folk like himself, looking for a home.

Crop Eared Wolf listened politely as my grandfather bumbled on, trying to dig himself out of the hole and recover some credit. He was a dozen years older than my grandfather, who had just turned twenty-eight, and he appeared to be enjoying their conversation; and, except for the fact that he knew he was sometimes talking foolishness, my grandfather was too. But since he didn't want to bore Crop Eared Wolf, and had no satisfactory answer to the question about why he had come to his country, and they had said enough about horses for now, he pretended he had somewhere to go. Which wasn't true, because he didn't even have anywhere to stay except the Macleod Hotel. So with courtesy, and a comfortable confusion of English and sign language, he said he hoped they would meet again one day, and they rode off in different directions, my grandfather northwest towards the Porcupine Hills and Crop Eared Wolf to his home on the Blood reserve at Stand Off, southeast of Fort Macleod.

. . .

My grandfather had come to Blackfoot territory for a lot of reasons, but one of them was curiosity. He and his brother Nat had gone to homestead on the Saskatchewan prairies three years earlier from their family home in Ontario, and had made a success of it. They even managed several hard winters living in a little sod house, with temperatures regularly dropping to forty below—so cold that it's the point where Celsius and Fahrenheit temporarily cross—and occasionally down below fifty. But they had heard about a warm winter wind called a Chinook which could come to the foothills in the midst of a cold spell and raise the temperature by as much as fifty degrees overnight, melting an inch of ice in an hour. They liked the sound of that after the last winter.

Signalled by a wonderful arch of cloud and a belt of blue sky, a Chinook is always a surprise; but, like many surprises, it can be hazardous, melting the rivers just when people have decided the ice is thick enough to take their horses and cattle across, or freezing melted groundwater so hard afterwards that the cattle can't get at the grass beneath. Jack had heard a Blackfoot story in which the Chinook was imagined as the breath of a beautiful maiden who had wandered from home and got lost in the mountains to the west; and he knew that beautiful maidens, in legend at least, are often dangerous. And then there was the local tale about a traveller who tied his team of horses to a post sticking up in the snow one night. A Chinook came, and in the morning his horses were dangling from the church steeple. Warm winds like the Chinook, blowing down the slopes of high mountains when the conditions are right, are known in a few other places around the world; but nowhere do they have the magical character they enjoy in the lee of the Rocky Mountains and the foothills of Alberta. And yet for all the legendary surprise of a Chinook, which so far my grandfather had only heard about, meeting Crop Eared Wolf was as wonderful a surprise as he could have imagined. Even more wonderful, though he didn't know it at that first meeting, would be the friendship that developed between them over the next twenty years. That friendship it is at the heart of this story.

And at the heart of their friendship was a gift that Crop Eared Wolf gave my grandfather some years later. It was a quirt—a riding crop or whip—carved and painted by Crop Eared Wolf in traditional Blackfoot iconography. It told the story of his tribal heritage and heroic exploits in war parties against old enemies such as the Sioux, the Shoshone, the Cree and the Crow, and of his courage on raids to bring home their best horses, which he did with such flair and finesse that his exploits were admired by the same officers of the North-West Mounted Police who were trying to wipe out that same venerable plains Indian tradition. My grandfather had arrived in Fort Macleod at a time when war parties and horse stealing were still taking place, though their days were numbered. By 1885, when they first met, Crop Eared Wolf's time as a warrior in that tradition was almost over, but he was a dangerous man to insult and you certainly didn't want him as an enemy, as several belligerent Indian agents later discovered. Along with his wartime exploits, his reputation was tied to horses, which he had "gathered in" or "brought home" from exile in the camps of his enemies—the very best horses, belonging to the most famous chiefs. He was very, very good at this, one of the best on the northern plains, and very, very good at boasting about it, his accounts among the most notable records of that time and place. Boasting and toasting and truth-telling, my grandfather said affectionately, knowing that these are at the root of such storytelling. That was the warp and woof of the fabric of Blackfoot horse culture—securing the horses and telling the story. Words and images, like dances and drumming, were not just *about* events—they were events themselves. Crop Eared Wolf's quirt was more than a witnessing to the things he had done in his life. It was a ceremony of belief in storytelling as well as a chronicle of events in Blackfoot history. He carried it in the ceremonial parades in the years before he took over as chief of the Blood tribe from his father, Red Crow; and then one day he gave it to my grandfather as a gift.

My grandfather kept the gift to himself for most of his life, its significance deeply personal but with puzzling responsibilities. He knew it was a kind of public trust, as well as a witness to Blackfoot history and to their way of telling and "writing" it. Writing without words is a narrative, lyric and dramatic tradition that goes back tens of thousands of years; it includes woven and beaded belts and blankets, masks and hats and chests, knotted and coloured strings, carved and painted trays, poles, doors, verandah posts, stone runes and rock paintings . . . and quirts. He knew he had to keep the quirt safe. It wasn't Sorreltop Jack's trophy; it was Crop Eared Wolf's testament.

He never displayed the quirt in the house where we lived, or even talked much about it . . . which was not like him, my mother would say with the smile of a daughter who had heard a lot of his stories. But after Crop Eared Wolf died in 1913, he kept it close; and he took it with him to the nursing home where he lived for the last months of his life, and where he died in 1947 at the age of ninety. The obligation that came with that gift and flowed from that friendship didn't die with him, and this book is my way of keeping it in circulation.

In one sense the quirt is a signature of *all* storytelling. Images, writing without words, carved and painted on an object—in this case, a riding crop—that has both functional and formal value, make it strange and familiar to us all at the same time; and those contradictions of strangeness and familiarity that it represents are, like those of belief and doubt, absolutely central to storytelling. We teach children about this when we say "once upon a time" and mean "right now"; and they soon learn to be surprised, each time as if for the first time, by the twists and turns in a story they have heard a hundred times before. This delight in the surprises of storytelling seems to be deeply human; and is certainly common across cultures. If we lose the custom or the habit of belief that sustains this contradiction between the familiar and the strange, we lose the stories. And if we lose some of these stories, we lose our sense of who we are and where we belong. And dreadful things happen.

Which is why this book is partly about certain kinds of stories and storytelling that give meaning and purpose to lives that are losing both or finding both, stories that do not take us away from reality but bring us back to it. And it is about stories that give us pleasure, a much misunderstood test of beauty and truth and goodness from time immemorial. Blackfoot storytelling, like our own, and like many peoples', is not simple, with past and future not so much separated by words and deeds and genealogies as they are connected by them through dreams and dances and declarations and memories and myths and medicine bundles that bring the real and the imagined into conversation. Science and art are interwoven with spiritual chronicle and cultural ceremony. This seems to have been recognized by many of those who came to settle in the foothills in the late nineteenth century, bringing their own strange storytelling with them and using it, as the Blackfoot did, to sustain their belief in themselves. They knew how precious that was; so there could be no excuse for the attempts that were made at the time to interfere with the Blackfoot spiritual ceremony that was the annual Sun Dance. When that was tried by several agents of Indian affairs, by some of the missionaries, and by a few—fortunately only a few—of the police, many people in the non-native community rallied to put things right. But when residential schools strove to stamp out both the languages and the stories of Aboriginal people across the country, almost no one rallied to put things right; and there is no excuse for that.

. . .

But for a brief time—largely in those two decades between 1885 and 1905—many people, native and non-native, tried to fashion a commonwealth in Chinook country that would accommodate Blackfoot sovereignty and new settlement and would give life to the spirit of the treaty made a few years earlier between the Blackfoot and the "Great Mother," Queen Victoria, on behalf of Canada. It was a time of uncertainty at every turn, with unfamiliar living conditions and livelihoods and unsettled sovereignties, as well as unpredictable weather. But it was also a time when many people in the foothills, awkwardly but ambitiously, looked for ways of getting along and getting on with the things that mattered to them all. Not everyone, of course, and not always; but often enough that their story offers hope for all of us today.

By the turn of the century the pace of settlement, the Crown's failure to acknowledge the sovereignty of First Nations that had been the condition of the treaty making, and the federal government's determination to maintain control of as much of the business of the west as possible—including the business of dealing with its First Nations by searching for a single answer to what was called the "Indian question," the curse of relations between natives and newcomers since their first encounters in the Americas five hundred years ago—were all beginning to overwhelm these ambitions. That part of

Canada, which had been on its way to creating a cosmopolitan culture that included markers of "civilization" recognizable to both the Blackfoot and the settlers, was instead becoming a hinterland to the metropolitan centres, a backyard—with some picturesque cowboys and Indians—to their stylish houses and fashionable front yards. In 1905, when the possibility of a single prairie province capable of countering the family compacts and imperial customs of Ottawa in the east lost out to the formation of the two provinces of Alberta and Saskatchewan, the promise of the territory and the promises of its treaties were forgotten. At least for a century or so.

For all his uncertainty in answering Crop Eared Wolf's question about why he had come to his territory, it seems my grandfather was looking for something. He never said—maybe he never knew—what that was; but I think he must have found it somewhere in Chinook country. His friendship with Crop Eared Wolf played an important part in that, to be sure. And, many years later, the quirt that Crop Eared Wolf gave to him has for me become a way of keeping alive a question my mother once asked, after telling me (for the umpteenth time) about the promise of that time between 1885 and 1905 in the foothills of Alberta when Sorreltop Jack was friends with Crop Eared Wolf: "What do we do now?"

This book is my visit to a particular place at a particular time with particular people who together offer something—some questions and possibly some answers—to the challenges we face in Canada now, and some hopeful ways of thinking about the opportunities we now have, one hundred and fifty years later, to fulfill the promise we made—the covenant we entered into— when the country was founded.

It's time to remember that promise, and that question: "What do we do now?" But first of all, we need to understand something of Blackfoot territory and Chinook country around Fort Macleod between 1885 and 1905. It's time to pay a visit.

1

LIGHTING OUT FOR THE TERRITORY

"I reckon I got to light out for the territory ahead of the rest."
MARK TWAIN, *HUCKLEBERRY FINN*, 1884

...

THE COWDRY BROTHERS—John and his older brother
Nathaniel, or Jack and Nat—had gone from Ontario in 1882 to
homestead in the district of Saskatchewan in the territory called
North-West. Nat was tall and trim, Jack was short and sturdy,
and both were just plain curious about all sorts of things.
Together they were a good match for the work that lay ahead of
them. They built a sod house with thick-rooted prairie grass cut
into bricks the size of doormats that they piled on each other to
make the walls, framed a roof out of pieces of wood from a dilapidated wagon, and then laid more sod on top. They were among
the first dozen or so settlers there, securing land at ten dollars for
a quarter section (160 acres) and ploughing it with a neighbour's
steel moldboard plough pulled by a Percheron mare they'd
bought along with a cart from a Red River trader, to start a small
farm near a little settlement called Pile of Bones by the banks of
Wascana Creek. The name Wascana was translated from the

Cree word for bones, *oskana*, and referred to the buffalo bones
piled by the banks—some say because of a belief by the Cree that
the buffalo would not leave an area littered with their bones. But
the buffalo were gone from the plains by the time the brothers
got there, and in due course settlers cleared the bones and sent
them east to be ground into fertilizer, for which there was a
ready market (now satisfied, in the unpredictable way of the
world, by Saskatchewan potash).

Jack and Nat settled fairly easily into their first season on the
prairies, looking up an uncle who had gone there as a surveyor a
few years earlier, and making friends with the other folks in the
neighbourhood, among them the Hudson's Bay manager at Fort
Qu'Appelle, Archie McDonald—he was called a "factor" in the
jargon of the fur trade—and his Métis wife, Nellie Inkster. From
them they learned how to live in the North-West, a region that
now included seven million acres—most of the land west of the
Great Lakes to the Rocky Mountains. They spent many eve-
nings talking with them and their other new Métis and Cree as
well as trader and settler friends about treaties and "Indian territory," and squabbling over whether the seat of government of the
newly configured North-West Territories should be Fort
Qu'Appelle or Regina—the new name recently given to Pile of
Bones in honour of Queen Victoria... much to the disgust of
many residents. In its first issue on March 1, 1883, *The Regina
Leader* described the name "Regina" variously as an insult, an
infliction and a curse. But the name held. And Regina won out
over Fort Qu'Appelle too, becoming the capital of the North-
West Territories.

They stayed on the dryland prairies around Regina for the
next three years, their farm surrounded by grassland stretching

out west to polar bluffs and sloughs around Qu'Appelle. By 1885, they had gathered together enough money from farming, and from the sale of some land they had bought when they first arrived, to give them a start in a new adventure. They had heard of opportunities farther west in the cattle country that lay in the foothills of the Rocky Mountains, now flush with the prospect of shipping by rail to eastern markets and on to Great Britain. And of course they had heard the stories about those warm winter breaks brought by the Chinook winds. The success of the ten-year-old North-West Mounted Police in bringing a certain sort of orderliness to the western prairies was encouraging, given the tales of Indian wars and vigilante violence that trickled up from the American west. And in my grandfather's mind, the reputation of the Blackfoot was a big draw. They were by all accounts the greatest horse culture and Indian nation of the northern plains, and word was that they had turned from fear-less warriors who rattled the other plains tribes into stern peace-makers who had signed a peace treaty with Canada a few years earlier and were already resisting its bureaucratic brutalities and calling the country to account for breaking its promises. He and Nat liked the sound of all that.

. . .

Much of the huge expanse of territory now called North-West had until very recently been referred to as "Rupert's Land," named in 1670 by King Charles II after his cousin Prince Rupert of the Rhine when he authorized a royal charter granting the "Company of Adventurers of England" a monopoly on the fur trade and control of all lands whose rivers and streams drained into Hudson Bay; the Hudson's Bay Company was thereby accorded rights to a million and a half square miles of western and northern Canada stretching from Labrador to the Rocky Mountains and south of the present Canada–U.S. border. Charles believed that the land was his to give because no other Christian monarch had claimed it; and it was an old joke that "HBC" stood for "Here Before Christ."

In 1869 the Hudson's Bay Company turned the charter over to the newly formed Canadian government, for a price of course, giving it control over a domain in the North-West five times the size of the original Dominion of Canada, which had just been constituted by the Fathers of Confederation. But the rights of the First Nations and the Métis had not been addressed by Canada in the course of that transfer, though they had certainly been asserted from time to time in the preceding two centuries. And Canada's responsibility to do so was clear, for it had inherited the British policy of making formal treaties with the indigenous peoples it encountered in its imperial undertakings, a policy that had been articulated some hundred and thirty years earlier by William Johnson, an agent for the British government living in the 1740s in what is now New York State and was then British North America. Fluent in Mohawk, Johnson came to know and admire the Iroquois; and he saw alliances with the Indian tribes as a matter mostly of expedience, though sometimes of necessity. His policy reflected that view. "I know that many mistakes arise here from erroneous accounts formerly made of Indians," he wrote. "They have been represented as calling themselves subjects, although the very word would have startled them, had it been ever pronounced by any interpreter. They desire to be considered as *Allies* and

Friends." If you call them "subjects," he continued, you had better have an army behind you.

. . .

So in the early spring of 1885, with some fairly incoherent ambitions and no careful planning, Jack and Nat loaded a wagon, hitched up four horses, trailed several more behind in what the cowboys called a "cavvy" (a bunch of horses that are not being ridden or harnessed), and lit out on the trail to Calgary and then south to Fort Macleod. Along the way my grandfather got thinking about their father, Thomas Cowdry, and about why he had come from the town of Great Torrington in the English county of Devon to Ontario thirty years before, first to Cobourg and then to Hogg's Hollow, north of Toronto. There he had built a house on land first settled by the miller and whisky distiller James Hogg after centuries of intermittent Aboriginal use by the Huron-Wendat, the Iroquois and the Mississauga. The settlement was sparse—Thomas built his house next to James's sons—but it was near a small village called York Mills, with a grist mill, sawmill and tannery, a post office and a school, as well as a carriage maker, stables and a blacksmith shop. Yonge Street, the main thoroughfare, was a notoriously muddy mess when the rains came, with a hill out of the hollow that was so steep and so slippery that heavy wagons had to take it in stages, resting the horses along the way. My grandfather had remembered this when he got to Saskatchewan and met the mud—"prairie gumbo" it was called—in spring.

Thomas had been a doctor in England, in practice with his father-in-law, Edmund Caddy, and for a while in Canada he continued his medical career; but he had a long-standing interest in the study of insects, which slowly took over from medicine. (Accounts of the 1850s in York Mills still identify him as a doctor, mostly I think because they were trying to increase settlement in the area and being able to advertise a "doctor in the house" helped.) He and one of his sons, called Edmund (known to everyone as Ned), helped found the Entomological Society of Canada, and he was later celebrated as one of "the pioneers of the science in the country." He continued to help in medical emergencies—especially those involving one of his cousins, his wife's brother Harrington Caddy, whom my grandfather always described as "a jolly fat old fellow, usually with a lot of liquor in him." Harrington did indeed love both his whisky *and* his housekeeper, the latter causing consternation in the family and the former testing Thomas's resolve, since he was routinely called to Grafton (just east of Cobourg) whenever Harrington was suffering with delirium tremens.

The year before young Jack headed off to Pile of Bones, his father had taken him back to England to sort out some family matters. His grandfather had been quite wealthy but also quite frail; and when he died, leaving Thomas and his two brothers, his wife remarried someone who (in Jack's words) "turned out to be pretty much of a rascal, and dissipated most of the property." The three boys had the estate put in Chancery and the rascal was placed in jail, where he eventually died ... but until he died he apparently fared quite well, having brought along a servant to look after him in prison. What was left of the inheritance eventually came to my grandfather's cousin Annie ... who gave it all away to charity, writing to say that there was so much poverty in England she thought that was only right. My grandfather was proud of her; but he also thought that he and his brothers could have put some of it to good use.

Thomas went back to England from time to time to see relatives, but he never considered returning to live there. Life was grim in England in the 1850s, the country's social and economic conditions chronicled to him in letters from his family, as well as by contemporaries such as the historian Thomas Carlyle whose tract *Past and Present* described the plight of millions of people trapped in what he called workhouse Bastilles and poor-law prisons. The family's home county, Devon, was particularly hard hit; and for several decades through the middle of the nineteenth century there was mass emigration to Canada, the United States and Australia. So my grandfather Jack grew up with stories told by his father of what was called "the condition of England"—hard times—and a conviction that going to make life elsewhere was a natural thing to do when your beliefs, or the brutalities of hunger and hardship, or simply boredom, made life unbearable—or maybe just uncomfortable. Besides, curiosity ran in the family, along with confidence that the world would always offer hope and possibility.

That confidence must have been tested for Thomas and his wife, Mary, for they had a hard landing in Canada. They brought with them five children, including Ned and Nat (both born in Great Torrington); but a year after they arrived, three of the children died, a son and a daughter of diseases at the young ages of ten and four, and an older boy of sixteen in a hunting accident. His obituary, a token of family grief, is pasted in the family bible. And yet Carlyle's counsel that "the eternal stars shine out again, so soon as it is dark enough" may have been on their mind, for the same year another daughter, named Aline (called Alley), was born and two years later, in 1857 in Hogg's Hollow, my grandfather Jack. Like three of his siblings, he was christened with only one name—John—which was unusual in families at the time. But as if to make up for their names, the support the family gave each other was unusually generous. That said, being the youngest among so many children may have had something to do with my grandfather's restless, independent spirit and his refusal to let life or its so-called lessons take over. He respected the surprises that life could bring, even though he knew they wouldn't always be welcome. Wonder, and wondering, seemed to be the way of my grandfather's world.

. . .

My grandfather was taught at home for several years; and when he was a teenager he rode his horse from Hogg's Hollow to attend Upper Canada College in Toronto. But he only stayed there a couple of years before he went out to work. Maybe because he and school weren't so well acquainted, or maybe because they were, one of his favourite novels was Charles Dickens's *Hard Times*, in which a teacher named Thomas Gradgrind interrogates his students—each of whom he calls by a number—insisting that what he wants is particular facts, presented in a particular language. In one infamous incident in the novel, he turns to a student named Sissy Jupe, whose father works with horses in the circus, and asks her for the definition of a horse. My grandfather loved horses; and he could recite this passage by heart. Although he had no idea of this at the time, Dickens's description of Gradgrind and his school turned out to be a grim precursor of later practice in many of the Indian residential schools.

> *"Girl number twenty," said Mr Gradgrind, squarely point-ing with his square forefinger, "I don't know that girl. Who is that girl?"*
>
> *"Sissy Jupe, sir," explained number twenty, blushing, standing up and curtseying.*
>
> *"Sissy is not a name," said Mr Gradgrind. "Don't call yourself Sissy. Call yourself Cecilia."*
>
> *"It's father as calls me Sissy, sir," returned the young girl, in a trembling voice, and with another curtsey.*
>
> *"Then he has no business to do it," said Mr Gradgrind. "Tell him he mustn't. Cecilia Jupe...."*

Then he asks her to give her definition of a horse.

> *(Sissy Jupe thrown into the greatest alarm by this demand.)*
>
> *"Girl number twenty unable to define a horse! ... Girl number twenty possessed of no facts, in reference to one of the commonest of animals!"*

Exasperated, Gradgrind turns to another student, named Bitzer, who responds:

> *"Quadruped. Graminivorous. Forty teeth, namely, twenty-four grinders, four eye-teeth, and twelve incisive. Sheds coat in the spring; in marshy countries, sheds hoofs, too. Hoofs hard, but requiring to be shod with iron. Age known by marks in mouth."*

> *"Now girl number twenty,"* said Mr Gradgrind. *"You know what a horse is."*

. . .

"But not the horses we depend on," thought Jack as he and Nat travelled west across the prairies to the foothills. When they came to a river, they would unhitch their horses from the wagon and ride them across. Then one of them would ride back and cut straddle logs to lash alongside the wagon to keep it afloat, while the other hitched up the horses and hauled it across with ropes. Tricks of the trade. Rope and rigging bound together more than equipment in those days. They were the duct tape and superglue of the plains. Horses provided the power . . . and the intelligence, my grandfather might have added.

The trip across the prairies wasn't especially hard for Jack and Nat, considering those winters in Pile of Bones, and the weather held cool and clear; but it was challenging, with wolves following the wagon on one stretch, and a group of young Blackfoot men making themselves evident as outriders when they got near Calgary. They weren't worried, though they were watchful . . . just like the Blackfoot. Sign language often made the difference and kept the peace, so they made signs as they had learned to do from the Cree. For hundreds of years, signing had been the lingua franca of plains Indians speaking very different languages—the Blackfoot, who spoke an Algonquian language, were surrounded by speakers of Athapaskan, which was radically different—and the signing reminded everyone of what they had in common, while they decided what they didn't. It was also a nice reminder that language itself may have begun with gestures rather than words. For my grandfather, the gesture that mattered was a handshake; but since he also loved to smoke a pipe, and knew about the long pipes of the Blackfoot and the significance of sharing one together, he had an idea how they might get halfway there with their new travelling companions. So he and Nat stopped their wagon, lit a pipe, and passed it back and forth between them. The Blackfoot men waved a welcome, and rode off in another direction.

Moving across the prairies to the foothills, the Cowdry brothers passed through miles and miles of native grasslands where the cattle had wandered over the winter. The buffalo were almost all gone, and ranching was about to take over the prairies. This was near-desert country, described in the middle of the nineteenth century by the geographer John Palliser as semi-arid grassland unsuitable for large-scale farming. The temptation to turn foothills country over to crops was a wet-season dream in a region whose most permanent feature was not that it was flat but that it was dry ... though some early visitors had a misleading welcome when they arrived during years of relatively heavy rainfall, and there were always exceptional stories. One farmer, growing Red Fife wheat on his ranch just west of Fort Macleod in the valley of the Old Man's River in the early 1880s became the first commercial wheat producer in Alberta.

But almost everywhere it was ideal for cattle, ranging across the open plains like domestic buffalo in spring and summer, herded in fall and winter into the foothills, where shelter and water were plentiful in the wooded coulees and native fescue provided feed except during the most drastic winters. The open range was the commons of sentimental song and story, a place where interests coincided and stewardship was shared. Keeping the short-grass prairies and the foothills in good condition benefitted everyone, for otherwise they would have to feed the cattle over the summer and winter on the home ranch, and many of them could little afford to do that; and even if they could, it wasn't always possible to secure hay in those early years. So keeping the range open and relatively unfenced became a high priority for the ranchers there.

The river that ran by Fort Macleod, where the Cowdry brothers were headed, was called Old Man's after *Napi*, the Blackfoot god who made the world. The reason the world is so full of wonders, the story goes, is that *Napi* was a trickster and a mischief-maker, just like the river. For the first decade that the newly created North-West Mounted Police had been in the region, Old Man's was responsible for intermittent spring floodings that plagued the original fort they'd built on an island in the middle of the river; just the year before Jack and Nat arrived they'd finally replaced it with a new barracks on the banks above Old Man's, in what would become the town of Fort Macleod. Willow Creek, close by to the north, had been the townsite preferred by the few dozen people in the district who were not in the police force; but agricultural priorities came before urban development—Willow Creek offered good farmland—and the new fort's location with its lovely prospect overlooking the Old Man's River was chosen. Though it was on, as one resident ruefully described it, "a piece of ground guiltless of ever having produced ought but a plentiful crop of stones," a contemporary newspaper's description of the view from the town was without irony:

Situated on the south bank of the Old Man's River, [it] com-
mands a view which, for variety, beauty and grandeur, is hard
to be excelled. Away to the north, at a distance of about a mile,
may be seen a small remnant of the old town in the shape of
a few log shacks yet resting upon the bosom of the waters....
To the northwest, almost in a line with the main street of the
town, rise wooded summits of the Porcupines, while away to
the west, and circling southward, the magnificent peaks of
the rocky range ... Chief Mountain standing out by itself a
conspicuous landmark, which can be seen at a distance of
200 miles. While to the north, and immediately in front of us,
the Old Man's River, winding through its changing scenes of
mountains, hill and dale, pursues its way....It is the finest
section of the North-West.

The new fort was sturdy, but some of the buildings that
sprang up around it looked as though they might fall down in
the winds that blew constantly in the foothills and across the
plains. A lady who arrived from the east and settled on a ranch
nearby described the townsite dismissively (after attending a
ball at the North-West Mounted Police barracks which she did
not enjoy, having been asked to dance by a man who "with his
half-breed wife had been cheering himself with more than one
drink") as "one of the last places to live in all the world ... covered with small stones which the never-ceasing wind drives
hither and thither with little clouds of dust.... How the people
live here happily I do not know and I don't think they are very
happy." And a grumpy twenty-year-old newcomer, who had
arrived a year earlier to open a drugstore, said the town "consisted of a crooked lane, it could not be dignified by the name

of street, lined with log stores and shacks, the former having square-faced frame fronts, and their whole appearance decidedly ramshackle and distressing." Within eighteen months, he was off to Lethbridge. But most of the other newcomers happily stayed, and had helped give the young town a more organized character by the time Nat and Jack arrived, with the fort barracks where the police lived to the north of a wide main street with a hotel and a trading post, blacksmith shop, shoemaker and several other stores, and stables and houses and a couple of churches in behind. Within a very few years, there were two blacksmiths, two butcher shops, fifteen stores, four churches, nine saloons, over fifty residences and nearly three hundred people.

Mail to that part of Alberta had been slow until quite recently, with contract delivery by cart and wagon and coach in summer, and sled and dog train in winter. Post destined for the east went from the North-West Mounted Police barracks in Fort Macleod, where it was stamped with U.S. postage, to Fort Benton and then onto the Missouri River on its way to Toronto or Ottawa or Montreal, or north to Winnipeg. In winter, when the Missouri froze up, mail to eastern Canada had gone from Fort Benton by stage to Helena and south to the town of Corrine, Utah, and the Union Pacific Railway.

But in 1883, when the railway reached Calgary, mail service improved dramatically. Weekly mail from Calgary to Fort Macleod began in January 1884 under contract to wagons from one of the local ranches and continued until 1893 when a railway spur line came down from Calgary. To carry dispatches, the North-West Mounted Police used riders and special mail wagons and sometimes Blackfoot runners like Deer Foot, who could make it from Calgary to Fort Macleod and back in two days, and return between Calgary and Edmonton in four.

One of the tributaries of the Old Man's River is called the Belly River, a direct translation of the Blackfoot word, for it feeds and waters the land where Red Crow's Blood tribe had traditionally made their winter home. It begins as a little stream up by the sacred Chief Mountain, which stands sentinel among the great mountains to the west that you can see from Fort Macleod, towering above the plains and foothills where the buffalo once roamed and where cattle now grazed. A legend tells of a great chief who grazed his horses, the finest and fastest in the west, on the flat land on top of the mountain where special grasses grow.

Nearby, to the west of town, were the coulees (dry ravines) where horses liked to gather under cottonwood trees as the wind whooshed and whispered across the prairies in every season. The summers were sometimes so hot that people said the flies walked instead of flew about; but that was when the berries ripened and were gathered—saskatoon berries (*okonoki*) and blueberries and chokecherries and baneberries and gooseberries and bull berries and bear berries, which were sometimes called *kinnikinnick*, a name that really means "a mix-up." The Blackfoot planted tobacco every spring, which they often mixed with *kinnikinnick*, and wild turnips that they dug up at the end of the summer.

Virtually every coulee and cottonwood grove in the territory had a Blackfoot name, of course, and the Blackfoot gave new names to many of the towns; but it is notable that none of them— in the words of Hugh Dempsey, one of the most knowledgeable and eloquent of Alberta historians—"reflects any antagonism or hostility towards the invading settlers. Some have humorous undertones, but most are logical and to the point." Fort Macleod was named *akápiyoyis*, which means "many houses," while the town of Gleichen, east of Calgary, was called *sokitsi*, or "fat stomach," after the owner of the general store in town. And sometimes the settler and the Blackfoot names were along the same lines. A town west of Fort Macleod, for instance, was named by a rancher with literary leanings after a line from Thomas Gray's popular eighteenth-century poem "Elegy Written in a Country Churchyard"—"the lowing herd wind slowly o'er the lea." Watching the cattle string out just before a winter Chinook and go to water at the big spring near town, and knowing that the bunch grass there provided excellent pasturage and that "lea" means "pasture," he called the town Cowley—keeping company, at least in natural history, with the Blackfoot name, which was *akái- sowkaas*. It means "many [wild] prairie turnips."

. . .

Coming into Fort Macleod on their wagon that spring, Jack and Nat needed a stable to put up their horses. They had heard there was one at the Macleod Hotel, which was already legendary in the territory, so they headed straight there. The owner, Kamoose Taylor, was part of the legend. The name Kamoose meant "wife stealer" in Blackfoot, and was apparently accorded him when he married an Indian woman whose family refused to let her go despite the dowry he offered of a horse, two pairs of blankets and some tobacco. Or so the story went, with about a dozen variations. Later, after she died, he understandably favoured his other name, Harry.

Like many people in those parts, Kamoose had tried a bunch of things before he settled on one. He had come to the west as a missionary, gone gold mining in the mountains of California, and when he came back to the foothills in 1874 had been the first man arrested by the North-West Mounted Police for bringing whisky into the territory from the United States. Down by the border was no man's land, and everybody's back-yard; and at a time when the boundary surveyors were still setting out their stakes, nobody paid much attention to the movement of products and people to and from the United States until the police arrived on the scene with orders to shut down the illegal whisky trade that was wreaking havoc in the Indian communities. But after Kamoose had paid his fine (having had not only his whisky but sixty horses and several wagons loaded with buffalo robes and other trade goods con-fiscated), he turned around and built a hotel in town where he welcomed friends and strangers and the police too with good (and this time legal) beverages, good humour ... and *fairly* good food, everyone said. In response to which, Kamoose posted signs in the lobby warning guests that "Assaults on the cook are strictly prohibited" and "Meals in your own room will not be guaranteed in any way. Our waiters are hungry and not above temptation." However, "The bar will be open day and night. All day drinks 50 cents each; night drinks $1.00 each. No mixed drinks will be served except in the case of death in the family." The two brothers, tired and dusty after their travels, were met by a sign at the entrance displaying the silhouette of a man's head and the notice "No Jawbone" ... meaning "cash only, no credit." Inside, the list of "house rules" included more instructions on how to behave:

All guests are requested to rise at 6:00 a.m. This is imperative as the sheets are needed for tablecloths.

Towels changed weekly. Insect Powder for sale at the bar. [Harry's answer to a patron who complained about the state of the towel hanging above the public wash basin was: "Twenty men have dried themselves on that towel and you are the first to complain."]

A deposit must be made before towels, soap or candles can be carried to rooms. When boarders are leaving, a rebate will be made on all candles or parts of candles not burned or eaten.

When guests find themselves or their baggage thrown over the fence, they may consider that they have received notice to quit.

Jewelry and other valuable [sic] will not be locked in a safe. This hotel has no such ornament as a safe.

Saddle horses can be hired at any hour of the day or night, or the next day or night if necessary.

Only regularly registered guests will be allowed the special privilege of sleeping on the Bar Room floor.

Refreshing themselves in the bar, the Cowdry brothers got acquainted with some of the local folks, including the stagecoach driver Frank Pollinger, known to everyone who travelled anywhere in the foothills as Polly. It was said that his horses could only understand him when he swore—like the men who drove the ox trains, called bull-whackers, who were renowned for their inventive curses. Polly's oaths were (as the local newspaper, the *Macleod Gazette*, described them) "never microscopic or feeble, but resounding and polysyllabic." It was said he could drive a wagon up a hill so slippery you could slide down it if you had a toboggan; and my grandfather liked him right away because he reminded him of the drovers who navigated the hills out of Hogg's Hollow when he was growing up.

They also ran into Francis Dickens, son of Charles, standing at the bar asking for "something quick at taking hold and slow at letting go," and my grandfather was delighted to meet this son of England's most famous author, who had died some fifteen years before. After running through his small inheritance, Frank—as he was called when he got to Canada—had signed up as an early recruit with the North-West Mounted Police. He had been stationed at Blackfoot Crossing (north of Fort Macleod near Calgary) for several years, but was in town this time on a brief visit from the battlefront with the Métis and the Cree at Fort Pitt in Saskatchewan, where he had been in nervous command when the fort was surrendered in one of the defining moments of the uprising led by the charismatic Métis leader Louis Riel. So of course the conversation, often agitated, was about the uprising, and the prospects of an Indian war in the west, and the leadership of Riel (whom my grandfather had met the previous year through his friends at Fort Qu'Appelle), and the bar was lively with opinions. Then my grandfather recited his favourite passage from *Hard Times* to Inspector Dickens, and started chatting away about the great novelist... but by that time Frank was well into his cups, a habit he cultivated more reliably than he did policing—or anything much else for that matter, for he was not as good a judge of character and plot as his father, and he had botched several assignments in the foothills before turning his uncertain attention to Saskatchewan. Nevertheless my grandfather, in his best Victorian turn of phrase, said he was pleased to make his acquaintance... to which the inspector mumbled a few words that sounded like something Polly would say to his horses, except it was microscopic and feeble. A year later, still in his early forties, Dickens left the force and was all set to follow his father's footsteps on the lecture circuit in the United States when he died suddenly of a heart attack.

As they settled into town Nat and Jack also found that a group of a dozen or so townsfolk, including a number of reformed whisky traders, gathered at mealtime around a long dining room table in the hotel, affectionately known as Taylor's Table, almost always with Harry presiding. Lively arguments were routine there too, and invariably the treaty signed with the Blackfoot eight years earlier would come up—praised as a peace pact with the most powerful Indian nation in the northwest—as would the recent selection by the Blood tribe of a new reserve in their old winter territory close to town, a move that pleased many merchants who looked forward to more trade with the Indians. But the conversation also covered the fences that were going up as settlement increased, protecting livestock and crops on the small farms but closing down the open range on which ranchers depended; the fires along the railway line, which dramatically increased the hazard of grass fires on the dry prairies; and of course the condition of Fort Macleod, which by general agreement was still fairly ramshackle. And Taylor's Table was the seedbed of some visionary speculation on the future of the North-West Territories, and it was there that the Cowdry boys got a quick but thorough education in how the territory looked from the vantage point of the foothills.

2

ON THE BANKS OF
THE OLD MAN'S RIVER

"In the province called Buffalo."
FRED HAULTAIN

...

DESPITE THE SEEMING self-confidence of the new nation of
Canada, the mandarins and their political masters in Ottawa had
a lot of anxieties about the First Nations in the west. The simple
fact—and (for the government) the worrying figure—was that in
1871 there were over thirty thousand Indians in the territories,
along with ten thousand Métis, and fewer than two thousand
Europeans or Canadians. So the new Euro-Canadians were
vastly outnumbered, and sometimes outclassed, by the great leaders of the tribal nations, men and women of stature and statecraft
refined through generations of dealing with other strangers and
settlers, including migrating Aboriginal ones. The Europeans
were often gifted, occasionally greedy, sometimes wise and generous of spirit; but they were more likely to be amateurs. In the face
of these odds, alliances and friendships were the order of the day.

And so the new Dominion, expanding the British practice of
treaty making that had begun well before 1867, proceeded to

negotiate a set of treaties with First Nations on the western plains. But they left the Métis out of the bargain, their central role in the life of the territory unrecognized, their sovereignty unacknowledged, and their civil status unclear. And for that piece of unfinished business, the country would pay dearly.

The treaties were, in principle, peace treaties to secure permission to enter and settle in First Nations' territories, and they included a solemn promise to ensure the continuing welfare of all the Indian tribes, in good times and bad. They were also intended to keep the Americans at bay until "Canadian" settlement was well established along the border. Whatever the treaties look like from the present day, and however many of their solemn promises were soon broken, treaty making on the prairies after Confederation did signal a recognition of both Canadian *and* First Nations sovereignty, overriding the ideology governing what the American courts had (in the 1830s) characterized as "domestic dependent" Indian nations. Canada explicitly undertook to "acknowledge the Indian title to his vast and idle domain, and to treat for it with much gravity, as if with a sovereign power"—a strong statement, to be sure, but as so often in the language used to describe Aboriginal lands and livelihoods, there is a catch. In this case, it is in the word "idle," which signals the misrepresentation that warped so much that followed, conjuring up the notion of "idle Indians" and an "empty land" just waiting for European agricultural (and in due course industrial) enterprise to make it "useful." Idle no more indeed.

Still, Canadian politicians and statesmen routinely celebrated the new Dominion's inheritance of the noble British practice of keeping your word (usually setting it alongside the sleazy American habit of breaking it). When treaty making started in

1871, Adams Archibald, the lieutenant-governor of Manitoba and the North-West Territories, wrote: "it is impossible to be too particular in carrying out the terms of the agreements made with these people [the prairie First Nations]. They recollect with astonishing accuracy every stipulation made at the Treaty, and if we expect our relations with them to be of the kind which is desirable to maintain we must fulfill our obligations with scrupulous fidelity." In other words, we must keep our word. As if to underline this, that same year the United States government had decided *not* to sign any more treaties, having failed to fulfill longstanding treaty obligations for a number of years and now facing the economic depression that followed the Civil War. It was an admission that they were unable, and if truth be told unwilling, to keep the promises they had made in treaties with their Indian Allies and Friends. Whatever our perspective, the Canadian–First Nations prairie treaties provide a framework, witnessed at the time by spiritual as well as secular leaders on both sides, for revisiting those promises and reconstituting the sense of alliance and friendship, as well as responsibility and respect, with which they were proclaimed in the rhetoric of the time.

The first of the treaties—numerically if not imaginatively labelled One to Eleven—were with some of the Chippewa and Cree tribes; the Blackfoot signed Treaty Seven in 1877. Of course along with their acknowledgement of First Nations sovereignty, the treaties were designed to clear the way for the railway, for settlement and for civil society in the narrative of the new nation of Canada, and to avoid the Indian wars that had devastated and demoralized the United States. And since the treaty-making displays of a serious-minded government might not be sufficient to remind the Americans that this land was Canadian, it was expected that the Canadian Pacific Railway would provide a bulwark against American territorial ambitions, binding the new country together with what historian George Stanley called "bonds of steel as well as sentiment" (and keeping a promise to British Columbia, which had joined Confederation in 1871—an ironic reminder that *some* promises to *some* people were kept). There was early opposition to the railway, as well as to the telegraph line that more or less accompanied it, from the Cree and the Blackfoot across whose territory the lines would run; but the treaties were supposed to address their concerns and establish conditions for both orderly settlement and First Nations self-sufficiency—though exactly what the latter might mean was unclear to everyone. Canada was in a teenage hurry, and the pace of construction of the railway line, for instance, was remarkably fast. One homesteader from Pile of Bones told about leaving in the morning to cut some wood, with no sign of the railway. When he returned that evening, he had to cross the tracks.

The Blackfoot had entered into several treaties with former enemies and future allies in the United States as recently as twenty years before they accepted a treaty with the Queen of Canada, so their leaders certainly knew about treaties and treaty making. Treaties were a time-honoured way of dealing with the crises the Blackfoot faced, including foreigners they disliked and the threat of war. But this was different, and not just because there was a crisis with the departure of the buffalo and the arrival of the railway and the settlers. The difference had to do with the territorial aspect of the treaty. For the Blackfoot, wars had never been about acquiring territory but about revenge or prestige, and this treaty with Canada was above all a treaty to prevent war and keep the peace. Using such a treaty to deal with territorial matters was completely unfamiliar to the Blackfoot, and more or less inconceivable. They said repeatedly that the Great Spirit, not the Great Mother, had given them the land and only that same Spirit could take it away.

But there wasn't much room for negotiation in the brief that the government negotiators had been given, and none at all when it came to that kind of territorial covenant. That said, there is plenty of evidence from the treaties entered into across the prairies that leaders on each side, however grudgingly, believed that what they were doing was for the best, and that the treaties bound both sides with promises to keep.

There is no question that the Blackfoot didn't understand some of the implications of the treaty. But they did understand keeping your word. So did the government negotiators David Laird, the lieutenant-governor of the North-West Territories, and James Macleod, recently appointed commissioner of the North-West Mounted Police, who three years earlier had led the force when it first arrived in the territory and built the fort named after him. In their view, the treaties were like a watching brief taken up by the Crown, ensuring that Canada would remain "seized of the issue," as lawyers say, in perpetuity, for nobody was sure what the future would bring ... except change. However mysterious the letter of the treaties to the First Nations and however uncertain their future, the spirit of the treaties to this end was clear both in the written account provided by the commissioners and in the oral record of the First Nations. *Both* sides became treaty people. Which means we are all in this together, non-native as well as native Canadians.

. . .

My grandfather used to repeat Henry David Thoreau, saying, "If I knew for a certainty that a man was coming to my house with the conscious design of doing me good, I should run for my life." Crop Eared Wolf and his father, Red Crow, certainly didn't need to be warned against "improvements" that would diminish being Blackfoot or encroach on the identity and integrity of their tribe. They refused to be browbeaten or belittled by the bureaucratic agents and missionary believers who came with designs to do them good; and instead of running, they fought for their lives with all their might and all their imagination. They were warriors, after all.

They were also peacemakers, making common cause and friendships with newcomers who respected their beliefs, and with whom they imagined a new kind of commonwealth in the foothills. That was what Treaty Seven was all about, and Red Crow had in an important sense accepted it because of his friendship with his neighbour, Commissioner James Macleod. "I entirely trust *Stamixotokon* [Bull Head, the Blackfoot name for Macleod]," he said. "He made me many promises—not one of them was ever broken"; and this was echoed by Crowfoot, who was chief of the Blackfoot Confederacy. They didn't use the word "commonwealth." But the word isn't a bad place to start understanding what was happening in a territory where many in the community believed that the contradictions of settlement and sovereignty could somehow be accommodated—a community comfortable with a confusion of medicine bundles and bibles, Blackfoot drums and piano recitals, Sun Dances and social dances, horse racing (at which the Blackfoot excelled) and polo (the first in North America, some say), and rodeos at round-ups to celebrate both the horse culture of the Blackfoot and the skills of the cattle range—a community in which conflicts would be settled by consensus in the territory, not by the politicians in Ottawa or bureaucrats in Middle-earth who knew nothing of the world they lived in or the people they lived with. The "wealth" in commonwealth meant first of all "well-being"; its contrary was what the nineteenth-century cultural historian John Ruskin called "illth" . . . not a bad coinage for the condition that threatened many First Nations peoples during this period, and came to pass afterward.

Although they were holding on to their heritage and history, the Blackfoot weren't living in the past. They never had; their way of life had always required stern attention to the present and to the future. They would have disappeared centuries earlier if that had not been so, if they had not been a thoughtfully adaptable people, or if they had not been ready for change. They had taken up with horses a mere hundred and fifty years before this, and stories about that radical transformation were told by elders who were still alive. Horses were a good surprise. The loss of the buffalo was not. But their stories told of both sorts of surprises.

The newcomers too lived by their own stories and songs and ceremonies and looked to the future rather than the past, though like the Blackfoot they held on to their traditions— both spiritual (in church services and the texts upon which they depended) and material (such as clothing and food), as well as in the arts and crafts that brought them together—because doing so centred them. But they knew they had to be ready for the next surprise in those uncertain times; and in this, the Blackfoot were an inspiration, and their acceptance of uncertainty a comfort. It was also an absolute necessity, for they were all like sailors at sea in the old days, navigating by the moving stars and aware (as good navigators must be) that they were always almost lost, ready to plot a different course at a moment's notice when a cliff loomed suddenly out of the fog, or the land-fall did not appear as expected.

. . .

The year my grandfather arrived in Fort Macleod, many things were uncertain for many people. For the Blackfoot, the world was changing in unfamiliar ways and at a bewildering pace, with the buffalo having disappeared, and danger everywhere. Some dangers they were dealing with, as newcomers came from every direction; but new diseases, brought by traders and settlers and whisky, continued to devastate their communities. And the Métis uprising that spring against the Canadian government introduced a new level of anxiety and violence on the western plains, unsettling relations not only between newcomers and natives but also among the First Nations themselves, with many people uncertain about their own loyalties, much less everyone else's. The Métis leader, Louis Riel, had declared a provisional government for the territories; and the plains Cree and Assiniboine nations, frustrated by the flagrant disregard of promises made to them under the treaty they had signed a few years earlier, rose up and joined the Métis. The Blackfoot did not take part in the uprising, remaining loyal to their treaty partners, the Dominion of Canada. But Riel's trial and execution kept tensions bristling across the country; and in November, the same month Riel was hanged, the Canadian Pacific Railway was completed from coast to coast, bringing more settlers to Blackfoot territory. New material technologies were also taking hold and new spiritual practices were taking over, and, in many ways, the next couple of decades presented challenges as great as any culture, indigenous like the Blackfoot's or more or less migrant like my grandfather's, had ever faced.

Anyone at that time who settled in the foothills of the Rockies realized that the Blackfoot—the *Niitsítapi*, or "the real people"—were civilized and sophisticated, and that they were not going anywhere. Most of the settlers, especially those involved in ranching (and one way or another that included almost everyone), knew that their lives and livelihoods depended upon cooperation with the Blackfoot, with whom they often developed surprisingly (and to latter-day postcolonial "experts," incomprehensibly) close working relationships, albeit occasionally punctuated by mischief and malice on both sides. They cooperated where they could, made friendships where they wanted, all the while transcending some of the boundaries and breaking down some of the barriers that the treaties unfortunately nourished. And although the treaties brought a particularly European energy and enterprise to the business of displacing and dispossessing people, the experience was not new to the Blackfoot, for they had tribal neighbours north and south of the border who from time to time wanted to wipe them from the face of the earth. But the Blackfoot survived; and now, with a new order upon them, they were determined to prevail. They were experienced both at making war and at making peace—the treaty had their signature on that. But surrender had never been part of their statecraft.

There were many friendships in this time and place, both among town residents and foothills ranchers and the North-West Mounted Police, and between many of them and the

Blackfoot. Some of these friendships were unequal, as friendships often are, with one party presuming superiority over the other. But the pride of the Blackfoot, nourished by leaders such as Red Crow and Big Swan and Crowfoot, saw them through those harrowing times following the decline and fall of the great buffalo herds on the northern plains and the new treaty with the upstart nation of Canada, and sustained their belief that they were the equal of anyone, and indeed superior to almost everyone. They needed this.

. . .

Back in the Macleod Hotel, around Harry Taylor's table, the conversation turned to the challenges facing everyone in Blackfoot territory. One of the most energetic regulars was Fred Haultain, a lawyer exactly my grandfather's age, who had come to Fort Macleod a year earlier and in that short time had defended a number of dubious clients with unfashionably stern attention to the presumption of innocence and the principle of reasonable doubt—not the strong suit of some folks in town, and sometimes (depending on the accused) bewildering to the Blackfoot. Fred Haultain and my grandfather became close friends—my grandfather named his first son (who sadly died) after him—and Haultain eventually became one of the most eloquent statesmen in the North-West, in company with several of the chiefs of the Blackfoot, for whom he had great affection. He was a champion of non-partisan politics in the territories, becoming its first (and only) premier in the days before provincehood; and he was a proponent of the single province, which he suggested—mischievously, some say, but my grandfather said perfectly seriously—be called Buffalo, a reminder of the natural and First Nations history of the prairies, instead of Alberta and Saskatchewan, named after Queen Victoria's daughter and a swift-flowing river in the dryland prairie. And, like the river on whose banks he had settled, Haultain did indeed have a mischievous streak, once conspiring with the local Indian agent to glue the Anglican parson's notes together before a service so that he read two sermons on different subjects without realizing what had happened. But he also had a humane sense of right and wrong, going to visit another churchman who had refused to conduct a funeral service for a young girl whose life had been . . . let's just say blemished. When he arrived at the reverend's door carrying a horsewhip, he got a solemn promise that a dignified service would be conducted the next day.

And Fort Macleod and the Blackfoot community were not worlds apart, despite the way the story of the territory is sometimes told. One ranch historian describes the town during this period with genial affection:

> *The varied backgrounds of the inhabitants of this plains out-post gave Fort Macleod a flavour unique in the northwest. There were probably more characters per capita in that little settlement than in any other centre on the Canadian prairies. Ex-whisky traders . . . went legitimate and rubbed shoulders with the Mounted Police, many of whom were just as adventurous as the old traders. Indians from the nearby Blood and Peigan reserves mingled with local ranchers, cowboys and assorted adventurers.*

All of them were making the best of opportunities, and making friends. Macleod Hotel played its part in this, for despite its entertainingly intimidating house rules it was in the business of hospitality. As new competitors came into the hotel business they all needed a reliable supply of reasonably clean linen. So laundries opened, many of them run by Chinese men and women who came to town; and one of them, Chow Sam, turned from a spell working at the Macleod Hotel to opening a succession of popular cafés in town, becoming a friend to both my grandfather and Fred Haultain, who later stood as godfather to Chow Sam's daughter Kathleen.

Around town, Jack met others who became his friends. Jerry Potts was one of the first. Born about 1840, Potts was the son of a Scots father and a Blackfoot mother named Crooked Back (*Namo-pisi*); his own Blood name was Bear Child (*Ki-yo-kosi*). He was not yet a year old when he was adopted by a saddler and trader after his father was killed in an altercation at his trading post on the Missouri River; but his new father had notoriously brutal habits, and after a few years he left the upper Missouri region rather quickly for parts unknown, leaving the young lad once again fatherless. Luck was now on Jerry's side: at the age of five he was adopted by another trader, an amiable man who taught him English as well as the ways of the settler society even as he learned the skills—the arts and the science—of living on the plains. From his teens, Potts was comfortable with the Indian and the white as well as the mixed-blood trading communities; and by the time he was in his twenties, his reputation as a warrior was well established and widely celebrated. On one occasion, while alone hunting buffalo, he met seven Crow Indians, deadly enemies of the Bloods. Four had rifles, and the other three had bows and arrows. They invited him to "visit" their camp nearby, and, having no choice (nor any illusions about the invitation), Jerry put on a cheerful face and agreed. So they set off, the three Crows with bows and arrows in the lead and the other four with their rifles behind. As they rode along, the Crows—not realizing that Jerry had learned their language while travelling with his father—began to talk about him, and he heard them discussing whether to kill him right away or wait until they got to the camp. Easier to do it now, they decided. As soon as he heard the telltale *click* of a rifle, Jerry slipped from his saddle, taking his rifle with him. The Crow leader fired at him, but missed; and before any of them got off a second shot, Jerry was down on his knees firing back, killing all four riding behind him while the three others with bows and arrows fled to their camp. Jerry caught his own horse, rode back to gather together a party of Blackfoot, Blood and Peigan warriors, and led them to the main Crow camp, which they demolished, leaving dozens dead and wounded.

Potts never looked the part of a great Indian scout, being short and stooped and what would have been called "uncomely" in the company of tall and handsome Blackfoot men, but his life was straight out of a novel. It could be dangerous if you tried to join the script and were not as gifted as he was—which few in the territory were. Fifteen years before my grandfather met him, Potts had been involved in an infamous battle on the Belly River near a trading post called Fort Whoop-Up, when the Blackfoot were attacked by their traditional enemies the Cree and the Assiniboine, who had heard of the devastation caused by a small-pox epidemic—which killed more than fourteen hundred Blackfoot—and thought the plains would be better off without them. Joined by the Peigan who also had repeating rifles, the Blood tribe defeated the Cree and their Assiniboine allies, slaughtering more than three hundred. It was the last major battle between any of the First Nations in Canada, though local hostilities continued for some time over the next twenty years. Potts's role in the battle, tactical as well as militant, became part of his story. At the time the North-West Mounted Police came through in 1874, Jerry was working out of a trading post in Montana for I.G. Baker—then one of the most important traders, transporters of goods (mostly by bull train) and cattle drovers in the northwest—and he was known as one of the best plainsmen in the territory. The Mounted Police took him on as scout and interpreter; he suggested the site for their original fort near what eventually became the townsite of Fort Macleod; and for the next twenty-two years Potts was an indispensable member of the force, guiding and cajoling the officers, winding them up and settling them down all at the same time, interpreting at every turn both the languages and the livelihoods, ancient and modern, of his Blackfoot people, and leading the police and some of the settlers through the territory that was for many of them to become a permanent home.

. . .

One interesting group of individuals around Fort Macleod and in the country nearby were so-called remittance men from Great Britain, sent out by their families to get them as far away from home as possible. As one newspaperman put it, they were often "deported for some small lapse of grace, which in the North-West would not afford gossip for ten minutes [such as] the unpardonable sin of preferring a pretty barmaid's society to that of a bespectacled aunt, coupled with a tendency to stay out all night." The tales of their escapades, including some courageous (albeit often foolish) adventures, provided entertainment all round—they may have been green, the reporter added, but they certainly were not yellow.

Many of them put on airs, as they were expected to. "Lord" Lionel Brook—the title was dubious, but genially upheld by the community—was a regular at Taylor's Table in the hotel. He had taken up ranching near Pincher Creek (thirty miles southwest of Fort Macleod) where, in the words of an old-timer in the district, "his picturesque appearance was always to be noted at race-meets and sports of the 1st of July and other times. He was invariably riding in belted Norfolk jacket, riding breeches and gaiters, wide-felt hat and monocle. The Indians called him 'Window Pane Chief,' and he has been a prince of graciousness to them."

The Blackfoot men get most of the attention from settler historians, but newcomers admired many of the women for their authority and judgement as well as their beauty and charm; and nobody who had any intelligence underestimated the Blackfoot women, with their unmistakable pride, their equitable presence of mind and their considerable influence over sacred as well as secular happenings. One of them, Red Crow's aunt *Natawista*, became especially notable in the 1870s, well beyond the Blackfoot tribe. She had first married Albert Culbertson, chief trader of the American Fur Company in Fort Benton, after a courtship that followed traditional protocols and an exchange of gifts that included a complete dowry for her from the Bloods—buckskin costumes, a new lodge, backrests and fourteen horses—and from the groom a wardrobe of silk, woollen and cotton clothing, as well as guns, blankets and tobacco for her father. When Culbertson later took to gambling and the marriage broke up, she became one of the Indian wives of a whisky trader and rancher named Fred Kanouse, who later ran a rooming house in Fort Macleod; and she remained a force to be reckoned with in tribal affairs. The following is a description of her by Richard Nevitt, a police surgeon in the early days of Fort Macleod, at a dance that followed a day of games and races.

The ladies came on horseback; only one, however, had a saddle and that was Madame Kanouse. You should have seen her dress. It was the Dolly Varden style, a large figured chintz just short enough to display the gorgeous stripes of a balmoral petticoat which in its turn was also just short enough to show two very small feet clad in moccasins and the end of a pair of leggings beautifully worked in beads. She also had on a heavy black velvet loose-fitting overcoat and over this a most brilliant striped shawl, the stripes being about three inches broad and alternately red, blue, green and red, with a narrow line of yellow between each colour. Her head gear consisted of a small plaid shawl. The other titled aristocrats were dressed also in gorgeous array, but perforce they yielded the palm to Madame.

Dressing up wasn't the sole prerogative of pretty women or remittance men, of course. Dances were very common and widely attended, with weekly dances in Stand Off on the Blood reserve, and regular local dances held throughout the territory in restaurants and private homes. Everyone would dress up in finery, with the cowboys putting on their fanciest trappings and gear for the occasion, and for the girls. Indeed, with all the demands of their life out on the range, cowboys were often gloriously extravagant in town, routinely spending wages from six months on the trail in as many days; and wearing clothes and gear that displayed a love of show—boots, spurs, chaps, shirts, hats (smaller in the foothills than in the American southwest, but, just as there, the best were often made by Stetson). There is a story about one roughriding cowboy who arrived in Fort Macleod from Pincher Creek for a ball, his evening clothes rolled up behind his saddle. When he got to town, he borrowed a clean and pressed white shirt, but was unable to get any shoes . . . so he went to the Hudson's Bay store, where all he could find was a pair of velvet slippers with red roses on the toes. He wore them all evening. This was a complicated and contradictory community; and anyone who thinks flowers are not a favourite of cowboys has not seen decorated cowboy shirts and vests and jackets, then and now.

. . .

My grandfather's first rancher friend was Edward (better known as Ned) Maunsell, who had come from Ireland some ten years earlier to join the newly formed North-West Mounted Police and was part of the first contingent that arrived in the foothills. Late that first summer season he saw the plains black with buffalo, moving in herds that seemed to go on forever; and over the next five years he watched their numbers dwindle to nothing. When his three-year assignment ended he left the police force, partly because he was bored with the inactivity after the police had effectively shut down the whisky traders—most of the smuggling now was to supply the police as much as the settlers, whose thirst routinely exceeded the regulated supply of liquor in the territories. At the time, consumption of liquor anywhere in the North-West Territories was legal only with a permit, and then only for "medicinal purposes"; and so the local doctor in Fort Macleod, who became my grandfather's next-door neighbour, was authorized to keep five gallons of whisky and two gallons of brandy in stock. But the regulations were impossible to enforce, and nobody tried very hard. The import and sale of booze was at the heart of the prohibition, with the territories offering an early example of the uneasy line that is still being drafted between the production and distribution and the consumption of drugs. In any case, the main reason Maunsell left the force was that he had dreamed of starting a ranch from the moment he arrived in the foothills. He saw, as did others, that the country that had supported millions of buffalo could also support large herds of cattle, provided the range was kept open for grazing. From Ireland he brought a knowledge of farming, which helped him supplement his income from ranching by growing potatoes to feed himself and oats to sell to the North-West Mounted Police; and from his time with the police he was at ease with the Indians, many of whom he knew well and trusted more than he did some of the settlers.

Ned Maunsell became my grandfather's close friend; and although they had different temperaments they both got along well with the Blackfoot, and saw each other through some tough times. The rancher's temper sometimes tested my easy-going grandfather, and probably the other way around; but all the same, in 1905 they took to ranching together, buying twelve thousand head of cattle—the entire stock of the famous

Cochrane ranch, founded in the 1880s and one of the earliest in southern Alberta—to take their place among the biggest ranchers in southern Alberta. But that's for later in this story.

. . .

When the Cowdry brothers arrived, Crop Eared Wolf's father, Red Crow, was the head chief of the Bloods in the Blackfoot Confederacy. He had earned the respect of the Bloods as a warrior with a storied war record and as a wise leader and statesman, and he had shown one way forward by turning from war to peace and from hunting buffalo to herding cattle, inspiring many in his tribe with his early success in farming and ranching while continuing to breed and build up his herd of fine horses and maintaining the traditions of secular and spiritual knowledge and of ceremony that had sustained his people for generations. He had also earned the respect of the police and the settlers and ranchers and townsfolk, and the sometimes grudging admiration of the Indian agents, to whom he always kept his word... not for their satisfaction, but for the benefit of his people. He was a peacemaker as well as a warrior, and stern in both roles.

The Blackfoot word for the Bloods, *Káínai,* means "many chiefs," and Red Crow was also chief of a smaller group—one of a dozen or so bands within the tribe—called Fish Eaters. It seems to an outsider a curious name, for the Blackfoot didn't usually eat fish; but in the old days when food was scarce they would catch fish from the rivers near Fort Macleod and in the mountains to the west, building fish traps that worked like the corrals into which they had herded buffalo. That kind of resilience and accommodation was one of their greatest strengths in hard times; and these times were becoming very hard for the *Niitsítapi*, the "real people" of *Nitawahsin-nanni*, their home-land—Blackfoot territory. They were used to traders, moving with the seasons as they themselves had done for centuries; so while the appearance of more and more settlers might threaten their sovereignty, it was the disappearance of the great buffalo herds that challenged their sense of the world.

Red Crow's stature as a leader of his people in Blackfoot territory was described by his friend the Methodist missionary, John Maclean, who had come to the foothills in 1880 and settled with the Bloods. Maclean quickly became fluent in the Blackfoot language, and versed in its subtleties. He had many close friend-ships in the Blood community—both with leaders such as Red Crow and Crop Eared Wolf and some of the rebellious younger men of the tribe, as well as with its everyday citizens, once tear-ing up floorboards of his little house on the reserve to make a coffin for a family who came asking him to bury one of their relatives. He provided food and medicine and loans and com-panionship and care to anyone who wanted or needed it, along with what he called "soul grub" on Sunday. This is what he had to say about Red Crow:

> *His mild demeanour gives no evidence of his warlike quali-ties. Yet he was, in the old buffalo days, one of the bravest warriors that lived upon the plains [with a war record of thirty-three raids against the Crow, Shoshone, Cree and Nez Perce]. I have listened to him at the Sun Dance eloquently relate his military adventures and successes [and] as he walks through the camp, arrayed in his stateliness and adored by his followers, he bears in his attitude the marks of a man of*

peace who loves his people and is ever studious of their wel-
fare. Sitting in his spacious lodge with the minor chiefs, he
discourses about the necessities of his tribe, lays plans for their
progress in the arts of civilized life, instructs them how to
maintain their law and keep inviolate the morality of the
natives. In the old days I have often gazed in astonishment at
the record of his brave deeds in the picture writing on his
lodge.... The scalp-locks were fastened upon it, and the writ-
ing in various colours ran around it, which detailed the history
of his life.... He is essentially a leader of men. Not by force of
arms, nor even through the influence of his position, does he
rule, although his official dignity is a strong factor in main-
taining his power over men; but it is his striking personality
which enables him to command implicit obedience to the cus-
toms and laws of the tribe.... His influence is no less among
the white people who have learned to trust him, assured that
he has always been friendly to their interests while guarding
the rights of his own tribe. It is to his friendship, intelligence
and good government that they are indebted for the peaceful
relations which have existed for many years between the white
and red races in the west.

Over a hundred years later, his great great-granddaughter
Annabel Crop Eared Wolf celebrated Red Crow's "wisdom,
foresight, courage, accomplishment and strong sense of commitment to the tribe and the ancestral lands [as] the standard of
káínaayo'ssini," the real *Káínai* way of life.

. . .

Back in the mists of time the Blackfoot had first moved onto what became their homeland, following the buffalo up to the North Saskatchewan River and beyond the Great Sand Hills in western Saskatchewan. There are various accounts of their migrations before the buffalo hunt gave meaning and purpose to their lives, long before horses came into their hands. But by the 1800s, the Blackfoot had developed extraordinary skills in horsemanship that caught everyone's attention and confirmed their reputation as the most powerful people of the northern plains, a reputation nervously acknowledged by early explorers and traders and by other plains tribes such as the Cree and the Crow and the Assiniboine and the Sioux. They had formed the Blackfoot Confederacy—a collective of three tribes called *Siksika* (their word for "black foot," supposedly a reference to the colour of their moccasins) and Blood (or *Káínai*) and Peigan (or *Pikuni*, a name celebrating a young man who was scorned for his shabby robe until he became a great warrior). All the Blackfoot spoke the same language, called Algonquian by linguists, and they had come together as Indian nations with their neighbours the Athapaskan-speaking Sarcee (who called themselves *Tsuu T'ina*, or "earth people") to form a confederation, a formidable defence against enemies on all sides. Not long before, they also had an alliance with the Gros Ventres in Montana, but a dispute over stolen horses had turned them against each other. In Montana too, the Blackfoot had (and still have) many relatives, who call themselves Blackfeet.

Their long and complex history as a great people is still told in stories and songs—often accompanied by dancing and drumming—and in carvings and paintings on skins and robes, and in parades as well as in other performances and protocols that certified their belief in their territory and their traditions. And their history stretches that territory into a world as wide as that which can be viewed from the ridge above the Milk River, southeast of Fort Macleod, where you can see rivers running north to Hudson Bay, east to the Gulf of St. Lawrence and south to the Gulf of Mexico—a world as wonderful—and as wonderfully strange—as any that can be imagined. But their history was also—and their world still is—in *Nitawahsin-nanni* itself, and is figured in the carvings and paintings in *Áísínai'pi*, now called Writing-on-Stone Provincial Park, about a hundred miles south east of Fort Macleod, which tell of material and spiritual happenings going back thousands of years in their homeland.

. . .

When Crop Eared Wolf's parents died in the mid-1850s from one of the waves of infectious disease that swept through many of the plains Indian communities during those years, his sister—who had married Red Crow—persuaded the chief to adopt her little brother. He did so, raising him as his own, and, before his death in 1900, appointing him his successor as head chief of the Bloods, having recognized his bravery and leadership on raids and scouting expeditions during the 1860s and '70s. He signalled his choice and Crop Eared Wolf's future responsibilities by giving him his favourite tipi design. Tipi designs, with their colours and forms and images and scripts and sometimes scalplocks, were among the most public forms of boasting and toasting and truthtelling, as well as of prayer; and this design, called Middle Painted Lodge, dated back to the beginning of Blackfoot spirituality and science and included a wide red band around the middle of the tipi with sacred otters painted on it. It told a story of the devotion to the spirits of his place and his people that was Red Crow's legacy, and would became Crop Eared Wolf's trademark. In return he promised his father to use all the power he had, and all that the spirits would give him, to defend the land they had chosen for their new home under the treaty.

During the 1880s, as the Blackfoot struggled to come to terms with the devastating disappearance of the buffalo upon which their spiritual as well as material nourishment had depended for generations, they held on to their horses—and their stories about them. Much is made of the enthusiasm of the indigenous peoples of the northern plains, particularly the Blackfoot, for stealing horses and telling stories about it. It was a way of gaining renown, to be sure, and of demonstrating success in war, like taking possession of an enemy's gun or shield or scalp. But it also had a very important place in the hierarchy of their mythical and historical consciousness. It was an act of mischief outside the law of civil society, and mischief was the signature of the Blackfoot creator hero *Napi*, the Old Man. Mischief can be a way of making enemies, so stealing horses—"bringing them in" or "bringing them home," to use phrases that were customary in Blackfoot accounts—came with considerable risks. Stealth and skill were crucial, along with a subtle and sophisticated knowledge of horses and how they behave, as well as of people and dogs. Much of this tradition of mischief-making is part of European culture too. Hermes, the messenger of the gods in Greek mythology, began his career when he was one day old by stealing cattle from Apollo, which he then barbecued but didn't eat, thereby making the point that some things are valuable not because they are useful but because they are special. Or, if you are a thief, because they belong to someone else. And in Hermes's case, in order to begin his life with a signature story. Having something to talk about, whether it had happened or was going to happen, was an essential part of being human, and being Blackfoot.

And then there was the pure delight of doing something difficult and dangerous just because it is there to do—in this case bringing in more horses than you need. Thoreau, in another passage that my grandfather admired, talked about the importance of "more than enough" (which Thoreau called "*extra vagance*," adding "it all depends on how you are yarded"), of the imagination pushing back against the pressure of reality and redefining it, of doing things that defy utility and sometimes even test morality. That was the argument made about the arts in the late nineteenth century by Oscar Wilde and others—art for art's sake—and it had its counterpart in the tradition of horse stealing that flourished in Blackfoot society into the 1890s. Given the respect accorded to horses in plains Indian society, fine horses—and more fine horses than enough—were like works of art as well as weapons of war, and in both cases figured as national treasures, their conformation and colour and character discussed with scholarly intensity.

. . .

During the 1880s, it was said that all trails in southern Alberta ended up in Fort Macleod. It was not a frontier town on the margins but a community at the crossroads, a centre of challenge and change. The street names, added as the town grew, give a sense of the stature of the characters in the town back then and how they shaped—and still shape—the community. First Avenue on the west side of town is now named after my grandfather, John Cowdry. From there, John Cowdry Avenue meets three boulevards: Chief Red Crow Boulevard; Colonel James Macleod Boulevard; and Jerry Potts Boulevard.

Directly to the east of John Cowdry Avenue is a street named for Fred Haultain, a man dedicated to a territory that respected the history of its First Nations as well as the hopes of its newcomers. Archie Maclean Street comes next; he was a horseman and cattleman known to everyone as "Honest Archie," and was one of the four founders of the Calgary Stampede in 1912. Colonel Sam Steele, like Colonel Macleod an original with the North-West Mounted Police, has the next street named after him; he served in various parts of the west before taking command of the detachment in Fort Macleod between 1888 and 1897. Then there is a street named for Annora Brown; born in 1899 (the same year as my mother), she taught school for several years and then turned to painting and became famous for her representations of the weather and the wildflowers and the Blackfoot and settler citizens of the foothills. Lillie Grier, who arrived in Fort Macleod the same year as my grandfather to take up teaching in its first organized school, claims the next street; she later travelled to the Yukon during the Klondike Gold Rush with her husband, D.W. Davis—sometime whisky trader, store manager, rancher and latter-day Member of Parliament in Ottawa (of whom more later), who helped the North-West Mounted Police build their island fort in 1874—before returning to Macleod as a widow in 1906 and living there for the next thirty years. And finally there is an avenue on the east side named after my grandfather's friend Edward Maunsell, one of the earliest ranchers in the territory.

So Fort Macleod is framed on the north of town by a great Blackfoot chief, a famous North-West Mounted policeman and a renowned plainsman who shared the blood of both; and on the east and west by a rancher and a banker.

3

AN UNUSUAL BANKER

THE BANKROBBER: *"Hand over the cash, or I'll shoot."*
JACK COWDRY: *"Shoot me, and be damned."*

. . .

WHEN THEY GOT TO KNOW each other better, my grandfather and Crop Eared Wolf used to laugh at the fact that a banker and a horse thief became friends.

The young Cowdry brothers had first thought about opening a livery stable when they got to Fort Macleod, because Jack knew about horses and Nat knew about grain and hay. Early on in their homesteading days, Jack had set off for Winnipeg to buy a couple of draft horses and found himself in the company of horse traders from what seemed like all parts of the world in a town that was fast becoming a centre of commodities trading. Winnipeg had just started its extraordinary late-nineteenth-century expansion; nearly ten thousand people had poured into town in the previous decade, and people were gathering there from south and north and east and west to trade. By the turn of the century, going to Winnipeg to deal in horses was like going to Istanbul to trade in rugs, and Jack became fascinated by the tricks of the horse trade and the criteria for success: learn everything you can about horses, expect surprises and trust your own judgement.

By the time they got to the foothills, Jack had given up the notion of going into the horse trade exclusively, but he thought a stable might be a way of keeping some contact with it. Except that there was already a good stable in town. Then a hotel came to mind, since Fort Macleod welcomed lots of travellers. But they decided there was no sense in starting out in competition with Kamoose, even though they figured a new hotel would gather good business and competition would no doubt keep both on their toes.

But it was their new friend Ned Maunsell who got them going in a different direction. Ned's elder brother George had worked for the Boundary Commission, surveying the new border with the United States, and when that was finished he joined the North-West Mounted Police, leaving when his tour of duty was done and joining Ned to gather stock and start a ranch. All they needed was money to buy some cattle; but they had decided to wait until spring so they would not have to overwinter the herd, which gave them some time to raise the cash. Their family in Ireland had promised to help them, and they wrote asking them for funds; sure enough, in late March, the funds arrived. Sort of. What actually arrived was a letter of credit promising that so-and-so would pay them such-and-such on demand—a cheque of sorts, but not one easily cashed in those times and in that place, because so-and-so lived eight hundred miles away in Deadwood, South Dakota, and the only way to get the money without going that far was to find someone nearby who would believe both in them and in the good word of so-and-so. "That's what banks are for," my grandfather said to his brother Nat. (In a nice coincidence, the Lakota Sioux name for Deadwood, *Owdyasuta*, means "to approve or confirm things.") Both Jack and Nat had worked as clerks in a bank before heading west, so they actually knew something about the business.

Unfortunately for the Maunsells, the nearest bank to Fort Macleod at the time was three hundred miles away in Helena, Montana. The few outfits that extended credit in or around Fort Macleod, like the trader I.G. Baker, had never seen a letter of credit and wouldn't give Ned the money. Still, three hundred miles to Montana was better than eight hundred to South Dakota, so Ned Maunsell headed off in late winter to get the money. His guide was Tony La Chappelle, who ran a tobacco and candy emporium in town with billiard tables and locally renowned cider in the saloon at back, where poker players gathered around a couple of tables day and night. If you asked the limit, you would be told "floor to ceiling." La Chappelle might seem to have been a curious choice, but he was one of the best guides in the territory, an ex–whisky trader who knew every trail between Fort Macleod and Fort Benton in Montana, and had often travelled on farther to Helena. On their way south, not far from Fort Macleod, a storm came up and they made camp; but their horses got away. So Ned went searching for them, and after a few hours he thought he saw them on a ridge in the distance and headed in that direction through the storm . . . but this was back in 1878, and they turned out to be a few stray buffalo. By that time, Ned was far from camp, and snow was blowing hard. He thought he knew the direction but couldn't see his way and stepped right through the ice into a river. He stumbled on, and by some miracle made it back to their camp; but by that time his feet were frozen. La Chappelle wrapped them in rags soaked in coal oil, and got him back to the hospital in Fort Macleod; but it took a couple of months before he got his feet back in circulation. All in order to cash a cheque.

Ned and his brother eventually got the money, bought the cattle and started a small ranch. Telling the story to my grandfather, Ned grumbled not just about the difficulty of cashing a cheque but also about the lack of a local line of credit for someone like him, still struggling half a dozen years later with the ups and downs of the cattle business. There were travelling bankers, working for the big banks based in the east, but they were more interested in operations with thousands of head of cattle; and they usually didn't know the local customers well enough to want to extend credit, especially without much (or often any) security.

James Macleod, too, grumbled about the lack of a bank in town. When Jack met him in 1885, Macleod had left the North-West Mounted Police but had just returned from resolving a dispute about policing the Canadian Pacific Railway construction camps in British Columbia. He told about riding all the way to Helena, Montana, in the early days just to pick up the policemen's pay. He also admitted that he had never been very good at bookkeeping, and when he was commissioner of the North-West Mounted Police from 1876 to 1880 the force had come under attack for mismanagement. A good banker would have been a good friend to have back then, he said. And now too, he added, for he was trying to juggle his duties as a magistrate with a small horse-breeding operation to supply the police force.

Nat was up for almost anything, and Jack knew they could work together. If Harry Taylor could build a hotel and Ned Maunsell could start a ranch and Tony La Chappelle could run a store and a saloon and find his way across the prairies in a snowstorm and Jerry Potts could—well, Jerry Potts was incomparable—surely they could open a bank. It would serve the community in the same spirit as Harry served his hotel customers, with a genial welcome and a good-natured warning about the rules. But Jawbone would be the rule, unlike at Harry's hotel. If you were going to do business with their bank, you had to be as good as your word.

It was clear that Fort Macleod was at the centre of a lot of activity for which a bank could be helpful. In the bar at Kamoose's hotel Nat and Jack heard a slew of complaints from cowboys who hadn't been paid on time (because the ranchers didn't have a bank to see them through with cash until they had sold their cattle), and from Kamoose and others in business who lost out because the cowboys didn't have money to spend. Even the missionaries, despite their well-advertised dedication to God rather than Mammon, were calling for a bank … and for advice about managing the donations they received, their paltry stipends from headquarters, and purchases from local merchants and tradesmen. And the officers of the North-West Mounted Police and the Indian agents responsible for fulfilling treaty obligations to the Blackfoot complained that they didn't have a place to deposit their wages and safeguard the funds they received from Ottawa to do their work. Small businesses needed all the banking help they do now, but at less cost, for it was the small businesses that supported the town with more than supplies. As one poncy ranching patron from England noted, after describing Fort Macleod as nothing more than "a wide muddy lane, with a row of dirty, half-finished wooden shanties flanking each side," the town did business which "would gladden the heart of many a shopkeeper in a country town in England, aye, if he could put his net profit at even one-fourteenth of that which rolled into the pockets of the possessor of one of those shanties." These were shopkeepers who needed capital to lend to the ranchers to buy the cattle and pay the cowboys as they struggled through hard times or expanded in good times. And the citizens of the town needed a hand, especially in those years, to build something more than a half-finished wooden shanty.

A few local merchants in Fort Macleod, including I.G. Baker, did offer loans to the folks they knew, but generally only for the purchase of items from the store . . . and as Ned Maunsell would tell you—he was not a shy man—even then they didn't always come through when you needed them. Some of the missionaries made loans to the Blackfoot for wagons and harnesses and horses, using money that came to them from "mission central" (invariably back east, which one devout wit said fitted the orientation of both their churches and the Blackfoot tipis); but they usually charged relatively high interest (though still only about half of what credit card companies do now). But all the settlers, the businesses in the region, the ranching community, the North-West Mounted Police, the Indian agencies and those Bloods and Peigan who came to town regularly hoped for a bank that wasn't owned by someone from somewhere else (like Halifax, Montreal, Toronto or Winnipeg). This wasn't just western distrust of easterners; there was some suspicion that a few of the regional and national banks based in those distant towns were vulnerable in the uncertain economic circumstances and high-flying business expectations that arrived with the railway. And they were right.

Almost without exception, Jack and Nat's new friends and acquaintances were encouraging. And after all, the brothers thought, they did have a little experience. So they started a bank, called Cowdry Brothers, with modest funds of their own. My grandfather used to say that "credit"—as in a line of credit or a letter of credit—means "he or she believes." To be a banker, he would insist, you have to believe... and dream a bit too, right alongside your customers. It seems they had a good instinct for whom to believe, and what to believe in, and when to dream, for Cowdry Brothers Bank prospered for the next twenty years. My grandfather also liked finding out how to do things—things that people needed money to do, like building houses and growing crops and raising cattle and milling wood and digging mines and starting or running businesses, which was good because almost all his early loans were to folks who had no security, and he spent a lot of time in these years visiting his customers in their homes and workplaces. His loans were usually for short periods of three or six months, which was typical for the time; but he almost always extended them when asked, often with suggestions about how to make things work better... or with sympathy when a hard winter had frozen the livestock, or a summer fire had burned the crop. Both happened regularly in the foothills, where uncertainty was a way of life and surprises came as regularly as the seasons. "You need to wait for a better year," he'd say, a fellow traveller both with his needy customer and with the depositors who were trusting him to safeguard their money (and thereby underwriting his loans); and then he would make the loan interest-free for the next stretch. He sometimes took chattel mortgages, but he almost never called them... and almost all his lawyer's bills were for the cost of removing chattel security. By all accounts from distinguished economic historians, the little bank played a big part in the success of ranching in the foothills, and in the economic development and cultural character of southern Alberta.

The word "chattel" is a reminder that banking originated in bartering, where actual commodities would be exchanged. Foremost among these always were horses and cattle, the latter derived from *chatel*, an Old French word for "property"; and the Latin word for "money," *pecunia*, comes from *pecus*, which means "cattle" (whence the Pecos River in New Mexico and Texas cattle country). Among the older generation of Blackfoot, wealth was still reckoned in horses into the 1920s, and the Indian agent on the Siksika reserve in Gleichen at that time tells of describing the interest they could earn by putting money on deposit as like "the colt of the money mare." To which one elder, pointing at the paltry interest entry in the account book, replied: "That's no colt. It isn't even a good egg."

Going back millennia, when commodities like cattle and horses were the currency, their agreed-upon value was the basis of commerce. In this, banking currencies have a lot of similarity to language. The visionary Marshall McLuhan once proposed that "by the meaningless sign linked to the meaningless sound we have built the shape and meaning of the world." He was describing how we believe in words, which are made up of arbitrary signs and sounds that are given meaning by conventions exactly like those we embrace when we credit a currency or a letter of credit, choosing to believe that a little coin or a small piece of paper has value . . . when it doesn't, really. Or rather it does, when we all agree to believe in it. The association of commerce with language is very old; and with coin and paper currency, just as with language, we depend on a collective belief in its value. One community's currency can often be another's curiosity, a counterpart to the "strangeness" of someone else's language, or customs. But custom itself, and especially the custom of belief in arbitrary signs and sounds, is shared across cultures. Understanding this is fundamental to understanding other people.

Many Blackfoot took to the new money economy as confidently as some of them took to the new language of English; but just as most of them kept their Blackfoot language, they also kept their traditions of bartering, trading horses or cattle as well as exchanging them for tipi designs and medicine bundles. Medicine bundles contained elements of sacred ceremony, such as sweetgrass, tobacco and paint, as well as individual objects including pipes, tipi flags, otter skins, war shirts and knives. They were opened and "read" after the first thunderstorm in spring, or on special occasions to transfer ownership or fulfill a vow. Almost all the Blackfoot balanced both traditional and new technologies quite comfortably in these early years, maintaining trade relations as support systems as well as commercial opportunities.

. . .

Banking conjures up coarse capitalist bogeymen, as well as biblical and qur'anic denunciations of usury. Back then, banking had a slightly better reputation; but it still attracted a familiar measure of scorn for its supposedly predatory instincts and its well-developed habit of scavenging the choicest morsels from the poor. But there was a moral philosophy that countered this during the nineteenth century, arguing that the poor who did not have any security to pledge needed access to money to get a start in life, or to pay for goods and services in a bad season. They needed someone to believe in them, and lend them money. In a preface to his play *Major Barbara*, written just after the turn of the century (about whether it was right for the Salvation Army to take good money from bad people), the socialist George Bernard Shaw wrote, "Money is the counter that enables life to be distributed socially: it *is* life as truly as sovereigns and bank notes are money. The first duty of every citizen is to insist on having money on reasonable terms." This rang true in Fort Macleod. Nobody had security in the foothills ... unless they had very rich backers (and then they certainly didn't need a loan from Cowdry Brothers). Most had only their good word, and with it a promise to keep.

Although it may seem sentimental today, "keeping your word" was a fundamental value for non-Aboriginal settlers as well as Aboriginal stewards in the foothills at that time, high-lighting the connection between language and currency. Here is how one of the earliest chroniclers of the foothills, the *Calgary Herald* journalist L.V. Kelly, opens his book *The Range Men: The Story of the Ranchers and Indians of Alberta*, published in 1913. It is, interestingly, one of the very few to put cowboys *and* Indians at the centre of the story of the foothills, not always with the respect we might wish for either of them, but recognizing that they were all in it together.

John Cowdry, who conducted a private banking business in the town of Macleod from 1886 until 1905, through the hey-day of the best years of the ranching business, never had a word of trouble from any of his customers. Often he advanced money on a man's mere word and never was his confidence abused. A man's word was his bond in those primitive days. The cowboys and ranchers were honest, clean and straight in all their money dealings even though they might pick up a calf [that is, mark a maverick calf with their own brand]. When Cowdry sold his private banking business (Cowdry Brothers) to the Canadian Bank of Commerce in 1905, the bank took over from the Cowdrys some four hundred and eighty-seven thousand dollars of loans, of which amount the Cowdrys had to guarantee fifty-two thousand dollars for [six] months. After the expiration of this time Cowdry was released from this guarantee, and out of that fifty-two thousand dollars he had to pay something under two hundred dollars, an astonishingly pleasing average to any banker.

. . .

One story, told in my family and in books about those early years, catches the character of this unusual banker. He was standing behind the counter in his bank, a little wooden shanty said by one contemporary to be known to every man and woman in southern Alberta. It was springtime, with warm weather blowing on a breeze that was making soughing sounds across the marsh marigolds by the river, while the snow-covered mountains to the west looked in the clear air like they were just next door. He was watching a group of Peigan Indians riding across the edge of town on their way home from south of the border, where they had been trading—some sceptics said stealing— horses. A few cowboys were about, getting supplies before heading north to their ranches and round-up.

And then a stranger came into the bank and looked around. There was nobody else there. He pointed a gun at my grandfather. "Hand over the cash," he demanded, "or I'll shoot."

Bank robbers were the stuff of frontier legend, but not yet of Fort McLeod. This one was young—who wasn't in those days?—and what we might call stressed out. My grandfather, who was only a few years older, was cool and casual. Or so the story goes. He turned around, kicked the safe door shut, spun the handles to set the lock, and swung back to face the stranger. "Shoot me, and be damned," he said. Then, before the young fellow could do just that, my grandfather scolded him for his stupidity, suggested that he should get on his horse and ride out of town before the Mounted Police came by, and then gave him twenty-five dollars out of the counter till to speed him on his way. He never said whether it was a cowboy, or an Indian, or one and the same. To my grandfather, it didn't matter; and saying who it was would imply that it did. The first bank robbery in southern Alberta was an unusual robbery. And the first private bank in southern Alberta was an unusual bank.

4

ENNAKEX/OTSITOTORPI/ AKÁPIOYIS: POLICE/WHEN THEY CAME/ FORT MACLEOD

"We thought we had more time."
BLACKFOOT ELDER

. . .

"WE WOKE TO FIND THE COUNTRYSIDE covered in buffalo," wrote twenty-year-old Ned Maunsell in the late summer of 1874, camped near what would become Fort Macleod on the Milk River ridge with his utterly exhausted fellow North-West Mounted Police officers, brightly attired in their red uniforms, towards the end of their long ride westward across the plain from Fort Dufferin in Manitoba. Their arrival was noted by the Blackfoot elder Father of Many Children in his "winter count" (kept on a tanned skin) as *"Ennakex/otsitotorpi/akápioyis"*—Police/when they came/Fort Macleod. A couple of years later, Father of Many Children recorded, *"Itakainiskoy"*—When there were plenty of buffalo. Three years after that, in 1879, he wrote, *"Itsistsitsis/awenimiopi"*—When first/no more buffalo. Then, in 1883, *"Istsienakas/otsitotorpi"*—Fire wagon, when it arrived. The buffalo had gone; and the Canadian Pacific Railway and settlers had come.

. . .

Soon after his arrival in Canada from his home in Ireland, Ned had signed up with the newly created North-West Mounted Police force, established the year before by the prime minister, John A. Macdonald, and inspired by the Irish Constabulary to bring "law and order" to the fledgling Dominion. Its commission had been hastened by the massacre of nearly two dozen Assiniboine in the Cypress Hills in Saskatchewan by liquored-up wolf hunters and a few Métis following the theft of their horses—probably by Cree raiders. And on another front, a dangerous kind of disorder was being caused by the whisky traders, illegally bringing rotgut spirits along with buffalo robes from the United States to trade in Canada. The border was just being surveyed at that time, and it certainly wasn't yet observed as a sovereign marker by the traders, whose scruffy style masked a shrewd and sometimes ruthless business instinct. Many of them became prominent figures in late-nineteenth-century society, as some of the Prohibition magnates did a few decades later; and when have traders ever been stopped by national boundaries anyway? As Thomas Jefferson said, prefiguring today's global economy, "The merchant has no homeland."

The government was also anxious to show the Canadian colours to the American neighbours but not to go into battle or provoke a civil war, as the United States cavalry and local militia in the western states of the Union seemed determined to do (though the later involvement of the North-West Mounted Police in Louis Riel's uprising could hardly be called peacekeeping). The new police force would parade the new Dominion's sovereignty to the First Nations and maintain the regime of law and order that they were sent to establish, appointing its officers as either stipendiary magistrates or justices of the peace. Although this overrode the long-standing British principle of an independent judiciary, it encouraged efficient and (at least in the early years) often surprisingly equitable enforcement of the law on behalf of First Nations, which nourished good relations—and disagreements that were straightforward rather than surreptitious—between the Blackfoot and the Crown.

Ned Maunsell and the North-West Mounted Police contingent had ridden hundreds of miles that summer season, heading west from the Red River with around three hundred men to patrol more than 300,000 square miles of territory. They saw buffalo herds that covered the land as far as the eye could see, and a prairie landscape that was as dry as the desert but blessed with creeks and rivers and hills and valleys along the way. For the men—many of them boys, like the cowboys they met—the unknown was the most fearsome menace on the ride westward; even though the region had been a part of the Dominion for seven years, it was foreign territory.

A plaintive song, "The Red River Valley," was going the rounds at that time. It was about a girl mourning the departure of her man, and most people north of the border no doubt assumed it was about the Red River settlement in Manitoba— though cattlemen might have realized it could be about another Red River, bordering Texas and Oklahoma. That southern river was a major crossing for the cattle coming up to northern railheads in Kansas and Missouri, or stocking the ranches around Fort Macleod, and they would have heard stories and perhaps sung songs about those great cattle drives, passing through "the nation"—a code for Indian Territory in Oklahoma—where a toll was charged per head of cattle by the Cherokee, Chickasaw, Choctaw, Creek and Seminole, the so-called Five Civilized Tribes. But there was none of that sort of gatekeeping on the Canadian prairies, where the sovereignty of the first peoples across whose land they were riding was being addressed—sort of—in the treaties that were being negotiated as the force rode west.

Although the North-West Mounted Police boys had some training, and a few of them considerable expertise in military routines, their knowledge of horses was limited . . . and their lives depended on their horses, since they certainly had none of the skills on foot over the open prairie that the Blackfoot or the Cree had inherited from their ancestors. Not knowing any better, they routinely camped down by the prairie sloughs and picketed their horses there to graze on the pond grass, because most of the grass up on the ridges seemed to have been eaten up or tramped down by the buffalo. But still their horses were in bad shape, and they couldn't understand why. As William Pearce, an experienced contemporary surveyor and articulate champion of ranching in the foothills (as well as an opponent of land speculation, called by his enemies the "Czar of the West"), noted,

> It was only necessary to give the horses enough time to fill themselves with the grasses on the ridges to enable them to stand the trip in first class condition. Throughout southern Alberta it was invariably reported that the North-West Mounted Police when they first came into the country could not understand why their horses were so foolish as voluntarily to seek the ridges for grazing where there was apparently little

pasturage in preference to the slough grass.... For some years
after their arrival the police seem to have had little knowledge
of the relative food value of the grasses.... If they had not been
able to procure a considerable quantity of oats from the
Boundary Commission ... they would have been paralyzed in
their movements on account of the condition of their horses.
As it was they were very greatly hampered. Looking back it
seems incredible that they were not wholly paralyzed.

They should have listened to their horses; but they were
lucky—helped along the way by the first peoples as well as some
of the second-comers on the plains, they made it to the foothills.
Their horses weren't so fortunate; many died on the trek, and
few of those that made it to Fort Macleod lived for more than
a few months.

During the years up to the early 1870s, antagonisms between
the tribes in the region north and south of the border—at the
time roughly marked by sod or rock pyramids about six feet
high—were complicated by the scourge of whisky. It was brought
into the territory by traders from the United States, and mixed
with anything available—opium, turpentine, vanilla extract,
various patent medicines and painkillers, red ink, tobacco and
slough water—to create liquor that wreaked havoc among the
settlers as well as the Indians, all of them keen to "oil up their
insides." (One easy recipe for lighter homemade refreshment
went as follows: make a washtub full of hot water into a lather
with washing soap, add a half dozen bottles each of Mustang
Liniment and Pain Killer, along with a quart of water in which
two plugs of blackstrap tobacco have been boiled.) The response
from many of the Blackfoot to the North-West Mounted Police

mandate to abolish the trade was surprisingly supportive, even though some of them had taken to drink. Or maybe *because* they had. Jerry Potts, for instance, liked to drink, and whisky was his frequent companion all his life; but he was sympathetic to the police mission because he hated the whisky trade, which had caused the death of his mother and half-brother in a drunken camp brawl two years earlier. (He got revenge a few months later, killing the murderer, ironically named Good Young Man.)

Even stone-cold sober, which he was most of the time on duty with the police, Potts was a character. His notoriously laconic style of speech became his trademark, and sometimes contrasted sharply with the earnest intent of others. Leading a party that included the governor general of Canada (the Marquess of Lorne) on a scouting visit to the west in 1881, Potts was asked by the impatient marquess—who had been riding all day and was getting exasperated that they hadn't reached their destination—"What's over the next hill?" No reply. So he asked again, "What's over the next hill?" Still no reply from the taciturn Potts. Finally the marquess repeated his question with all the imperial authority he could muster. "Now say there, my man, what's over the next hill?" "Another hill," replied Jerry and returned to his musings. The marquess must have been listening to some other things that Jerry said, however, for later he spoke out—and in the minds of the government, spoke completely out of turn as governor general—in support of the Blackfoot when their rations promised under treaty were being cut back by a government in Ottawa that was having trouble balancing its books, and by Indian agents in the field who were happy to have an excuse to show who was in charge.

. . .

After leaving their camp on the Milk River ridge, one of the first stops in the foothills for the North-West Mounted Police contingent was to be the infamous Fort Whoop-Up, near to what is now Lethbridge. It had been a trading post for whisky and robes for fifteen years and it had a wild west reputation worthy of its name, burnished by stories like the following, taken from a letter written by a resident of the fort named Snookum Jim—his name at least is true—to a friend in Fort Benton, Montana, the year before the North-West Mounted Police rode by.

Dear Friend,

My partner, Will Geary, got to putting on airs and I shot him and he is dead. Your potatoes are looking well.

Yours truly,
Snookum Jim

Fort Whoop-Up was near where the St. Mary and Belly Rivers join the Old Man's. Even though whisky traders had their own "personal trails," forts like Whoop-Up certainly weren't hidden—after all, they were trading posts, dealing in buffalo robes and other commodities even if some of their trade was illegal—and anyway nothing was hard to find if you had Jerry Potts along, as the police did at that point. The post had been established by two Montana traders, John Healy and Alfred Hamilton, in 1869, Healy being married to the daughter of one of the Blood chiefs, Many Spotted Horses, who gave him permission to build in his territory. He adopted a young Blood child who became known as Joe Healy; Joe's parents had been killed in a raid in Montana, and he later became a notable figure in the community, regularly called upon as an interpreter. When Crop Eared Wolf died in 1913, he was even a serious, though unsuccessful, candidate for head chief of the Bloods. This was a community full of unusual connections and surprising alliances.

As they rode up anxiously to Fort Whoop-Up, the North-West Mounted Police saw the Stars and Stripes flying from its flagpole, which didn't help calm their nerves. But after a comically dramatic flourish of setting up their field guns and preparing for battle, Potts led Colonel Macleod towards the fort, his nonchalance prompting some members of the force to put his intelligence into question. But that was always a mistake; and in this case he almost certainly knew more than he let on, for they found only one man there, along with several Indian women; and instead of a fight they got a good dinner for the entire troop. D.W. Davis, the American trader in charge of Fort Whoop-Up on behalf of I.G. Baker and the Fort Benton traders, was temporarily absent; but some weeks later, when the North-West Mounted Police returned for a mop-up, D.W. (as he was known) served them another hearty dinner that many wrote home about, complete with vegetables from his garden. No matter who you were, hospitality was a trademark in the foothills … unless you came to kill your enemies or steal their horses. Living in a world of courtesies was crucial. D.W., like many others in the whisky trade (such as Kamoose Taylor), quickly turned legitimate. He became manager of the large I.G. Baker store in Fort Macleod, which is where my grandfather first met him in 1885; and encouraged by his friend Kamoose, D.W. stood the very next year for election to the parliament in Ottawa, where he would very effectively practise his skills as a dealer for the next decade.

. . .

Although the Blackfoot may have been uneasy at the arrival of the North-West Mounted Police, they could see that they overwhelmingly outnumbered the newcomers; and without any notion of how many white people there were in the world, they were not too worried. In fact, given what they quickly understood to be the mandate of the force—to eliminate the whisky traders—they were quite happy to help. The whisky trade had ravaged the Blackfoot community—one trader reported that at least seventy Bloods had been killed in drunken quarrels in the winter of 1871–72 alone—and few of the Blackfoot chiefs themselves had been free of drunken tragedies, so there was hope that the police would be able to stop the trade. Which they did, and remarkably quickly. It was, depending on your point of view, a triumph of community policing or the introduction of a police state on the western plains. In either case, it worked, and almost everyone except the traders was glad.

The Belly and St. Mary Rivers are tributaries of the Old Man's River and, riding northwest from Fort Whoop-Up, the North-West Mounted Police reached the banks of the Old Man's River, making camp on an island in the river where Potts recommended that a fort be built, right in the heart of his homeland, between Blood and Peigan territory. It would be easy to defend, if that ever became necessary; wood for building and fuel was close by, and hay could be grown in the river bottom in summer; and the river had plenty of fish, with deer and elk and small game in the brushlands and antelope and buffalo still roaming the grasslands. They called it Camp Macleod after their commanding officer, set up a corral for the horses, and then built a stable before turning to construction of the fort (supervised by the resourceful D.W. Davis) on October 13, 1874. Having split up the troops along their way across the prairies to set up other forts, they now had only a hundred and fifty men. Three years later, with scheduled departures (such as Ned Maunsell's) and defections, they were down to 113, with as many horses, maintained across the North-West Territories at the relatively modest cost of $1,000 per man and horse per year, compared to $1,500 for a cavalryman and horse in the United States. A small medical unit was attached to the fort and became the first hospital in southern Alberta; they built a larger one ten years later when the new fort was constructed on the townsite. And within the next few years, a hospital (run by the Grey Nuns) was opened on the Blood reserve, celebrated in the local newspaper as "the first Indian hospital in North America." A year later it received the gift of a pipe organ from one Eusèbe Brodeur, an organ builder from St. Hyacinthe, Quebec, teacher of the craft to the Casavants, and brother of the Sister Superior. The curious customs of the newcomers fascinated the Blackfoot, who sometimes responded to them as others would to the curiosities of primitive peoples.

. . .

Despite his early reputation as a warrior, and his habit of standing a good distance from a friend of his while they took pistol shots at each other to shave their whiskers, Jerry Potts was a mostly genial presence in and around town, and became a very good friend of my grandfather's in the late 1880s and '90s. His taciturn manner was the subject of many anecdotes, but he was not nearly as hot-tempered as some stories suggest, and he always took the easiest way. If that meant a measure of violence, so be it. But one of his favourite stories showed a different side. In May 1875, over thirty of his horses were stolen by Assiniboine raiders, who took them to Montana. A year earlier he would have mounted up and gone on a raid to recover the horses, and remove a few scalps if anyone interfered. But, alert to the new order of things, he secured a letter of introduction to the U.S. Cavalry from Colonel Macleod and went south, where he was escorted into the Assiniboine camp by a cavalry officer and gathered up his horses, mercilessly mocking the infuriated horse thieves, who were as unaccustomed to such a bloodless coup as he was.

Jerry's abbreviated style of speech in English made it easy to underestimate him when it came to the subtleties of civilization, and he sometimes seemed at a loss when institutional or legal jargon came into play. But my grandfather said that for all his seeming disengagement from whatever was going on around him, he was always on the watch and was a very good listener, one who could make you make sense by the quality of his attention... provided he felt you had something interesting to say.

After the police had built the fort and settled in for the winter, Potts insisted, in his straightforward fashion, that since they were camped in Blackfoot territory they should meet with the most widely respected statesman-chief of the Blackfoot as soon as possible. So on the first of December that year Colonel Macleod rode north to Blackfoot Crossing on the banks of the Bow River to meet Crowfoot, head chief of the Siksika nation at the time. My grandfather didn't arrive there for another ten years, but one of his favourite stories, widely told in the histories of the western plains, had to do with that meeting. Surrounded by nearly two thousand Indians, their tipis spread out for miles across the prairies, Macleod spoke first, paying tribute to Crowfoot and his people, asking permission to come into their country, praising the chief's statesmanship, promising to safeguard the Blackfoot tribes from the scourge of whisky and their lands from settlement before a formal treaty was made between the Great Mother and the chiefs, and to maintain the peace for all people. And he said that his word would be his covenant with them, and that he would always keep his word. He spoke for about three minutes, conscious of ceremonial protocol as the guest. "We are glad to be here," he concluded. Jerry Potts translated, and Crowfoot listened carefully.

Then Chief Crowfoot began a long speech, in Blackfoot, during which he picked up a handful of earth and held it to his chest while he pulled out the grass and flung it in the direction of Colonel Macleod, motioned to the river flowing east and to the mountains in the west, pointed at the Mounted Police horses with unmistakable scorn, and described a herd of buffalo going over a buffalo jump and then a buffalo hunt on horseback, eyes flashing and feet stomping and arms waving and voice rising. Macleod, who had not yet learned Blackfoot and couldn't understand a word, got nervous. Worried by the chief's energetic—and maybe belligerent?—gestures, Macleod turned to Potts and asked, "What's he saying, Jerry?" "Damn glad, too," replied Potts.

That meeting between Colonel Macleod and Chief Crowfoot, for all its apparent incongruity, marked the beginning of a remarkably good relationship between the Blackfoot and the North-West Mounted Police, which meant between the

Blackfoot and Canada. And this extended to Red Crow, chief of the Bloods, whom Macleod recognized in the community around Fort Macleod as a leader to be reckoned with, and to be trusted. And he himself was respected by Red Crow. Friendships helped, as they almost always do; and the friendships that developed between Macleod and Crowfoot (*Isapo-Muxika*) and between Macleod and Red Crow (*Mékaisto*) owed much to Jerry Potts, and played an important part in the successes of that period. So did keeping your promises.

Did those two ways of welcoming, from two conventions in which courtesies and candour counted but were bound into different languages and different ceremonial traditions, mean that Colonel Macleod and Chief Crowfoot lived in two worlds? I grew up with this question; and I still think the answer is yes and no. Customs shape the way we live in the world, and govern everything from codes of conduct to political actions. They also influence our scientific and religious stories, our histories and myths. We instruct our children in the complicated customs that govern these—which is to say that govern and guarantee belief—and they sometimes seem very strange to those from another community. But that strangeness I described earlier paradoxically gives us all something in common—the arbitrariness of words and signs, those "meaningless signs linked to meaningless sounds" through which we build the "shape and meaning" of the world that McLuhan talked about. Translations like Jerry Potts's underscore this by their apparent inadequacy, highlighting the artifice of every ceremony, including the most familiar of all, the ceremony of language. Aside from his exceptional skills as a scout, one of the reasons Potts became such an important figure in the foothills during this time was not his quirky character or his laconic style but the way in which, perhaps by instinct and perhaps by design, he both drew attention to the strangeness of different customs and found a way of accommodating them by offering his own strange mediation. He was an avant-garde artist as well as an idiosyncratic (and at times somewhat confusing) interpreter, alerting everyone to the artifice of all communication. Certainly my grandfather thought that much of his apparent bumbling was deliberate. Defamiliarization, the modernist literary critics call it. Making the familiar strange and the strange familiar . . . that's what the arts do all the time. Jerry was just before his time. Or maybe right on time. Recognizing the strangeness in his people's stories, he helped the newcomers see and hear it in their own. And he helped them recognize how every chronicle of events, as a record of what happened, must also be a ceremony of belief if it is to be taken as true.

5

THE ARISTOCRATS
OF THE PLAINS

"Some great wonder, that he could believe...."
KING ARTHUR, IN *SIR GAWAIN AND THE GREEN KNIGHT*

...

"IT WOULD HAVE BEEN AS EASY to count or to estimate the leaves in a forest as to calculate the number of buffalo living at any time during the history of the species prior to 1870," said the American zoologist William Hornaday a decade later. Long bull trains freighting supplies across the plains, with six or more wagons and a couple of hundred oxen hauling up to a hundred tons, often had to be bunched together and remain quiet for several hours to permit the buffalo to pass; and wherever they were encountered in herds the buffalo would blacken the plains, moving as though one unbroken robe sometimes twenty miles in width and sixty miles in length—the sight overwhelming observers and defying accurate description, with counting made more difficult by the fact that at certain times of year, such as after the fall rut, the smaller autonomous herds would come together in mega-herds.

The Milk River ridge, where Ned Maunsell and the North-West Mounted Police were camped, is a good place to start talking about the buffalo that once ruled the plains and whose departure transformed the Blackfoot and all the other Aboriginal peoples of the region. The Milk is a tributary of the Missouri, the "Mighty Mo" of song and story, and is the only river in Canada that is part of the great Mississippi drainage basin; and that vantage point on the ridge, from which you can see rivers running north and south and east to the corners of the earth, offers a historical as well as geographical perspective on the great plains of the northwest, reflected in the myths and the movements of the Blackfoot following the buffalo through the seasons. I should add that the proper scientific name for buffalo is "bison"; but since we are going with nicknames in this story, I'll stick with buffalo.

Iinii was the Blackfoot name for buffalo. Buffalo had roamed the plains for half a million years in one form or another—originally giant, then by evolutionary steps smaller—with what many of us now call plains buffalo (identified by naturalists in wonderfully emphatic language as *Bison bison bison*) flourishing around ten thousand years ago, in numbers estimated to be as high as seventy-five million.

Sometimes as tall as six feet at the shoulder and ten or twelve feet in length, and weighing upwards of a ton, one buffalo alone commanded respect, and thousands running in a herd were an awesome sight. And an absolute necessity. Buffalo gave the plains Indians everything they needed by way of food and clothes and footwear, along with hides for tipis and shields and all sorts of tools and glues, as well as sinews for thread and bowstrings, stomach liners for water and food containers, ribs for sled runners, and skins to write on and rattles to dance with. (I wonder what definition Mr. Gradgrind would have come up with.) As well, the spirit of the buffalo informed their lives in many ways, and their seasonal migration dictated the movement of the tribes when the buffalo moved around the hills and across the plains in vast herds that blackened the whole country and blocked out the grass. Buffalo hunts became national events, and often nourished rare cooperation among the First Nations of the western plains.

Aboriginal people, more or less ancestral to the Blackfoot, had been in southern Alberta for more than thirteen thousand years. Blackfoot culture, like all human culture, originally moved on foot, and this influenced the small size of their social and economic units, and the ways in which such bands could come together in tribal communities to improve hunting capacity. That turned out to be an effective arrangement even after they took to horses, but there were certainly inconveniences when they only had dogs. Tipis had to be small, so that they could be hauled on a travois by the dogs; and limited movement meant that they were much more vulnerable to the weather, and much less able to modify their lives or their livelihood than they proved to be when horses came along. Before horses, the Blackfoot followed the buffalo on foot, creeping up on them downwind or surprising them from behind a bluff, spearing them or shooting them with bows and arrows. Sometimes they would chase them along prairie driveways—marked with stones and shrubs and sticks draped with coyote or wolf hides—into makeshift corrals or "buffalo pounds," or (perhaps as recently as the 1860s) run them through narrowing pens over natural rock outcrops, called buffalo jumps, at the bottom of which they would slaughter them with clubs and spears. Even when the Blackfoot became accustomed to horses, they remembered the stories of older times that they had grown up with, stories of making their way across the plains on foot—exaggerated, of course, like those I told my children about walking ten miles barefoot to school and back, both ways uphill, with temperatures so cold that words froze as they came out of people's mouths and you had to break them off one by one so you could tell what they were saying. But the Blackfoot stories, unlike mine, ensured that the lessons of survival were not lost. And scouts still went on foot to assess the movements of enemies or the migrations of buffalo, or when and where the berries were ripening, well into my grandfather's time in the territory.

In the early years of the nineteenth century, the Blackfoot were frequently camped in the United States at the head of the Missouri and in the rich valleys of the Judith mountain range, moving back and forth across the not-yet-established border to follow the buffalo, as their ancestors had done for millennia; and they were often described by traders and explorers as "American Indians." But by the 1840s, the Blackfoot were more often at home in the foothills of Alberta, prompted by trade in furs with the British, plentiful berries in the foothills and the availability of wood and water and shelter from the weather, as well as from the tribal warfare that had left many of their community dead; shelter too from the grass fires that were the occasional scourge of the plains, bearing down with what the naturalist John Macoun described as "the speed of a fast horse.... As [one] came near us the whirling smoke and flames seemed to take the forms of living things that were in terrible agony."

. . .

Wolves—and dogs—were said to have taught the Blackfoot how to hunt the buffalo in groups or packs, as Crop Eared Wolf told my grandfather, but wolves also taught them (with transparent self-interest) that animals with hoofs and horns were all right to eat, but those with paws and claws should be left alone. Horses were never keen on this, but when the Blackfoot got big horses in the early eighteenth century and called them *ponokaomitai-ksi*, or elk-dogs, horses felt a bit better, because this put them in the company of the dogs that were important to the Blackfoot—they had hauled the belongings of plains Indians on travois for well over five thousand years, and were still used that way in some Indian communities on the prairies when my grandfather came there—and elk antlers were used in sacred rituals, with women sometimes wearing elk tooth ornaments on their dresses.

Even allowing for the importance of buffalo hunting on horseback, the horse soon meant something much more to the Blackfoot. And the Blackfoot are certainly not alone in their respect for horses, both real and imagined. For millennia, horses have provided a ceremonial centre as well as a commercial and military asset for civilized societies—a still point in a turbulent world. One of the most famous of these equestrian ceremonies, profoundly influencing social, economic, political and religious life in Europe and beyond, was chivalry. The name brought together the French word for horse, *cheval*, with *chevalerie*, signifying knighthood; and it came to define an archetypal horse culture, combining gentleness with force and the secular with the sacred, and creating an ideal of wandering within the reality of a settled society, the chivalric knight having one eye on the horizon and the other on his home. Like the nomadic warrior of the Asian steppes or the romantic wanderer of ancient China or the buffalo hunter and warrior chief of the plains tribes, the medieval knight was a carefree rebel living within a strict set of courtesies that maintained a balance between freedom and discipline, love and war, life and art. One of the great moments of European literature, from the medieval poem *Sir Gawain and the Green Knight*, takes place when King Arthur, hosting a Christmas feast, asks for *sum mayn mervayle, that he myght trawe*—some great wonder, that he could believe—and through the door rides a giant of a knight on horseback, beautifully adorned and dangerously powerful.

The Blackfoot believed in such horses, and such horse riders. They had saddles and bridles and all sorts of other horse tack richly woven and worked for both war and peace, and for the ceremonies of each that had become part of their culture. And they were certainly aware of the other great plains Indian horse breeders of the time, being avid and envied breeders themselves. They would not have known about the Persian horses with leopard spots; but the great mid-nineteenth-century Blood chief Many Spotted Horses had a herd of over five hundred paints and pintos, many of which would have been Appaloosas, bred along the banks of the Palouse River by another famous horse culture, the Nez Perce. Other horses would have been raided from the Crow or the Cree or Assiniboine, or the Shoshone or the Sioux. Blackfoot breeding both for performance and for conformation was renowned; and they loved particular colours. Like sorrel.

Horses were first brought to the Americas by Christopher Columbus on his second voyage in 1494—he arrived with twenty-four stallions and ten mares and a significant number of cattle. Some say he simply brought horses *back*, for there were stories (scientific, it turns out) about ancient "dawn horses" that roamed the rain forests and swamps of the Americas for millions of years before some of their descendants travelled across the land bridge to Asia and Europe and north Africa, while those that stayed behind disappeared around ten thousand years ago, victims of climate changes and predators, including humans. But some insist that a few remained, hiding in the box canyons and highland gorges of the west until their kin came back with Columbus. In any event, on the island of Hispaniola where Columbus landed, the horses he brought over thrived, creating in remarkably short order substantial herds along with skilled horsemen who adapted Spanish equestrian techniques and equipment to the new environment. When the Spaniards moved on to the other parts of the Caribbean, Central America, Venezuela and Brazil, they found the horses were slow to adapt to the tropical regions; but when they got to the pampas of Argentina and the plains of the American southwest, the horses knew they were home again. In times when feed was scarce, the Spanish set the horses free to roam; and within a few years the pampas were, in the words of one observer at the beginning of the seventeenth century, "covered with escaped horses in such numbers that when they go anywhere they look like woods from a distance." They were spreading out too across the North American plains, and a traveller reported in 1777 that in the Rio Grande area of Texas there were so many horses that "their trails make the country, utterly uninhabited by people, look as if it were the most populated in the world."

The indigenous people took to horses in different ways. Initially, the Spanish were careful not to let horses into enemy hands. But the remarkable uprising of the Pueblo Indians against the Spanish conquerors in 1680, which drove two thousand of them from the Santa Fe area and killed hundreds, resulted in large numbers of horses escaping into the New Mexico desert. Even so, the Pueblo Indians responded cautiously. By contrast, within a generation of acquiring their first horses (some by happenstance but many by theft), the great warrior tribes of the Apache and Comanche were doing things on horseback that astonished even the skilled Spaniards, and horses were soon in the hands of other plains tribes. There is a story that the Shoshone and the Nez Perce rode horses before they ever met a white man; and an Indian named Shaved Head was said to have been the first to "discover" horses among the mountain Indians and bring them to the Blackfoot in the mid-1720s. When the horse arrived the Blackfoot changed their hunting techniques, surrounding the buffalo with a large number of horsemen and shooting the animals as they milled about in a circle, or chasing them, with each rider singling out a buffalo to kill. By the 1830s the Blackfoot were almost exclusively hunting by the chase, still using lances or clubs or shooting with bows and arrows until breech-loading rifles became available in the 1870s (since muzzle-loading muskets were very difficult to reload while on a running horse). Racing along beside a herd at high speed past the slower bulls to the cows in the lead, the rider would bring his horse close to the buffalo he had picked out, slot an arrow (from the couple of dozen in his quiver) to his bowstring and aim at a spot described by William Hornaday as "from 12 to 18 inches in circumference ... immediately back of the foreleg with its lowest point on a line with the elbow." As the arrow was shot, a well-trained horse would swerve away from the buffalo to avoid disaster if she collapsed in front of them, and swing back if a second shot was required. The rider would have coiled the long end of his bridle rope under his belt, so that if he was thrown and not seriously hurt he could retrieve his horse and continue the chase. There were still some Blackfoot hunting on foot, their speed and stamina amazing to everyone; but with horses the Blackfoot became not only skilled buffalo hunters but also fearsome warriors and exquisite connoisseurs of the horse ... especially those belonging to their enemies.

Hunting on horseback required great skill, as well as a knowledge of the anatomy and physiology of the buffalo and their different instincts and movements when running in a herd or running alone. It also required fast horses, selected and bred for speed and agility; and Joe Healy, who had followed the last of the buffalo herds into Judith Basin in Montana in the late 1870s, told my grandfather over dinner in the Macleod Hotel one night about how a couple of first-class buffalo-hunting horses would be kept in each band, with hunters riding other horses out to the hunt. In another account by a contemporary, the buffalo horses "seemed to know better than the men what to do amid the dangers of a hunt, for when suddenly a buffalo turned upon them they sprang aside to escape the danger and pursued afresh." The Bloods, it was said, were often in charge of a hunt because they had the fastest horses.

The sophisticated arrangements that sustained buffalo hunting both before and after the arrival of horses, with other tribes joining in depending on where the buffalo were and how they were congregated, generated economic and social conditions that often surprise those who hold on to stereotypes of hunting and gathering societies, especially nomadic ones like the traditional Blackfoot. Subsistence was never a minimal condition for the people of the plains; nor was it for any of the Aboriginal peoples of the Americas; and subsistence and surplus were certainly not competing conditions in Blackfoot society. Subsistence meant having everything you needed, spiritually as well as materially; it was a condition of sovereignty within nature rather than dominion over it. And surpluses were relatively common, with buffalo meat and berries dried and stored for distribution during the winter season.

There had long been a regular accumulation of capital in the form of medicine bundles and dances, as well as sacred and secular songs, in Blackfoot society, but after the early eighteenth century, horses as emblems of prestige and power became another kind of surplus quite consistent with a subsistence economy. Of course there were periods of hardship and scarcity, as there are in all times and places; but capitalism and socialism are European "isms" and schisms, not those of the plains Indians; and surpluses, while not exactly routine, were a familiar part of life, nourishing the kind of balance between work and play, and between the demands of the day and the display of beauty in visual and verbal arts as well as dance and music, which we all cherish.

. . .

The disappearance of the buffalo must have seemed inconceivable to those who had grown up watching tens of thousands of animals pass by in a season, though we should all know what that feels like from watching once-familiar species become extinct in our contemporary world. The buffalo collapse was foreshadowed by some of the Blackfoot seers, and by those who had followed the seasonal movements of the buffalo, with runners and scouts bringing back information more sophisticated than contemporary GPS technology, information that included detailed reports on the flora and fauna upon which the buffalo depended, and the size and health of the calf crop.

By the 1870s many Blackfoot saw it coming, though not nearly as quickly as it did; and there is little doubt that the Blackfoot agreement to Treaty Seven was brought about in part because some signs of trouble were clear. The government negotiators painted a gloomy picture, noting that the continuing presence of buffalo on the northern plains contrasted starkly with the situation south of the border, where the buffalo had almost disappeared from many of their traditional grazing lands. The Blackfoot knew this, for they moved back and forth and had many close kin there in Montana Blackfeet country. But as one elder said, "We thought we had more time." They didn't. Nor did the buffalo, who were gone from the northern plains within a decade.

Some warning signs had been noted, but just as in another environmental disaster—the collapse of the Atlantic cod fisheries at the end of the twentieth century—they were often dismissed, or misconstrued. In the case of the cod, many of those who spent their lives harvesting them, and even the scientists with nothing at stake (except their reputations), got it wrong. But beginning in the nineteenth century fishermen had noticed that the oil content of cod livers—a lucrative product—depended on where the fish were caught. This worried them, and they wanted more attention paid to local habitat and spawning cycles to counter the widespread belief that cod roamed throughout the northern Atlantic relatively unaffected by regional catches. Even as notable a scientist as Charles Darwin's friend Thomas Huxley, alert to the concern but oblivious to its urgency, proclaimed (in an address to the Great International Fisheries Exhibition in 1883 in London) that, while it might be possible to exhaust some inland fish species such as river salmon, the number of ocean fishes such as cod was "so inconceivably great that the number we catch is relatively insignificant, and . . . the magnitude of the destructive forces at work upon them [in their natural environment] is so prodigious that the destruction effected by the fishermen cannot sensibly increase the death rate." Barely a hundred years later, the great cod fishery had been virtually eliminated.

Just so, the buffalo dominated the plains until the 1870s, their numbers also inconceivably great and seemingly inexhaustible, even though it was clear that their range was being encroached upon and their habitat imperilled by human settlement and by fences, a menace for almost any wild animal. But other troubles were mounting as a lucrative trade in buffalo hides and robes attracted both skilled plains Indian and Métis hunters and an assortment of enterprising non-native buffalo hunters from across the continent. Their collective enterprise devastated the herds and destroyed a way of life that had defined plains Indian culture for millennia, just as the earlier trades in sealskins and whale oil had come close to wiping out entire species along with many island and coastal cultures around the world. In all these cases, the slaughter was aided and abetted by new technologies. In the case of the buffalo, horses certainly played their part, but it was the trade in robes—fostered by the demand for buffalo skins for machinery drive belts, improved tanning methods (with strong lime), and contemporary clothing fashions—that did them in, with railways providing easy transportation to markets and the repeating rifles used by both Indian and white hunters bringing an industrial-scale enterprise to the hunt. Well-equipped and brutally wasteful Euro-American hunters played a major role in the carnage, as they set out to gather up a valuable commodity as fast as they could, in any way they could, and with nothing like their own way of life at stake. One of them, Josiah Wright Mooar, was said to have killed over twenty thousand buffalo between 1870 and 1879, in his case mostly along the Texas Panhandle; and in 1876, sixty thousand hides were shipped down the Missouri River to eastern markets from Fort Benton. Certainly the arrival of the North-West Mounted Police, followed within a couple of years by the treaty commissioners and the opening of the territory for settlement, signalled a momentous change in the life and livelihood of the Blackfoot in the foothills of Alberta; but the breathtakingly fast demise of the buffalo changed their world more than strangers ever could. And to make it more traumatic, they went hand in hand.

The national governments in Canada and the United States took note but did next to nothing, intermittently passing legislation that was unenforceable, and encouraging slaughter that was unsustainable and settlement that was throttling the life out of the buffalo's range. Instead, the Canadian government spent time and energy exaggerating Indian hostility south of the border in order to implement treaties designed to pacify First Nations on the Canadian prairies, and to justify the expenditure involved to a mostly eastern public that was grumbling about their taxes.

Whom and what to blame? As the scale of the devastation became apparent, the Blackfoot occasionally blamed the Cree, with whom they had historically belligerent relations, and the Métis, who did not have their sense of the territorial protocols of the buffalo hunt. Many said that the Sun Spirit was angry because they had let the white men wreak such havoc. But the Blackfoot recognized that they were parties to the trade, and thereby to the slaughter. However they interpreted this particular crisis, the Blackfoot were acutely aware that both natural and supernatural powers were infinitely greater than human ones, for better or for worse, and that the will of the Creator, unfathomable as it might be, governed both ordinary and extraordinary events. They believed in "acts of God," though with much less self-interest than our insurance companies. Indeed, in ways acknowledged by some of the early missionaries, the Blackfoot had the kind of faith—though not the specific forms of belief—that Christianity espoused, recognizing that the same power that could say "every beast of the forest is mine, and the cattle upon a thousand hills," in the words of Psalm 50, could strike off those multitudes of forest animals and take away the millions of buffalo that once roamed the foothills. Since the scale of the loss wasn't apparent until two years after Treaty Seven, some of the Blackfoot thought they were being punished for signing the treaty, pointing to the fact that three of the Blood chiefs who signed it died before the year was out. But overall, the Blackfoot response to the disappearance of the buffalo during the decades after 1880 demonstrated their ability to change while remaining the same. Hugh Dempsey, who has listened to many stories told by those who were around back then, reports that "their tales of the last days of freedom and the destruction of their old ways of life were not filled with bitterness or anger. They were told plainly and simply as facts that could not be changed through the passage of time."

The Blackfoot had come into this time as the most powerful people of the northern prairies, "the aristocrats of the plains," and one of the great horse cultures in the world, rivalling those of the Asian steppes and the Arabian desert millennia earlier, and the chivalric culture of medieval Europe. With their powerful status among the great Indian tribes of the west came a wealth of experience in the ways of the world, which for them included centuries of wars and diseases and climate changes that had intermittently altered their tribal and territorial alliances. To be sure, this seemed like no other time in their history. But their storytellers told of other drastic events that they had survived, and after which their sovereignty had sometimes even been enhanced... as was the case when the horse transformed their lives a mere hundred and fifty years earlier, within the memory of grandchildren... just like the story I am telling.

The frightening difference, of course, was that this was happening at a fearsome pace, that it was happening everywhere in their homeland, and that it was happening to the buffalo, who for thousands of years had provided sustenance and health to body and soul for the Indians of the plains.

And although the collapse of the buffalo was devastating, and happened brutally quickly, the Blackfoot knew from stories passed down to them of climate changes that had transformed not only the plant and animal populations but the geography of their whole world, the waters rising and falling and land thrusting up and wearing down all over the plains, some of it happening long before human habitation on the planet and linked to their stories of the creation of the world as we know it. Stories were told of inland seas (out of which horses emerged millions of years ago, some said, which is not far from the scientific account of the evolution of the horse in the Americas) and of upland volcanoes like the Mazuma eruption that geologists tell us happened seven or eight thousand years ago in the Cascade Range in Oregon, forming Crater Lake and being followed (as Blackfoot stories tell it) by a time of darkness and dry snow. And there were much more recent memories, told by men and women who were alive back then, of the "little ice age" of the seventeenth to nineteenth centuries. As Dempsey writes, "elders related stories that encouraged conformity to band mores and a common understanding of the band's place in a charged supernatural world." Which isn't that different from what many of us are taught. We learn early that there are some things we cannot control, and must surrender to. The weather. Disease. Death. For some, religion teaches us to accept such things. Science shows us we don't always have to. Balancing the stories of religion and science, and admitting that sometimes both get it wrong, is something we have not yet learned to do very well.

. . .

Every tribe in the Blackfoot Confederacy was divided into bands, each with its own chief. This was a practical organization, as well as a matter of traditional principle, for the small number of men and women and children in a band—say twenty or thirty families—was an efficient group for travelling and camping, and the bands got together when the buffalo were moving in large herds, as well as in the winter camps and during wartime.

Each tribe, in turn, had both a war chief and a peace chief, though the distinction seems to have been easily misconstrued by outsiders, for both would have war records, and either could claim authority by the force of his argument on a particular subject. That said, one of them would be acknowledged as the head chief, and his decisions held on most everyday matters. But in times of serious trouble, the war chief would come to the fore.

The lines of authority were relatively clear, and disagreements would normally be talked through until a decision was taken... and then the authority of one or the other was (usually) strictly observed. Recognizing this, and admiring its effectiveness, the police fostered close and constructive relations with the chiefs, relying on them to maintain order and good governance in their community at a time when these traditional lines of authority were still respected. Over and over again, conflicts and controversies that had the potential to be divisive and possibly dangerous to the wider community were dealt with by the chiefs, sometimes sternly. The key was the continuing presence and the power of customary tribal sanctions and incentives. When these were subverted or destroyed, as they were by the relentless social engineering of the Indian Act and its field agents, things spun out of control in many communities.

Traditionally, life in camp was centred around the tipis, made with long poles tied together in a cone, covered with buffalo hide and decorated with designs telling of events and powers both material and spiritual. The tipis could be taken down and put up easily when the families moved between their summer home out on the plains and their winter residence closer to the mountains; a fire kept the tipi warm in winter, while a flap at the top let out the smoke and kept the inside cool in summer. The simple style of the tipi masks a sophisticated sectioning of space that caught the elements of curve and cone which defined the dwelling itself, with private and public areas clearly defined and decorated accordingly, comfort being paramount. Indeed, the interior was certainly as comfortable as a Victorian parlour, with cushions and carpets and blankets and backrests, and when family and friends came, the hosts would offer food and share a pipe to

make them welcome and give thanks. The floor plan was ellipti-
cal rather than circular, with the skin cover held down by large
stones that would be left in "tipi rings" from year to year when
the tribe moved between winter and summer camps. The
entrance to a tipi always faced east to the rising sun, and that side
of the tipi was the public space, while the west side was private
and used for sacred ceremonies. The north was the men's quarters, the south the women's, and the beds were along the tipi
walls, with occasional adaptations for particular occasions. The
hearth was always in the centre, with a tie-down peg to which a
rope around the lodge poles would be attached in high winds,
not unusual on the plains and in the foothills.

And from early days right through my grandfather's time,
fun in camp was a feature of Blackfoot life. There were games
for children and adults; singing and storytelling; drumming
and dancing: the tea dance, for instance where men and women
would compete to see who could drink the most tea and still
keep on dancing; and the laughing contest dance, when two
groups would choose a man from one side and a woman from
the other to see who could get the other to laugh first by singing and telling stories and making funny gestures, the loser
providing the meat and bannock and other food for the dance
the next week. And there was the most important dance—
indeed the most important ceremony—in the Blackfoot community, the sacred annual Sun Dance, sponsored by a woman
and held after the Berry Moon in summer when the saskatoon
berries were ripening.

The significance of the Sun Dance was first of all religious;
but the line between the secular and the sacred was not neatly
drawn in Blackfoot society . . . indeed in some respects there

wasn't any line at all. Spiritual powers as much as material sustenance nourished both individual and collective well-being, as
they often have in the history of humankind; and the Sun Dance
was as important as a celebration of the tribal communities as it
was a consolidation of individual welfare. In that sense, it was
much closer to Judaism than to Christianity, just as the sense of
covenantal promises was, though the Sun Dance shared
Christianity's acknowledgement of the sacredness of suffering,
signified in the Crucifixion and the sacrificial torment under-
taken by select—usually self-selected—men. And the way in
which all this was interpreted was through song and story ... just
as it is in the Bible. So when some of the missionaries and police
opposed the Sun Dance on grounds that it encouraged the telling of stories of enemy raids and horse captures, always under-
taken at risk and sometimes (as with Crop Eared Wolf's
experience) occasioning injury or even death—because it would
encourage young men to try for themselve—they caught its
importance while missing its significance ... unless they paid
attention to the readings of the Old Testament and New
Testament at church the next week.

6

TREATY SEVEN

"To acknowledge the Indian title . . .
and to treat for it with much gravity,
as if with a sovereign power."
DUNCAN CAMPBELL SCOTT, 1913

. . .

COURTESY COUNTS FOR MUCH, especially when customs differ. It creates responsibility, and respect. When the leaders of the Blackfoot Confederacy gathered at Blackfoot Crossing on the Bow River in mid-September of 1877 to consider the offer of a treaty from the government of Canada—or more precisely from the Great Mother, Queen Victoria—courtesies were the currency of the formal exchanges between them and their counterparts, the government negotiators James Macleod, commissioner of the North-West Mounted Police, and David Laird, lieutenant-governor and Indian superintendent of the North-West Territories. They masked both anxieties and ambitions, and they characterized the rhetoric on both sides.

The timing was set to coincide with the seasonal routines of the confederacy. (In fact some of the Blackfoot such as Joe Healy, and a few leaders including the Peigan chief Big Swan, were away hunting what buffalo they could find when the negotiations began.) The gathering was originally to be in Fort Macleod, at the centre of Blood and Peigan country; but Fort Macleod was where the North-West Mounted Police were located, and Crowfoot refused to meet in a white man's fort, insisting instead on his Blackfoot (*Siksika*) tribe's homeland territory at its traditional gathering place, Blackfoot Crossing.

The tribes in the Blackfoot Confederacy acted together in agreeing to what was presented to them by the new Dominion of Canada on behalf of Queen Victoria, while they struggled with conditions that were variously incomprehensible, inconceivable or misunderstood.

The first misunderstanding, however, was the government's assumption that Crowfoot was chief of the Blackfoot nation; but there was no such thing as a single Blackfoot nation. It does not seem to have been deliberate (though it almost certainly made success more likely) but it indicated something about the boilerplate character of treaty making. The treaties, by British and European tradition, were nation-to-nation agreements. Yet the Blackfoot was a confederacy of tribal sovereignties, each with its own political and constitutional dynamics. The misunderstanding was particularly ironic, given that Canada itself had followed the United States in departing from the eighteenth-century European idea of absolute and indivisible sovereign power residing in independent nation-states, opting instead for divided sovereignties flowing from the people and vested in provincial or state and federal governance, a concept some say the Americans borrowed from the Iroquois Confederacy. The Blackfoot Confederacy may not have had the same clarity as the Iroquois did to outsiders; but it had its own political formalities and courtesies which the

North-West Mounted Police appreciated even if they did not always comprehend, and upon which they based their practice of dealing with the chiefs of band and tribal jurisdiction.

So when Crowfoot was singled out by the government as *the* chief, a status that emerged because of his considerable diplomatic skills in dealing with the newcomers and his undeniable leadership abilities, some of the other chiefs—several of them with greater influence among the Blackfoot tribes than Crowfoot—were understandably irritated. Red Crow of the Bloods, for example, had a larger following and often exercised greater authority in decisions of the confederacy; and the Bloods and the Peigans were both unhappy with the change of venue from their territory to Blackfoot Crossing, and were strategically late in arriving for the negotiations. Indeed, Red Crow initially thought that the presence of the Blood tribe's war chief and one of its great orators, Medicine Calf, would be enough, and there would be no need for him to attend. And many from throughout the confederacy were not at all sure about the treaty. Some (such as Medicine Calf) were strongly opposed; many were confused by its commitments; and some just didn't think it was all that significant. The winter count for that year kept by Blackfoot elder Father of Many Children recorded "*Itsiparkap-otomiop*"— when we had a bad spring. No mention was made of a treaty; and even the next year was described simply as a "mild winter."

David Laird opened the gathering with a tribute to both the Great Spirit, who in his words "has made all things, the sun, the moon, and the stars, the earth, the forests, and the swift running rivers," and the Great Mother, the Queen, "who by the Great Spirit rules over this great country and other great countries."

And now the Queen has sent Colonel Macleod and myself to ask you to make a treaty. But in a very few years the buffalo will probably be all destroyed, and for this reason the Queen wishes to help you live in the future in some other way. She wishes you to allow her white children to come and live on your land and raise cattle, and should you agree to this, she will assist you to raise cattle and grain, and thus give you the means of living when the buffalo are no more. She will also pay you and your children money every year, which you can spend as you please. By being paid in money you cannot be cheated, as with it you can buy what you think proper.

Discussion took place over several days, and the chiefs of the Blackfoot tribes conferred among themselves, often seeking the advice of elders. Crowfoot turned to one named Pemmican, whose wisdom, spiritual as well as material, he respected. Twice he went to his lodge, and twice Pemmican would say nothing. Then, on a third visit from Crowfoot, he spoke:

I want to hold you back because I am at the edge of a bank. My life is at its end. I hold you back because your life henceforth will be very different from what it has been. Buffalo makes your body strong. What you will eat from this money will have your people buried all over these hills. You will be tied down, you will not wander the plains; the whites will take over your land and fill it. You won't have your own free will; the whites will lead you by a halter. That is why I say don't sign. But my life is old, so sign if you want to. Go ahead and make the treaty.

Crowfoot was disturbed; but shortly afterwards, Red Crow came to him with the decision of the Bloods, who were by no means unanimously in favour. As for Red Crow, he was cautious, but he trusted his friend Colonel Macleod; and having gained the support of his tribal council—not an easy task with some powerful chiefs opposed—his message to Crowfoot was that the Bloods would sign if he and his followers would. That afternoon, Crowfoot gave his famous acceptance speech to the commissioners.

While I speak, be kind and patient. I speak for my people, who are numerous, and who rely upon me to follow that course which in the future will tend to their good. The plains are large and wide. We are the children of the plains, it is our home, and the buffalo has been our food always. I hope you look upon the Blackfeet, Bloods and Sarcees as your children now, and that you will be indulgent and charitable to them. They all expect me to speak now for them, and I trust the Great Spirit will put into their breasts to be a good people—into the minds of the men, women and children, and their future generations.

The advice given me and my people has proved to be very good: if the Police had not come to the country, where would we all be now? Bad men and whiskey were killing us so fast that very few, indeed, of us would have been left today. The Police have protected us as the feathers of the bird protect it from the frosts of winter. I wish them all good, and trust that all our hearts will increase in goodness from this time forward. I am satisfied. I will sign the treaty.

He was followed by Red Crow, who expressed confidence in his friend James Macleod, rather than in the paper document. For him, being as good as your word was the test, and Macleod had passed it.

> *Three years ago, when the police first came to the country, I met and shook hands with Stamixotokon (Colonel Macleod) at Belly River. Since that time he made me many promises. He kept them all—not one of them was ever broken. Everything that the police have done has been good. I entirely trust Stamixotokon, and will leave everything to him. I will sign with Crowfoot.*

And for his part, Macleod was well aware not only of his personal responsibility but also of that which the Blackfoot had conferred upon the government.

> *You say that I have always kept my promises. As surely as my past promises have been kept, so surely shall those made by the Commissioners be carried out in the future. If they were broken I would be ashamed to meet you or look you in the face; but every promise will be solemnly fulfilled as certainly as the sun now shines down upon us from the heavens.*

It is easy, given the past century and a half, to doubt the good faith of the commissioners; but I believe they meant what they said, just as the Blackfoot leaders did.

. . .

The occasion of Treaty Seven was remarkable in many ways. It was an occasion that seemed, even more than the numbered treaties that preceded it, to signal something special and to symbolize not only all the promises of the other treaties but the participation and collective promise of the non-Indian people of the plains, in this case the rancher and settler community that had come to live in Blackfoot territory. As one later commentator noted, "probably never in the history of the North-West Territories had so many people assembled in one place at the same time." The Blackfoot and Sarcee, along with several bands of Stoneys to the north towards the mountains, were signatories, and made up the majority of people present; but almost all of the residents of Fort Macleod attended, along with many from Fort Calgary (as it then was) along with missionaries, traders, police and plains Indian and Métis observers from across the territory.

A description by Frank Oliver, from Fort Edmonton, gives a good sense of the gathering.

> *There was a numerous and miscellaneous assortment of unattached Indians, half-breeds and whites from the more Northerly plains and the Edmonton settlements on the North Saskatchewan and other Northern points, who were without any special reason for their presence except a desire to see what was to be seen and to tread hitherto forbidden ground. Of these I was one. Eastward from the camp, the valley for miles was full of horses which seemed to be unguarded. But if the herd were approached, a Blackfoot head promptly popped up from among them. This was accepted as notice to move in another direction. Horses were wealth, power, prestige, quick transport that made Indian life on the buffalo plains most*

pleasant and desirable. They were the most valued possession of both Indian and whites, and were guarded accordingly.

Another observer, North-West Mounted Police inspector Cecil Denny, brought a more informed eye to bear on the scene, though one that also overflowed with settler sentimentality. Something was happening to—and with—the new country called Canada as it entered into a covenant not just with "some people," but with an ancient civilization. It was a moment of decision . . . and of what an observer schooled in the tradition of British romantic poetry would have called dread.

There must have been at least a thousand lodges in camps on both sides of the river. . . . Their horses, herded day and night, covered the uplands to the north and south of the camp in thousands. It was a stirring and picturesque scene; great bands of grazing horses, the mounted warriors threading their way among them, and, as far as the eye could reach, the white Indian lodges glimmering among the trees along the river bottom. By night the valley echoed to the dismal howling of the camp's curs, and from sun to sun drums boomed from the tents. Dancing, feasting, conjuring, incantations over the sick, prayers for success in the hunt or in war, all went to form a panorama of wild life vastly novel and entertaining, and seen but once. Never before had such a concourse of Indians assembled on Canada's western plains; never had the tribes appeared so contented and prosperous.

And never before had they been so worried, he might have added. Laird and Macleod—Macleod especially, because he lived there—recognized the challenges of life in that time and place where the settlers were the wayfaring nomads and the Indians were the homeland custodians dealing with unpredictable turns of fortune.

. . .

Treaty Seven was the last of the treaties to be signed during the 1870s, fulfilling (from the government's point of view) the commitment Canada had made when it acquired control of Rupert's Land, as well as the promise to British Columbia when it entered Confederation in 1871 that a transcontinental railway would be built across the great sweep of land held by the Indian tribes. To do that, the government knew it would need to make large land concessions to the company building the railway and later allow for immigration and settlement all along the line; but that could not happen until the land was ceded by the Indians. And so the prairie treaties.

There is no question, when all the rhetoric is set aside, that the government commissioners were agents of settlement in the west. But they were also dedicated to the well-defined principles of international treaties between nations, and well aware they had inherited those principles from the tradition of British–Indian treaty policy enunciated over a century earlier by William Johnson, principles assumed by Canada on Confederation. One of these was articulated in 1913 by the most reliable early twentieth-century historian of Indian affairs (and one of its most controversial officials), Duncan Campbell Scott, as the absolute obligation "to acknowledge the Indian title ... and to treat for it with much gravity, as if with a sovereign power." Another principle was reiterated by Colonel Macleod at the gathering for Treaty Seven, and had been signalled earlier by Adams Archibald, speaking as the lieutenant-governor of Manitoba and the North-West Territories when the first numbered treaty was being negotiated, reminding the new Canadian government that "if we expect our relations with the [First Nations] to be of the kind which is desirable to maintain we must fulfill our obligations with scrupulous fidelity." This was a peace *and* partnership treaty.

The Blackfoot tribes were experienced in international negotiations and treaty making with both allies and enemies; twenty-two years earlier, its chiefs had made a treaty with the "Long Knives," their name for the United States government, a treaty that included the Gros Ventre, Flathead, Pend d'Oreille, Nez Perce and Cree tribes. So they knew what treaties were about. They were about peace—for now, at least. But they had good reason to be anxious as they gathered at Blackfoot Crossing. They had been devastated by the smallpox epidemics that had swept the plains after the coming of the new settlers, the state of the buffalo was deeply troubling, the encroachment by the Cree and the Métis on their hunting grounds was a constant bother, and the scourge of other diseases had become a frighteningly unpredictable threat, having reduced their population by almost half over the past several decades. And as if these were not enough to worry about, that American treaty had long since been broken and they were understandably uneasy about this one, especially with a government that was just ten years old.

. . .

With hindsight, they were right to be anxious, and the reasons go profoundly deeper than some of the actions—or inactions—

that would be sanctioned by Ottawa, which included its sometimes deadly failure to provide the rations mandated by the treaty. *Canada did not keep its word.* That is at the heart of the matter, a breach of faith which has had profound, and poisonous, consequences for both Canada and Chinook country. But precisely because of that it may provide a context for revisiting the treaty now, for recalculating (rather than reconsidering) its promises, and for recovering respect. As an early signal of this possibility, and at a time when the old British Empire was giving way to independent commonwealth nations around the world, Charles, the Prince of Wales and next in line for the throne, attended the hundredth anniversary of Treaty Seven in 1977 on behalf of the "Great Mother," offering an indication of its status among Canada's treaties with First Nations and the unique promise it represents on behalf of all Aboriginal people in Canada. I attended the 125th commemoration at Blackfoot Crossing—*not* a celebration, I was sternly told by several Blackfoot—and there was cautious optimism in the air, some of it the result of a realization that the people had survived and were celebrating not the treaty itself but a new historical interpretive centre and other initiatives by the Blackfoot tribes. The premier of Alberta, Ralph Klein, was there, speaking (to my surprise, but not the Blackfoot's) remarkably fluent Siksika for several minutes, returning the (again, to me surprising) respect accorded him by the Blackfoot. I talked afterwards to Siksika chief Adrian Stimson, and asked him whether he would have signed Treaty Seven had he been here back in 1877. He chuckled, and said probably not; he came from a warrior line, and two of his forebears who were there—Old Sun and Heavy Shield—had not wanted to sign. But they did, persuaded by Crowfoot. That kind of accommodation needs to be remembered, and a new accord reached; for many would now say that Old Sun and Heavy Shield and Medicine Calf were right in their distrust and dissent. Canada needs to find a way of showing that the Blackfoot were right in following the lead of Crowfoot and Red Crow and Big Swan, who signed as a Peigan chief.

There were many problems in the structure and style of the negotiations—if one can give the government proclamations and Blackfoot protests that name—and many, many shameful actions and attitudes followed the signing of the treaty. But there were also moments of surprising promise. At its best, the treaty promised a new kind of covenant between that prairie world and the people who lived in it, as well as with the spirits of the past and the future that inhabit and inform it. And it clearly represented a formal acknowledgement of the sovereignty of the tribes of the Blackfoot Confederacy and the Stoneys. It is often said, usually to underline the duplicitous nature of the negotiations, that this sovereignty was not acknowledged; but it *was*, both by the spirit of treaty making and in the letter of the treaty. The anthropologist and historian Michael Asch, in a very important new book called *On Being Here to Stay*, catches one important indication of this beyond the eighteenth-century principles of treaty making I have referred to, when he notes that the language of the prairie treaties accords the chiefs and headmen the same status to sign a treaty on behalf of their people as the commissioners had on behalf of the Crown. And there was *no* indication that Treaty Seven would change this; indeed, there are plenty of indications in the other numbered treaties, which Treaty Seven echoes, that the sovereign relationship between the Crown and the signatories would be a continuing one. The Supreme Court of Canada has turned to this point often in its recent judgements; and Asch quotes from the preface to its judgement in a case called *Badger* (after the accused, a Treaty Eight Cree arrested for hunting for food on private property), in which the Court outlined certain principles to be applied in interpreting a treaty.

> *First, a treaty represents an exchange of solemn promises between the Crown and the various Indian nations.*
>
> *Second, the honour of the Crown is always at stake; the Crown must be assumed to intend to fulfil its promises. No appearance of "sharp dealing" will be sanctioned.*
>
> *Third, any ambiguities or doubtful expressions must be resolved in favour of the Indians and any limitations restricting the rights of Indians under treaties must be narrowly construed.*
>
> *Finally, the onus of establishing strict proofs of extinguishment of a treaty or aboriginal right lies upon the Crown.*

And yet there is something more. For all the nation-to-nation dynamics—or some would say deceptions—of the treaty, it was also a *sacred* agreement, entered into by both sides with a very real sense that it was made under the authority of a higher power, with the Great Spirit presiding beyond the politics of either the Blackfoot or Canada; and the promises made on both sides were guaranteed not only by a specific treaty liturgy but also by sanctions equivalent to swearing on the Bible or smoking a sacred pipe. In that sense, the spirit of the treaty *is* the treaty, for it was the spirit that underwrote its commitments. Orality plays its part in this, and this is just beginning to be acknowledged as fundamentally important (which should be much easier than it seems to be, since the major institutions of our Euro-Canadian society—our courts and churches and parliaments and schools—are arenas of orality in which performance often trumps print). In the case of the treaties, the presumption that they are mutually binding contracts rests on the knowledge that there has been prior mutual consent; and since the agreement was reached orally before the treaty was signed, the full extent of the oral agreement needs to be taken into account . . . and can even claim precedence.

Finally, the "letter" of the treaty, its language, included terms that were either poorly translated to the Blackfoot or untranslatable, and the implications for territorial authority, which up until then had been challenged only in tangible ways by those ready and willing to risk war, were never given the attention they required. While Crowfoot may have been the most aware of all this, he was also the most hopeful that the treaty would benefit his people, facing the loss of the buffalo and the inevitable flow of white settlers onto their lands. The translation of languages, and the naming of lands, has long been recognized as an exercise in power, and by no means only in the Americas. There is a play by the Northern Irish writer Brian Friel called *Translations*, about the mid-nineteenth-century British Ordnance Survey that plotted the Irish countryside and translated local Gaelic place names into English. One of the local inhabitants of a fictitious town called Ballybeg (from the Gaelic *baile beag*, meaning "small town" . . . like Fort Macleod) comments on the Gaelic language in a way that seems to catch the character of the rhetoric used by both chiefs and government officials in the Treaty Seven negotiations. "It is a rich language, full of the mythologies of fantasy and hopes and self-deception—a syntax opulent with tomorrows. It is our response to mud cabins and a diet of potatoes; our only method of replying to inevitabilities." And then, conscious of the damage that can be caused by changing the names of places, and even more so the language of a people, the Irishman continues, "It can happen that a civilization can be imprisoned in a linguistic contour which no longer matches the landscape of fact."

. . .

When Crowfoot agreed to Treaty Seven, he was still accurately describing his people in declaring: "We are the children of the plains, it is our home, and the buffalo has been our food always." And he gave thanks for "the mountains, the hills and the valleys, the prairies, the forests and the waters, and all the animals that inhabit them." His eloquent celebration of the place he called home could be dismissed today as rhetorical or romantic, but it was a linguistic contour that at the time *did* match the landscape of fact. And the rhetoric had muscle. Listen to the Montana philosopher (as well as sometime mayor of Missoula and speaker of the Montana House of Representatives) Daniel Kemmis, talking about the preambles to the constitutions of the state of Montana and the United States. He points out that they both begin with the words "We the people"; and the preamble to the United States Constitution then proceeds immediately to identify the specific purposes of government of which the constitution is to be the instrument. Montana's preamble, however, before getting down to the instrumental details, has this to say: "We the people of Montana, grateful to God for the quiet beauty of our state, the grandeur of its mountains, the vastness of its rolling plain," and then goes about ordaining and establishing the constitution. Kemmis remarks as follows:

Why did the authors of this constitution pause to express their gratitude for the Montana landscape? It would be possible to argue that they were simply being long-winded in a document which should be lean and concise. But it could also be argued that [they] said not a word more than they had to say, but that [what] they had to say [was] that the way they felt about the place they inhabited was an important part of what they meant when they said "we the people."

This is covenantal as well as constitutional language. David Laird spoke in the same covenantal language as Crowfoot when he acknowledged that "the Great Spirit has made all things—the sun, the moon, and the stars, the earth, the forests, and the swift running rivers," reinforcing the sacred bonds of family by continuing: "The Great Spirit has made the white man and the red man brothers, and we should take each other by the hand. The Great Mother loves all her children, white man and red man alike; she wishes to do them all good." Crowfoot too was speaking the words of a new covenant as well as the preamble to a new constitution, for that is what the treaties were, binding for the Blackfoot and the banker and everyone else in the territory. A covenant and a constitution for people who were all bound in good faith by a treaty.

But Canada did not keep its word.

. . .

And a crisis was looming. At least one key figure, James Macleod, recognized this; and the crisis he feared arrived just two years later, early in 1879, when the plains tribes faced terrible starvation. The buffalo were gone and promised rations were reduced or withheld. In the spring Macleod made a lengthy visit to Ottawa to discuss the situation with the recently re-elected John A. Macdonald government. He returned to the west in July, bringing eighty new recruits as well as food supplies for distribution to the Indians. Edgar Dewdney, the newly appointed Indian commissioner of the North-West Territories, travelled west with him, and they spent much of the last half of 1879 visiting the Indian agencies throughout the territories. Despite the fact that Macleod's health was beginning to deteriorate under the strain—he had Bright's disease, in his case a severe form of kidney inflammation—he travelled more than 2,300 miles by horse that year to conduct his police work, as well as to fulfill his judicial responsibilities as a stipendiary magistrate. But most of all, he travelled to almost every corner of the territory to assess the dreadful circumstances of many of the plains tribes. Macleod's understanding of the government's obligations towards the Blackfoot and other treaty nations—he had, after all, been its commissioner for Treaty Seven—seems to have been significantly different from that of the administration of Prime Minister John A. Macdonald. Put bluntly, they had promises to keep, and their honour to uphold. When Macleod got to know my grandfather, he told him that he was appalled by the government's failure to keep its promises and furnish foodstuffs for the destitute Indians, adding that the Ottawa idiots seemed to think that the Blackfoot could still gain their livelihood by hunting, "as if everyone didn't know that there is nothing for them to hunt."

. . .

As though this wasn't enough, there was another threat to peaceful coexistence in Canada, sponsored by the Sioux leader, Sittting Bull. In 1876 the Sioux had fought General Custer and won the Battle of the Little Bighorn in Montana. For several years before that, Sitting Bull had had his eye on Canada, and had been trying to persuade Crowfoot and other Blackfoot chiefs to join him in a war on the encroaching settlers and the American army; and it is an open question who would have won. The Indians were skilled fighters, and in most instances outnumbered the settlers; in contemporary nineteenth-century phrasing, "occupation rested upon the savage."

But the Blackfoot in Canada refused, partly because, with long memories of treachery, they were still fighting some of their own battles against the Sioux, but mostly because they had come to know and respect the North-West Mounted Police. After his victory over General Custer at Little Bighorn, and in retreat from a much expanded American cavalry, Sitting Bull fled to Canada with over five thousand Sioux followers and tried to organize the tribes to wipe out the settlers on both sides of the border. But mistaking the constabulary (non-military) style of the North-West Mounted Police for weakness, and misjudging the mood of the Indians on the northern plains, he had few takers. After visiting Crowfoot and making peace with his old enemies the Blackfoot, Sitting Bull decided to wait it out and see what would happen.

The presence of the Sioux in Canada intensified competition for an increasingly scarce food supply, and threatened to lead either to conflict among the plains tribes or collaboration among them against the settlers. Commissioner Macleod was frustrated by the dilatory efforts being made to persuade the

Sioux to leave the territory, so he and Sam Steele (who was later put in command of the North-West Mounted Police detachment at Fort Macleod) went to meet with Sitting Bull shortly after the signing of Treaty Seven. Negotiations produced little satisfaction for Sitting Bull, though he did receive permission to stay in Canada if he obeyed the law … but there would be no treaties, no reserves and no rations for his people. He remained for a few years in the Cypress Hills near Fort Walsh in southwest Saskatchewan, where he had regular contact with the police stationed there; but in 1881 the exasperated Sioux chief finally left the Cypress Hills to return to the United States, where he faced a sad comedown, working for a while with Buffalo Bill's Wild West Show—also a refuge, later, for Louis Riel's lieutenant, Gabriel Dumont.

. . .

The early years after the treaty were grim for the Blackfoot, with starvation not far from the door. Fresh meat ran out, so dried meat and bacon and pemmican were substituted, with flour that was often black because it had been made from frozen wheat. The situation was made worse by the measles and scarlet fever that now took many of their children. Among the Bloods, disease was devastating for the next couple of decades. In 1881, there were 3,560 Bloods collecting the annual treaty money; by 1890 that number was halved, and by 1896 it was down to 1,300, with annual deaths double that of births. The arrival of relatives from the United States, many in wretched shape, to join their Blood families complicated the situation; and the Canadian economy was struggling too, though treaty provisions should have been a protected budget. The result on the Canadian prairies was desperate hunger, starvation for some of the First Nations, and unrest among them all, with cattle thefts widespread. With their signature sense of humour, the Blackfoot name for Commissioner Dewdney, who kept promising day after day that food would arrive, was *Apinau-kusi*, which means "Tomorrow." The language of Treaty Seven turned out to be, in the words of that play *Translations*, "full of the mythologies of fantasy and hopes and self-deception—a syntax opulent with tomorrows."

. . .

My grandfather's rancher friend Ned Maunsell was at the Treaty Seven negotiations, and his experience in those years gives a sense of how this played out for everyone on the ground . . . ground that was still sparsely settled. The Indians were eating dogs and snaring gophers; and Ned and his brother, living in a log cabin they had built the previous summer to start their ranch, had much sympathy for them but little food for themselves. One day a local Blood man came by, and they did what anyone would do in the foothills at that time, gave him tobacco and a meal. The next day he came back with his wife and child. Again they fed them. For weeks after, every time they lit a fire Indians would see the smoke, take it as a signal, and arrive at their door. Soon the Maunsells were nearly out of food, and couldn't keep up the hospitality; but neither would they eat in front of the starving Blackfoot. So they took to eating cold bacon and bread in the bush.

They eventually got some food from a neighbour—there were only about a dozen settlers between Fort Macleod and Lee's

Creek (now called Cardston) at that time—and finally had a meal; and the next day, in one of those wonderful coincidences, the cattle they had bought when they finally got that letter of credit cashed arrived on the trail from Montana. After a long day branding over a hundred head—one hundred and three, to be exact—and herding them to the cabin, they went in to get the dinner that was left over from the night before; but the Indians had paid them another visit, taking some of their food ... but courteously leaving them enough bacon and tea and flour and sugar for a few more meals. The only other thing they took beside food was an illustrated bible. They knew all about writing without words.

During the next few weeks, their new herd was raided several times—fresh meat!—and they lost a good number of cattle which they could ill afford to part with. By the end of the season, they were down to fifty-nine head; and in exasperation, Ned and his brother—both being former North-West Mounted Police officers—went with several other ranchers to meet Colonel Macleod and see what could be done. "If you can identify the Indians who killed your cattle, they will be punished," Macleaod said, knowing full well that was impossible (and adding that in his experience some of the settlers were stealing more cattle than the Indians, because everyone was hungry and because some the newcomers were scumbags). "If we corral our cattle together at night, can we defend our property?" the ranchers asked. "If any of you fellows kill an Indian, he will be hanged," replied Macleod. "Then will we receive compensation for the cattle killed by the Indians?" "No," answered Macleod. "This country is not yet open for settlement [the ranchland leasing regulations were not in place until 1880] and you brought the cattle in entirely at your own risk."

Maunsell wasn't happy; but he said that this whole experience made him more than ever conscious of how they were all in it together, especially when it came to getting enough to eat. Under the same circumstances, he admitted to my grandafther, he and his brother "would have stolen themselves, if they found a place to steal from, and something to steal." And although the song was not yet written, the two Irish brothers would have sympathized with the lyrics of "The Fields of Athenry," which offers a wife's lament in mid-nineteenth-century Ireland for her young husband, who has stolen "Trevelyan's corn" so his children "might see the morn," and is about to be sent away from his homeland on a prison ship that will take him to exile in Australia. Trevelyan was the British administrator responsible for providing—or more exactly, not providing—relief during the Irish famine. *Apinau-kusi.* Tomorrow.

. . .

The Blackfoot Confederacy was as complex, as fluid, and as full of tensions as the Canadian federation, but the Blackfoot responded to the departure of the buffalo and the arrival of the new immigrants to their ancestral territory by bringing centuries of craft and culture and statesmanship into conversation with new realities and new imaginings, signing that peace treaty instead of going to war (which would have been their first instinct, and at which they were very experienced), even as they took stock of the changes that were upon them, changes brought about by forces they did not fully understand. At the same time, and as a kind of assurance that everything was not lost, they continued some traditional practices (such as stealing horses and joining the occasional war party) right through the 1880s and even (it is said) into the 1890s, and most importantly, held with fierce determination to their religious ceremonies and to their authority as the custodians of sacred as well as secular knowledge and practice.

Disoriented and disabled by the treaty and dislocated by its reserve provisions and the restrictions on customary practices that were imposed by capricious Indian agents, the Blood tribe turned its attention to the changing location of their reserve. "Location, location, location" was as much the mantra for land selection then as it is now, and it catches something of the imaginative as well as real crises that they faced . . . and imaginative crises can be as deadly as disease. For it was territory, *not* neatly surveyed plots of land, that the Blackfoot saw as their rightful heritage.

The Dominion Lands Policy that staged the settlement of the west was designed to create homestead parcels; but arrangements in the foothills, with large ranching leases on the open range and substantial landholdings under treaty, maintained the imaginative illusion—if not the reality—of a domain that was territorial rather than proprietary; and the Blackfoot were very much part of this imaginative domain. The rancher "users" were privileged, to be sure, for they had special consideration in the government's granting of leases; but in the main they were good stewards, keeping the grasslands in remarkably good condition . . . and keeping settlement away from the open range, for a while at least. Both forms of land tenure—individual proprietorship and communal custody—had their awkwardnesses; but the second was much more congenial to Blackfoot understandings of a homeland, and it was also in line with the ranching culture of the foothills. In turn, the settlers' antipathy toward "idle" land protected for grazing instead of promoted for ploughing made for common cause between the ranchers and the Blackfoot, for whom the open range and the Indian reserve were fundamentally important.

The Blackfoot's strong survival instinct made them determined to find ways of securing self-sufficiency by sustaining their cultural heritage—the imaginative reality of the "real people"—even as they adapted their lives and livelihoods to deal with the new circumstances. For some, this meant compromising their traditional territorial connections. Led by Chief Crowfoot, the Siksika tribe chose a reserve bordering the railway, while the Peigan took land closer to their traditional hunting grounds near Pincher Creek and the Porcupine Hills. At first the Bloods had gone along with the Siksika, and accepted land adjoining their reserve; but with memories of their hunting and gathering lives and the movement of summer and winter camps still fresh in their minds, the railway must have made them feel like the prisoners in Johnny Cash's song "Folsom Prison Blues" who hear the train rolling round the bend and are tortured by the fact that it keeps moving while they don't anymore. Also, they just didn't fancy the barren plains along the Bow River.

So they requested a change, and in a move that should have been replicated across the country as First Nations took stock of the reality of their treaty and reserve life, the Bloods chose a new reserve in 1883 near to their traditional winter camping ground by the Belly River. This land turned out, not surprisingly given its close connection with the annual buffalo migrations, to be at the heart of ranching country; and at over 545 square miles, the Blood reserve remains the largest in Canada, with the second largest Aboriginal population (next to the Six Nations Reserve near Brantford, Ontario).

The government attempted to secure what it called, in transparently aggressive language, the "surrender" of some of their reserve land, but in the Blood territory of Chief Red Crow, his son and successor Crop Eared Wolf, and his son Shot Both Sides (who in turn became chief), all resisted this, Crop Eared Wolf with a fierceness and effectiveness that has been inspiring to Bloods for a century now, and which I will tell about later. The Peigan maintained the size of their reserve as well, though coerced into a couple of surrenders, later reversed. And between 1912 and 1918, the Siksika took a decision to surrender land that reduced the size of their reserve but for a time made them the wealthiest Indian community in the country, and much wealthier than many of their settler neighbours in and around Calgary. The confederacy held together by allowing partners to go their own way ... something they had learned long ago.

7

THE ROUND-UP

"Well, it was an ordinary, everyday steer with a leg on each corner."
FRED STIMSON

...

BEEF WOULD DO EVERYTHING, it was said. It would feed the Indians. It would provide a relatively safe return on investment ... except during the occasional bad winter. It would fill the freight cars of the new railway and foster both national commerce with eastern Canada and international trade with the United States and Great Britain. It would nourish a good local market and contribute to the economic success, the popular ideology, and the political sovereignty of Alberta. And it would save the native grasslands in a region where drought was the long-term norm; if you put too many cattle on the grass for too long, you destroyed your ability to winter your stock. And that would wipe out you and your ranch. It was that simple.

The 1880s marked the beginning of the "beef bonanza." In 1881, there were nine thousand cattle in the whole of the North-West Territories. Just five years later, by 1886, there were a hundred thousand in the grasslands of the foothills alone; by the turn of the twentieth century, a half million. And Fort Macleod was at the centre of this new cattle-ranching community, right in the heart of the foothills.

Cattle ranching in the foothills brought together the plains cultures of the Americas with the heritage of horse and cattle ranching from Spanish America, and the traditions of the cattle trail and the cowboy became a kind of chorus to Blackfoot horse culture. Range-savvy cattle were at a premium, and the best of them were brought in from south of the border, with both cattle and cowboys from Texas and Colorado, Wyoming and Montana coming to the grasslands and ranches of the foothills. Eastern stockers—cattle bought to finish for market rather than to build up a herd—often turned out to be poor at wintering on the western range, a euphemistic way of saying that they died in large numbers. Newfangled ways of "spoiling cattle" by feeding them through the winter with hay and grain were regarded with suspicion, if not contempt; one rancher boasted that if he could get through a winter on whisky then his stock could survive on snow. The ability to rustle for food, cows that were good mothers to the calves, and calves that were weaned early so the cows were strong enough for the next season were the most important attributes of a good herd.

My grandfather's love of horses made him comfortable with both the Blackfoot and the cowboys (some of them Indians, of course) around Fort Macleod. The best of them were very good horsemen—whether herding cattle (often purchased south of the border) back to the home ranch, or checking the cattle on the winter range, or gathering them in the spring round-up. They had to be. They spent most of their waking hours in the saddle, day after day, month after month, year after year. They worked and played with riding and roping skills that were necessary on the ranch and in the rodeo, just as they worked and played with language, creating a lexicon of technical terms—many of them from Spanish—twisted and translated into cowboy lingo: *criollo* was applied to cattle and horses as much as to people; *la reata* migrated to "lariat," *vaquero* to "buckaroo," and *dar la vuelta* (wrapping the end of a rope around the saddle horn) to "dally." A "willow" was a range mare, a "waddie" a cowboy riding one (or anything else, for that matter), and a "slow elk" a cattle beast poached by a waddie out of work.

The singing of a cowboy also fell between work and play, and my mother said my grandfather knew more cowboy songs than there were stars in the sky. He said that singing a song, or just the sound of a human voice, helped settle cattle—a notion still current in dairy barns around the world; and at night especially the cowboys would sing to the herd. When they ran out of tunes, they would launch into a litany of profanities, often comically contradicted by some religious humming; or they might recite the words on a coffee label or a can of condensed milk. And during the day, they would whoop and yell and hoot and holler to move the herd along. The importance of cowboys' songs as part of a specifically literary as well as a broad cultural heritage throughout the Americas was illustrated later when the American folklorist John Lomax was invited to speak—and to sing cowboy songs—at the annual meeting of the prestigious Modern Language Association of America in New York in 1909. He had just completed his graduate work at Harvard under George Kittredge, a distinguished literary scholar who was successor to the university's first professor of English, Francis James Child. Child, in turn, was the editor of the famous collection *English and Scottish Popular*

Ballads—the Child Ballads, as they were often called. Together, Child and Kittredge shaped Harvard's Department of Modern Languages, insisting that what is sometimes marginalized as folklore and folk song belonged with the Norse and Icelandic and Celtic and Germanic folk traditions, and with the stories and songs of Old and Middle English and eighteenth- and nineteenth-century America. Lomax published the ballads he collected in his *Cowboy Songs and Other Frontier Ballads* in 1910 (with an introductory letter from former president Theodore Roosevelt, to whom the book is dedicated). Like all literary texts, these songs were about lives and livelihoods, longing and lamentation. Their casual tone defied the circumstances they often portrayed, confusing nonchalance and intensity in what T.S. Eliot once proposed as a sign of good poetry. And they were defiantly communal. In the epigraph to his book, Lomax quoted from a song called "The Jolly Cowboy":

What keeps the herd from running,
Stampeding far and wide?
The cowboy's long, low whistle,
And singing by their side.

The "folk revival" in the 1950s and '60s owes much to Lomax and his son Alan, a reminder that songs such as these—like the border ballads of England and Scotland, and the oral performances of people all over the world for thousands of years—are an integral part of the cultural and imaginative life of nations. Including the Blackfoot nation, whose songs are much less well known—except to the Blackfoot, for whom they are part of their national literature. This has a specific importance in Canada, where the absence of written literature has often been taken as a signal of "underdevelopment" (a politically correct word for "primitive"). Lord Durham used it in his famous 1839 report on rebellions in Upper and Lower Canada, recommending responsible government for a united colony but dismissing French Canadians as a people who should be assimilated, since they had no literary tradition and no history. Much more recently, the same account was given of the Gitxsan and Wet'suwet'en peoples in British Columbia in a major Aboriginal rights case called *Delgamuukw* in the 1980s, where they were dismissed by the trial judge as "unorganized societies . . . roaming from place to place like beasts of the field" because they had "no horses, no wheeled vehicles, no written literature." (His judgement was later rejected by the Supreme Court of Canada on those and many other grounds.)

. . .

In the late spring of 1885, the newly arrived Cowdry brothers witnessed the start of the biggest round-up that the Canadian west had ever seen, with sixty thousand head of cattle gathered up from their winter ranges just south of Calgary all the way down to the Montana border. The cowboys mustered at Fort Macleod and moved out from there, one group (led by Jim Dunlap from the Cochrane ranch) riding west towards Pincher Creek and another north to Willow Creek. There were fifteen mess wagons, each with fifteen riders, and a large herd of saddle horses from which the cowboys would choose their mounts each day for the weeks they would be out, sleeping in a bedroll covered with a tarp. At night the horses would be turned loose to graze, watched over by a young—or sometimes creaky old—cowboy called a wrangler (from the Spanish *caballerango*).

The captain of the round-up heading to Willow Creek was George Lane. Born in the United States, Lane had worked on some of the best-run ranches in Montana, where he learned about the methods of open-range "cattle drive" ranching that had been practised for a couple of centuries farther south in Texas and Mexico and throughout parts of South America; and he had also picked up the newer midwestern techniques, with their careful breeding and intensive feeding programs. He brought his experience of both to Alberta, where he became foreman of a ranch called the Bar U, northwest of Fort Macleod. The Bar U was one of the first big ranches in the Canadian west, managed in its earliest days by Fred Stimson, a character who combined a comedian's wit and an aristocrat's elegance with a rancher's initative and a cowboy's flair—he admired and collected the regalia and equipment of cowboy culture throughout the Americas, as well as those of the Blackfoot, with whom he had very good relations; and he and George Lane and others developed a Canadian ranching compromise that drew on continental ranching experience but suited Chinook country and the conditions of its cattle industry. And he was a tough competitor, no matter what the occasion. In court one day, he was being cross-examined by Paddy Nolan, a Calgary lawyer known for his own quick wit, whose client was accused of stealing some cattle. The exchange went like this:

MR. NOLAN: Your name is Fred Stimson, I believe.
MR. STIMSON: It is.

MR. NOLAN: You spend most of your time riding the
   range, do you not?

MR. STIMSON: No, sir. I spend most of my time in bed.

MR. NOLAN: You are very short-sighted, I believe,
   Mr. Stimson.

MR. STIMSON: No, sir, I am not.

MR. NOLAN: Then why do you wear glasses [actually,
   a monocle]?

MR. STIMSON: Oh, just for effect.

MR. NOLAN: Now, Mr. Stimson, you claim my client
   misbranded one of your cattle?

MR. STIMSON: I do, sir.

MR. NOLAN: Please describe the animal in court.

MR. STIMSON: Well, it was an ordinary, everyday steer
   with a leg on each corner.

And with that, Paddy Nolan gave up.

. . .

One account of the round-up, reported in the *Macleod Gazette*,
celebrated a particular cowboy with praise that invokes the combination of skill and strength and sense of humour that defined
a civilized horseman on the prairies:

   If there is a man on the round-up who keeps up the spirit of the
   boys more than another and who provides more amusement
   to break the monotony, this man is John Ware. John is not only
   one of the best natured and most obliging fellows in the coun-
   try, but he is one of the shrewdest cow men.... The horse is not

running on the prairie which John cannot ride, sitting with his face either to the head or tail, and even if the animal chooses to stand on its head or lie on its back, John always appears on top when the horse gets up, and smiles as if he enjoyed it—and he probably does.

The writer of that praise song was C.E.D. Wood, the editor of the *Macleod Gazette* newspaper (and its co-founder a couple of years before). The early issues of the *Gazette* were printed on a drum cylinder press operated by a crew of Blood Indians who had the job of turning the handle, which was sufficiently heavy work that they had to trade off regularly to let someone else have a go. John Ware was well known to Wood, as he was to many in the community, for his courtesy, his craft as a cowboy, his love of comedy and his courage—and newspaperman Wood was notorious for being quick with his opinions and open with his prejudices.

So it is interesting that he did not mention that John Ware was black. Because it didn't really matter, at least not in ranching country. In some of the towns, though not Fort Macleod, it was another matter; Calgary had displayed an intimidating round of racism earlier that year when a black man was suspected of murder. He was later convicted after a proper trial; but for a time both before and after that Calgary was very unfriendly to blacks. Ware had been told he was not welcome, and a black man named Henderson, visiting Calgary, had been run out of town. (He went to Lethbridge, where he apparently settled in just fine.) The situation in the foothills was, as always, riddled with complications. Many of the white men had Blackfoot or Cree or Métis wives, so the domestic scene was reasonably accommodating;

but still, like was seeking like. *Céad míle fáilte*, proclaimed the *Macleod Gazette* in 1882—Gaelic for "a hundred thousand welcomes"—when news came of the arrival of a few more white women in the foothills.

In truth, there was a dog's breakfast of prejudices along lines of race and gender and religion and everything else imaginable, not only in the towns but throughout the territory, where ignorance and stupidity maintained the same time-honoured hold on human behaviour as it still seems to have in so many places around the world. But in the foothills and on the prairies, what mattered most was performance, and a kind of class that comes with confidence and craft. Of course, Wood's account may have been influenced not only by Ware's leadership at the round-up but also by the fact that a quarter of the cowboys on the western plains, from Texas and Oklahoma up through New Mexico and Colorado to Wyoming and Montana and north to Canada, *were* black, freed from the curse of slavery after 1865 and bringing with them a knowledge of horses that went back for generations on the plantations, and was immensely valuable in the ranching business. And although the life of a cowboy was hard, it was also free—freer than most other livelihoods available to them, especially in the United States, at that time. The myth of the western plains and prairies, Canadian as well as American, needs adjusting. John Lomax, with extensive experience in the cowboy and ranching communities in the American west, noted that it was not at all unusual to find "negros"—using his word—in a cow camp. Mel Brooks was onto something with *Blazing Saddles.*

John Ware was born into slavery on a South Carolina cotton plantation, and after emancipation first came to Canada on a cattle drive, having been hired on the word of a friend to bring a herd north from Montana to Alberta. With no apparent experience on the trail, he was assigned duty as night herder and pick-up man at the back of the herd—a dusty, dirty and boring job, the lowest on the hierarchy during a trail ride. And he was given an old nag to ride, and a ragtag saddle. After several days—and cautiously, because he wanted to keep the job—he asked his trail boss for "a better saddle and a worse horse." Now, some folks might think he was looking for a lazier horse and a cushier seat. In fact, it was quite the opposite. He wanted a livelier horse and a working saddle. In the way of that world, the cowboys on the trail decided on a little mischief and got him a rank horse that nobody would, or could, ride. His being black might have encouraged them; but they would typically play games with newcomers of all sorts and sizes, and dozens of cowboy songs celebrated how often the mischief-makers were shown up as fools.

As they were here. Ware knew horses, and was immensely strong and skillful. "Cheeking" the horse when he mounted—using the cheek strap of the bridle to pull the horse's head towards the saddle to prevent it running or bucking as he got on its back—he settled in the saddle. Immediately, the horse swapped in, spun round, frog-walked and fishtailed, went up to the heavens in one direction and came down to earth in another, and tried everything else in an outlaw's copybook . . . but John rode it to a standstill, the routine in rodeos in that day before they adopted the wimpy eight-second rule that is now the norm. From that day on, Ware's reputation was assured, and he lived up to it at every turn.

A few weeks before the round-up, newspaperman Wood had been serving as the recorder of brands—most folks served in several capacities, which confounds the purists but sustains small communities—and he was visited by Ware, asking to register a mark for his cattle. Asked how many cattle he had, Ware said he hadn't any yet, but planned to have some soon; and he wasn't going to steal them, he added, not because he was black but because he was a cowboy (and might, by mistake of course, mark a maverick—an unbranded calf—with his own brand at round-up time). Then Ware asked for the number nine as a brand, since he had enough money to buy nine cows. When Wood asked whether he wanted a single nine, Ware said no, he'd like four, because he planned to have a whole lot of cattle. And so it was. He went on to become a rancher of renown in the district, one of the very few who commanded the kind of respect that George Lane did, and whose experience and skill were widely sought after and universally acknowledged . . . with the brand 9999—for "big cattle," as Wood said when he approved it.

John Ware also became known for his singing, and it was said that he could sing a herd to sleep like nobody else, a reminder that music itself also brought black cowboys across the northern plains into public recognition—not blues or jazz, as we might expect, but the cowboy songs that Lomax collected, and that cowboys sang. Some of the most familiar songs of the period, like "Riding Old Paint," were in fact composed by African Americans—in that case, by one Charley Willis from Texas—and many others were sung by cowboys to the herds to quiet them through the night. "Riding Old Paint" ended up being one of the anthems of the west, as popular as "Home on the Range," and still played as the last song at country dances in the ranching country of Alberta and British Columbia when I was growing up.

John Ware did not forget an insult, and for a while after his "unwelcome" he had refused to go back to Calgary. But when he died in early September 1905, just over a week after the breakup of the North-West Territories into the provinces of Alberta and Saskatchewan, when his horse stepped in a gopher hole and fell on him, his funeral was the biggest Calgary had ever seen, with news reaching far and wide even in the short two days since his death. He was celebrated as one of the greatest stockmen of his time, which was prime time—a rodeo cowboy and rancher around whom wonderful stories swirled, like the time he walked across a corral of range bulls by stepping from one back to another because it was the shortest and easiest way. In his eulogy, the Baptist minister said: "To know John Ware was to know a gentleman, one of God's gentlemen. He leaves us with the thought that black is a beautiful colour—one which the Creator must have held in particularly high favour, because he gave it to His most beautiful people. Make no mistake about it, black can be beautiful." In a move that would have delighted John Ware for its humour, and always amused my grandfather, the Calgary lawyer R.B. Bennett (later prime minister of Canada) was directed to sell Ware's ranch—his wife, Mildred, known to everyone as Mother Ware, had died earlier that same year. So Bennett sold all the horses first... and then had to hire some horses to round up the cattle. Calgary never really was a ranching town like Fort Macleod.

. . .

Much of the success of the Blackfoot in facing their future and securing a measure of self-sufficiency after the collapse of the buffalo herds had to do with horses. Even with the buffalo gone, the Blackfoot continued to breed horses for speed and for show but also for the new livelihoods of settlement, in which size and strength mattered, and they began to crossbreed with draft horses brought in by some of the ranchers and farmers. And the horses they had, with buffalo-hunting stamina and speed and agility, were perfect as cow ponies.

It is little wonder that the Bloods, skilled at herding buffalo with horses, took to cattle ranching without skipping a beat. The Methodist missionary John Maclean, who lived on the Blood reserve, estimated that there were two thousand horses there in 1887 for about 2,300 Indians . . . and about the same number of dogs (which, he wrote in his notebook, should not be advertised too widely). Ranching, which flourished in the territory during the last two decades of the nineteenth century, depended upon horses at every turn, from the rigging that reflected the heritage of the *pampas* and the *llanos* of southern indigenous and Spanish America, as well as the plains and the prairies and cowboys and Indians of the north, to the songs and stories in which horses were celebrated as, variously, rank outlaws and righteous saviours. "After God, we owe our victory to our horses," said the Spanish conquistadors. So did the plains Indians. Up until the treaty, it was victory over their enemies. In the 1880s, it was victory over despair.

So the Blackfoot continued to put horses at the centre of their lives, giving them pride of place in their civic and ceremonial lives. And by the time my grandfather arrived in Fort Macleod, many Blackfoot, including the Blood chief Red Crow and his son Crop Eared Wolf, had turned from buffalo to both farming and ranching, with nearly sixty acres in potatoes and grain. Their familiarity with the seasonal round in that dryland environment put them in a good position to succeed where some of the settlers had not, and their experience with the native grass species of the plains and foothills, where the buffalo had grazed from fall to spring and parts of which (for the Bloods and the Peigan at least) were now included in their reserves, provided the knowledge and know-how to build up large herds of cattle and horses, which were flourishing on their grasslands by the 1890s.

Fort Macleod was not only at the centre of the ranching community but in the lead when it came to the fairs and rodeos that celebrated farming and ranching life—and in the case of Macleod, Blackfoot culture. There had been an exhibition rodeo with local cowboys and Indians for the Marquess of Lorne at the Strong ranch just west of Macleod on his visit to the foothills in 1881. Fort Macleod then took the lead with a fall fair in October 1886, the week my grandfather and his brother opened their bank, and Cowdry Brothers supported the annual fairs and accompanying rodeo events for the next twenty years. They always opened with a parade of Blackfoot riders dressed in their beautiful leggings and shirts and vests and headdresses, the horses adorned in beaded saddles and bridles and blankets and breast bands and saddlebags.

But the permanence of the Blood reserve as the new homeland was hard to accept, especially for a people bewildered by the notion not of settling down but of staying put. Nobody stays put all year, their stories told them; stay put, and you will starve. Which they almost did in those terrible years immediately follow-ing the treaty. But they had agreed to settle on their reserves; and they did, more or less. Many of them, including Red Crow and Crop Eared Wolf, kept their tipis, which were important for gathering together family and friends and were painted with religious designs inspired by dreams or war experiences; and they also built houses, fencing the land to corral their horses and cattle and keep them away from their crops. Being close to the land that had once been part of their seasonal routine was immensely important; and no one who has visited the country by the Belly and Old Man's Rivers around Fort Macleod could doubt that it would foster a consciousness of higher powers, especially for people who had lived there for centuries. Its beauty was a rare confusion of the wild and the domestic, the sacred and the profane.

And there were always songs and stories about horses. More than anything else, and sanctified by the ceremonies of the horse dance and the horse medicine that was secure in the keeping of its custodians, these helped the Blackfoot resist the pressures of a reality that might otherwise have become overwhelming. In that sense, all stories are resistance stories, giving us a way of creating a centre of belief from which we can move out to live in a world of events. For the Blackfoot, horses were at the heart of many of these stories, taking over from the buffalo. In Mongolia, the birthplace of horse cultures and the home of some of the greatest horsemen and horsewomen in the world, the word for spirit—*takh*—is also the word for a wild horse. The same spirit shaped Blackfoot culture. And it brought together native and newcomer alike, for as the prairie historian Lewis G. Thomas insists, "there can be little doubt that a love of horses was a most important element in the creation of a sense of community in southern Alberta." That, and storytelling, in a wide variety of forms.

My grandfather in 1882 sitting on a Red River cart near Pile of Bones (now Regina), where he and his brother had just built a sod house on their new homestead. He used the cart to travel to Fort Qu'Appelle, where he would go regularly to see friends and pick up supplies from the Hudson's Bay post.

"Kamoose" Taylor standing in shirtsleeves in front of his hotel, wearing a bowler hat. "Polly" Pollinger, the masterful driver of the Concord stagecoach, is looking back towards the camera as he gets ready to urge the horses on their way to Fort Benton, Montana, with his celebrated polysyllabic curses.

The main street of Fort Macleod in the spring of 1885 as my grandfather saw it when he and his brother arrived—a wide, muddy lane on a bed of gravel. The new Macleod Hotel is the first white two-storey building on the left.

Colonel James Macleod, commander of the North-West Mounted Police, was one of the two commissioners at Treaty Seven in 1877; this photograph was taken two years later in Ottawa where he'd gone to berate the government for not keeping its word, leaving the Indians without the help promised them in the bleak years after the collapse of the buffalo.

Fort Whoop-Up, the notorious whisky trading post (though it also traded in buffalo robes, wolf pelts and Indian ponies, as well as axes, knives, tobacco, sugar, flour and tea), was the first destination (near what is now Lethbridge) for the police when they arrived in southern Alberta. When Macleod rode up and saw a homemade American flag flying above the ramparts he expected trouble; instead they found one trader and a welcome dinner.

Red Crow, head chief of the Bloods, wearing his Treaty Seven medal and the ribbon given to him as an honorary guest at the ceremony in Brantford, Ontario, commemorating Mohawk chief Joseph Brant. Red Crow had signed Treaty Seven, so while a fearsome warrior in earlier days he appears here as a peacemaker, holding a tobacco pipe.

These bones, piled west of Regina, are more organized than those at Pile of Bones when my grandfather arrived there in 1882. Through the following decade, settlers across the prairies gathered the buffalo bones as a cash crop, sending them east on the recently completed Canadian Pacific Railway to be ground into fertilizer.

This is Red Crow's famous Middle Painted Lodge, sometimes known as the Single Circle Otter Tipi, with six sacred otters—three on each side of the tipi—painted in black on the broad red horizontal band. Its design is said to go back to the beginning of Blackfoot religion. Red Crow (*Mékaisto*) transferred it to his adopted son and future Blood chief Crop Eared Wolf (*Makoyi-Opistoki*) in 1892, probably at the Sun Dance that year. This photograph (like the later one of the Sun Dance lodge) was taken by Robert Wilson, a former North-West Mounted Police officer and trader, and contentious Indian agent.

Perhaps no one epitomized the complicated character of the foothills during this period more than Jerry Potts, son of a Scots father and a Blackfoot mother. He was a legendary plainsman, a warrior with a formidable reputation, a police scout and an interpreter who never wasted words. He knew his way everywhere in Chinook country, and, known to the Blackfoot by his Blood name, Bear Child (*Ki-yo-kosi*), he was a friend to people from all walks of life.

This was taken just after Crop Eared Wolf became head chief of the Bloods upon Red Crow's death. He is about to take up his warrior heritage by resisting the persistent, punishing demands from the Indian agent—Robert Wilson—to surrender part of the Blood reserve land. Crop Eared Wolf had promised his father he would never surrender; and he kept his word.

The Blackfoot name for the Bloods is *Káínai*, meaning "many chiefs." The Blood chiefs gathered here in 1905 include (back row, left to right) the interpreter Joe Healy and Chief Running Crane. Front row: Blackfoot Old Woman, whose ambitions troubled Red Crow; Day Chief, whom Red Crow had instead promoted as chief of the bands down river on the reserve; and head chief Crop Eared Wolf. Blackfoot politics were stern and sophisticated.

The Blackfoot visit to Ottawa in 1886 was sponsored by John A. Macdonald in gratitude for their not participating in Riel's uprising. Back row, left to right: Father Albert Lacombe, an Oblate priest who mediated between the Blackfoot and the government, and the renegade interpreter Jean L'Heureux, who pretended to be a priest and promoted the interests of the Indians. Middle row: chiefs Three Bulls and Crowfoot (both Siksika) and Red Crow (Blood); in the front row: North Axe (Piegan) and One Spot (Blood). Later this day they met with the Prime Minister at Earnscliffe, his official residence.

In 1894 my grandfather took a trip to Toronto with his children Gus (three) and Mary (seven), after Amy's death that winter, to see their grandparents, the Whitneys. The picture catches something of my grandfather's life as a single parent, for both his young wives—the second being my grandmother, Gussie—died in childlbirth. He spoiled his children, because he could; and he gave them his spirit of fortitude and his sense of fun, because he knew they would need them.

8

THE UPRISING

"Evening prayer gives more pleasure
in heaven than all the military music
played by the North West Mounted
Police outside my cell window."
LOUIS RIEL

...

WHILE THE ROUND-UP THAT SPRING of 1885 was full of
promise, the news that was swirling around Fort Macleod was
not. It came as no surprise to my grandfather, though he had
hoped for a better turn; but it came quickly, first by word of
mouth and then by mail—not for another year would a telegraph
line be built to Macleod, from Dunmore, just outside Medicine
Hat on the main line of the Canadian Pacific Railway. (There
were one or two telephone circuits in town already, though
proper local telephone service would not be in place for another
decade.) But by whatever means available, word was widespread throughout the foothills that spring about the troubles
back in Saskatchewan.

The Métis had been almost completely left out of the treaties, leaving them vulnerable both to the certainty of settlement and to the uncertainties of local influence. Language and
religion, specifically the French language and the Roman

Catholic religion, played a part in this malign neglect of the west, but so did ignorance (of the northwest by the policy mandarins in Ottawa) and stupidity (seldom in short supply when people are in a hurry, as Canada certainly was). For renewed unease among the Métis was hardly surprising to anyone who was paying attention. Under the leadership of Louis Riel, they had proposed a provisional government for the North-West Territories back in 1869, but it was pre-empted by the purchase of Rupert's Land and the creation of the province of Manitoba. Increasingly frustrated and fearful over the next decade, Riel's Métis supporters—urged on by white settlers angry that their appeals to Ottawa for a representative government had been ignored—had called him back in 1884 from exile in Montana to lead them in proclaiming their grievances.

It was in this setting, on March 19, that Louis Riel once again announced a provisional government for the territories. March 19 is the feast of the patron saint of the Métis, Saint Joseph, and the declaration set in motion a righteous uprising inspired by the bible as well as buffalo hunting. The Cree and Assiniboine rose up on their own behalf before joining the Métis... and the "rebellion," as the government liked to call it, was underway.

In the following weeks a series of confrontations took place, with Cree and Métis forces fighting a combination of redeployed North-West Mounted Police and Canadian military troops, the latter sent in open carriages by train around Lake Superior. There were battle victories on both sides, but the war was won by the government; and those Métis and Cree who weren't killed were held for trial. Louis Riel was accused of treason, and his trial began in late July.

Although my grandfather had just arrived in Fort Macleod a few months earlier, he turned right around when he heard the news that Riel would be tried in a Regina court and went back to support him. Because time was short, he rode on the new Canadian Pacific Railway from Calgary. He knew that the railway represented much that Riel opposed, as he himself probably did. But my grandfather also believed in the idea of a powerful, independent, representative government for the people of the northwestern plains, which is essentially what Riel had proposed; he believed in the hopes and possibilities of its first peoples; he was quite sure the government in Ottawa wouldn't understand, and wouldn't care; and he knew that the eastern papers were not only full of malicious nonsense about the rebellion but were also portraying the Indians as primitive peoples who recognized their inability to govern their own affairs and welcomed "civilized" intervention.

My grandfather and his brother felt the nervousness of their fellow settlers at the uprising, but they were above all angry at the federal government's seeming disinterest in the changes overwhelming the northwest, and the precarious position of the Métis in a part of the country without any kind of responsible government. Indeed, the call for a new order in the territories was widespread, and not by any means limited to Métis concerns; delegates to the territorial council (which had been established in 1876 and consisted of what one observer described as five able men disabled by limited authority) regularly demanded a shift in responsibility from Ottawa to the west.

One of the most strident, though not always the most sensible, voices was that of Frank Oliver, who had painted that picture of the huge gathering at Blackfoot Crossing for Treaty Seven eight years earlier. He had founded the *Edmonton Bulletin* in 1880 (the first newspaper in Alberta), and then served as a member of the territorial assembly; he would later become federal superintendent-general of Indian affairs from 1905 to 1911; but here he is in August 1885, writing in his newspaper:

> *The North-West Territories in Canada have sometimes been termed in derision, British Siberia, on account of the northern Latitude which they occupy. But the resemblance in political institutions is even more striking than in soil and climate. While Canada as a whole, and the different provinces of which it is comprised are united under a system of responsible government, the North-West is under a despotism as absolute, or more so, than that which curses Russia. Without representation in either parliament or cabinet, without responsible local government, the people of the North-West are allowed but a degree more control of their affairs than the serfs of Siberia.*

A year earlier, he had written an even more incendiary column, suggesting that "if history be taken as a guide, what could be plainer than that without rebellion the people of the West need expect nothing. While with rebellion, successful or otherwise, they may reasonably expect to get their rights."

It was in this spirit that folks like my grandfather supported Riel, but without some of the hyperbole—though having said that, I recall my mother saying he always put a premium on Riel's arguments, which included a good measure of Old Testament rhetoric. In any case, both Oliver and Riel reflected the frustration felt by many in the northwest. The Blackfoot didn't support the uprising itself, in part because they didn't like the Cree, who had led the attack against them just fifteen years earlier, but mostly because they trusted people like James Macleod and others who had seen them through times of trouble since the treaty signing. Their leader, Red Crow, didn't hate war; and he was afraid of no one. War, for him, had simply outlived its usefulness. But he was not Métis.

. . .

My grandfather was joined by a few of his settler and Métis friends at the trial, held in the recently built and still scruffy Regina courthouse before a jury of six English and Scots Protestants. (An Irish Catholic in the jury pool was rejected for not being of British stock.) Some of my grandfather's acquaintances did not support Riel's methods, or were not convinced by his divine inspiration; others considered him unstable at best, uncontrollable at worst. Nonetheless, many in the territory felt common cause with his resistance to Ottawa's ambition to fashion the new western hinterland in a way that would do little more than serve the interests and feed the enterprises of the metropolitan east. They were proud when Riel proclaimed that even as the eastern provinces were great, the North-West was greater. And when Riel insisted that he was not just a Métis leader but a leader for good in the country called Canada, they recognized that his uprising signified unfinished western business. *Real* business, my grandfather would say, playing with both the mispronunciation of Riel's name that was common back east and the Blackfoot word for themselves—*Niitsítapi*, the real people.

It was just at that moment that the sorry legacy of mistreatment of Indians in the United States since 1776 was being chronicled in Helen Hunt Jackson's widely read *A Century of Dishonor*, published in 1881. It was used by the Opposition during the year of Riel's uprising to castigate the government; but it also provided considerable self-satisfaction in Canada—particularly ironic given the circumstances surrounding the prairie treaties—to those who wanted to celebrate the British practice of "keeping your word" ... a British word being always more reliable than an American one, even—so it seemed—when you were in the process of breaking it.

With faith in Catholic martyrdom and the fortitude of Métis stoicism, Riel rejected the defence of insanity which his counsel pleaded; in short order, he was convicted of treason and sentenced to be hanged despite the jury's recommendation of mercy. My grandfather railed against Riel's guilty verdict and the sentence of capital punishment until the day he died in 1947; and he might well have agreed with some of the arguments put forward by the Catholic archbishop Taché, who in the shadow of the trial and execution called for a new kind of government and (overriding his own strong opinions) a new kind of non-partisan understanding and commitment to peace in the North-West Territories, warning (in the words of an earlier letter, published in the *Globe* newspaper, from the Oblate missionary Father Alexis André to Riel's lawyer) that otherwise "we shall have in the North-West a new kind of Ireland in which the two races will cordially detest and treat each other like sworn enemies."

After the trial my grandfather stayed a week or two longer in Regina, long enough to realize that his friends from Fort Qu'Appelle—the Hudson's Bay factor and his Métis wife who had helped him and his brother Nat settle into the new life when they first arrived—had a surprising involvement with Louis Riel. Understandably so, for theirs was *the* story of the northwest. For over a century, such couples had been involved in the fur trade, and a new people—the Métis—had emerged from unions between Scots and Irish and English and French traders and (mostly) Cree women ... who in turn became key players in the trade, often running it more or less as a family business. But it was their daughter, a young Métis girl of thirteen, who was most deeply affected by the uprising and by Riel's sentence, and who made her involvement personal by somehow getting permission to visit Riel in prison while he awaited execution, travelling to Regina regularly to do just that.

How she managed this, and even why, is a mystery. Later, her daughter Margaret wondered whether she might have been a thirteen-year-old go-between carrying messages to the great Métis leader—I heard this because Margaret became my own mother's best friend. My mother thought maybe she had a crush on Riel. Whatever the reasons, like many teenagers Margaret's mother kept a journal which she carried with her to his jail cell; and in it Riel—who imagined himself as the psalmist David, dashing down his enemies with words and music—wrote remarks like "evening prayer gives more pleasure in heaven than all the military music played by the North West Mounted Police outside my cell window." Margaret became my godmother, and when I was growing up she would read me her mother's journal like holy scripture.

I often wonder whether my grandfather had a hand in persuading Margaret's grandfather, who as Hudson's Bay factor had helped arrange transportation for the army troops, to show solidarity with his wife and allow their rebellious daughter to visit the condemned rebel . . . or upriser. And who knows, maybe her father was the enabler himself; he certainly knew Riel and had spoken of him agreeably to Jack, and may indeed have asked Jack to come back for the trial. These were contradictory times, and everyone knew soldiers who had fought on both sides, and often had opinions that embraced each in turn. Whatever the case, all his long life my grandfather held a special affection for Margaret's mother, and for what Riel said to her and wrote in her journal; and he mentioned her in the last letter he wrote to my mother just a few days before his own death.

. . .

Instead of returning to Fort Macleod right away after Riel's trial, my grandfather went back to Ontario to propose to the sweetheart he had been courting, mostly at a distance, since he left to go homesteading three years earlier. Her name was Emma Whitney, though she was always called Amy; and it is a measure of their love, and her sense of adventure, that she said yes when he proposed. He had nothing arranged yet in Macleod, though he told her he was all set to start a bank. She was keen on him, but cautious about the bank. "With what?" she asked. "With my brother," he answered. But he was a good storyteller, and had almost certainly entertained her and her parents with tales of life in the foothills, and his new friends. And spoken of the territory as a homeland, not a frontier. A Blackfoot homeland first of all, he would always say; but one that he hoped to make his and Amy's. Even amidst the unsettled economic and political circumstances that followed Riel's uprising, he believed that he and Amy could make a good life in the foothills. He believed in their future together; but "nobody has any future there if the Blackfoot don't," he would add . . . and then go on to say that he was sure they did. Even in the short time he had been there, he had seen and heard something of their refusal to be reduced in spirit, or bullied by the bureaucracy that followed the treaty.

9

SETTLING INTO THE FOOTHILLS

"This was my country once."
RED CROW

...

MY GRANDFATHER AND HIS new bride were part of a long line of settlers in the foothills. Newcomers had been arriving in southern Alberta for centuries: from the east and north, following the beaver and the buffalo; from the west across the mountains, hunting and fishing in summer and fall; from the south, seeking the shelter of the wooded coulees and benchlands in the front range of the Rockies in fall and winter. The newcomers were Cree and Assiniboine, Sioux and Shoshone, Kootenai and Shuswap; traders, dominated by the French and British and Métis cartels; and, in the decade before 1885, the North-West Mounted Police, a band of missionaries, small-herd and several big-time ranchers, some traders turned merchants, a few folk in the legal, medical and educational professions, and others looking for new opportunities.

John Cowdry was one of them. He didn't have a trade or a profession, and although he knew horses he didn't yet know the cattle business. But he had some modest funds, a brother whom he trusted, and a fiancée who believed in him. So when he returned to Fort Macleod in August, with a wedding date set for December, he turned to the task at hand. A house for him and Amy could wait until the fall; right now, he had to decide about the bank.

The town itself expanded considerably in the late 1880s, with I.G. Baker one of the main shops, selling not only groceries, dry goods and hardware but also ranching supplies such as saddles and harnesses and wagons. Tony La Chappelle's candy and tobacco store and billiard parlour continued to be a local gathering place; a former trader started another blacksmith's shop, while a boatbuilder for the Hudson's Bay Company in the north opened a carpenter's shop, and an ex-policeman a bootmaker's shop, the second in town. More gambling establishments opened up, with faro and poker the preferred games and high stakes the preferred limit—my grandfather liked cards, and had a gift for numbers which he passed on to my mother, so he was a regular—and over the next couple of years more lawyers came, a barber shop opened next to the shoemaker's, a dentist came to town for ten days each month; and soon there were several more hotels and saloons and grocers, as well as stores offering a wider range of horse tack and wagon rigging and general agricultural supplies, as well as household appliances and homemaking goods.

Jack and Nat chose a site between the Queen's Hotel and the Athletic Saloon on Main Street, and built a small banking shop with boards from the river bottom (where some of the timber from the old fort had ended up) which they hauled up on foot, or hitched onto any wagon that passed by. They had help on the building from the local tinsmith and hardware merchant Al Grady, the jack-of-all trades D.W. Davis, and Ned Maunsell, who brought along a couple of his friends from the Blood reserve. They were joined by the North-West Mounted Police surgeon George Kennedy and Big Swan, the Peigan Indian chief, whom my grandfather had met on one of his rides to the country around Pincher Creek where many of the ranches were located. By the following summer they were ready. They opened in the fall with advertisements soon appearing in the *Macleod Gazette* for "Cowdry Brothers: Bankers and Financial Agents. Drafts Issued on and Collections made on all Available Points. Drafts, Cheques and Sterling Exchange Bought."

They began their loans in town with the local livery stable, as crucial then as a gas station and automobile mechanic are now in a small town; my grandfather had checked out the stable carefully long before the bank opened. And soon they extended their business not just to ranchers—who became their mainstay—but to grocers, auctioneers, hardware merchants, saddlers, builders, undertakers, lawyers and druggists, among others, many of whom brought money in as well as borrowed it. These relationships continued even after the arrival in the foothills later in the 1890s of the chartered banks, which could sometimes offer lower rates... but not better service, or the flexibility that was Cowdry Brothers' trademark. Loyalty and friendship played a part in their business, of course; but their hardscrabble customers would not have stayed with them if it put their livelihood at risk. They had a few fairly secure institutional customers, lending funds to the government-run Indian agency on occasion; and during the 1890s they routinely underwrote the payroll of the

North-West Mounted Police. But most of their business was with ranchers and merchants and the men and women holding households together.

As for the Blackfoot, the town was substantially dependent on them, for the treaty had given Fort Macleod as much life and purpose as the railway and the ranchers did. Treaty payment day in November was a special occasion. After bonus payments the first year, payments of five dollars were made annually to each man, woman and child on the reserves, with the minor chiefs and councillors receiving fifteen dollars and chiefs twenty-five dollars; and then, as David Laird had said in his address to the tribes during the Treaty Seven gathering, "you can spend as you please [and] buy what you think proper." Which they did, with pleasure and to the delight of the town merchants, as a description in the *Macleod Gazette* in 1888 confirms.

One of the important annual events in this part of Alberta is the treaty payments to the Blood and Peigan Indians, or rather the trading in town which follows.... The Peigans came first. On Saturday the Blood procession began, and all day Sunday they arrived in droves of hundreds.... On Monday morning it was estimated there was close onto 2000 Indians in town. The stores were simply packed with men, women, children and dogs. During almost the entire morning it was absolutely impossible to get from one end of I.G. Baker and Co.'s store to the other. It is safe to say that no city in the Dominion of Canada presented the same stir as Macleod did on Monday last.

The merchants and the Blackfoot both looked forward to the treaty day trips to town: the local newspaper announced payment days with great enthusiasm despite the occasional grumble about the small-town inconvenience of large crowds. The local ranchers also benefitted from the treaty, for its ration commitments (now the buffalo had gone) gave them a reliable local market (and they certainly did not welcome the intermittent reduction of rations which caused severe hardship to the Blackfoot and antagonism between them). In normal times, the Bloods and the Peigan (whose reserves were closest to town) consumed over two thousand head of cattle in a year, along with 3,700 sacks of flour—1½ pounds of meat and ¼ pound of flour per person per day—and when ranching and farming became well established on the reserves, Fort Macleod continued to be the main centre for their agricultural supplies. There was provision in the treaty for an annual purchase of ammunition, and rifles and suits of clothing had been provided for chiefs and councillors, along with axes, handsaws, augers, files and whetstones. A few cows were provided to families who wanted them, or hoes and spades and scythes and pitchforks, along with a plough and harrow, for those who wished to take up farming. And teachers' salaries were to be paid.

There were Indian Department buildings on both reserves, the construction of which enriched the town and its trades, and the Department of Indian Affairs provided settler employment to a number of trades and professions as well as to the Indian agents. As employees of the federal government, responsible for the application of the repressive Indian Act, the Indian agents were insulated from local influence, but they were far from headquarters in Ottawa and had to manage relations with the Blackfoot, as well as with other federal authorities such as the police, on their own... which fostered some very personal and occasionally pernicious conduct. The presence of some of these agents disturbed the Blackfoot; but there were exceptions, and even in the darkest hours some bright lights.

The North-West Mounted Police also represented a significant presence in the town, spending a good amount of money from government funds for supplies, and for goods and services from their own salaries; and like the ranchers and merchants they too often found themselves on side with the Blackfoot. During the latter part of the 1880s, it was estimated that over $100,000 (around two and a half million dollars in today's currency) was spent annually from these sources in and around Fort Macleod.

Overall these revenues—treaty payments and promises aside—benefitted the newcomers to the territory. As for the Blackfoot, reserve life and broken promises hardly seemed a fair exchange for having "ceded, released, surrendered, and yielded up" to the Government of Canada the rights, titles and privileges to their hunting grounds—language that was not appreciated by them at the time, and nearly a hundred and fifty years later is still not accepted as representing the spirit of the treaty. But they had agreed to keep the peace, an agreement they have kept. The treaty may have been a good deal for the town, but it became clear it was not a good one for the Blackfoot.

My grandfather was well aware that if there had been no Blackfoot there would have been no Fort Macleod. And no banker. And no opportunity for Cowdry Brothers Bank to play a significant part in the success of ranching in the foothills, and of the businesses in that part of the territory; or, over the period from 1885 to 1905, to become what one economic histo-

rian called the "the largest and most dynamic bank in Alberta."
But one with few opportunities to help the Blackfoot, except . . .
well, we shall see.

· · ·

My grandfather was an enabler by instinct, and relied on a word
and a handshake. And he was seldom disappointed. He listened
to the talk of the town, often providing funds for ventures written off by others, or to individuals whose reputation was down.
Nobody's perfect, he would say . . . and go ahead, if he felt, well,
confident. Well, maybe not entirely confident, but at least cautiously optimistic. That was one advantage of a private bank—
you had nobody to answer to except yourself . . . and your
brother. Over the twenty years that he ran the bank, very few of
the bank's loans went bad; and there were only a couple of occasions when he found himself in court. One was almost comical:
it was to accept a proposal, called a "discontinuance," from Ned
Maunsell to cancel a legal action that Maunsell himself had
started, in a bad mood, having to do with a loan. When it was
done, my grandfather turned around and loaned him some
more money. The other time involved a lawyer who, as one contemporary observer remarked, "found a quibble and dwelt on
it." It came to nothing.

Of course, some of his clients *were* a bit slippery . . . but not
with my grandfather. One of my favourites—and I think his
too—was Dave Cochrane, a successful rancher and renowned
maker of mischief. He had been notorious as a whisky smug-
gler, and continued his craft long after the police had shut down
the trade. He knew the routine of the North-West Mounted

Police well, since he had joined the force in the early days; and after he left he would frequently fool the officers by drawing attention to himself after making handoffs to others, so that he would be arrested and distract the police until his associates could make their way to market in town (often selling to the very same police officers).

Dave also liked taking things, "liberating" anything that wasn't tied down … and untying some things that were. There was a story that he once took the shingles off a neighbour's house while the owner was inside; but an even better one, and unquestionably true, involves a North-West Mounted Police stove. It seems a new stove had been delivered to the barracks, and was sitting out back while the police did some renovations inside to make room for it. Dave liked the looks of that stove. Everybody did. But it was very heavy, and much too close to the building for anybody to move without being seen, even someone as experienced at freeing up merchandise as Dave Cochrane. So he devised a plan. Every few days, while passing by the fort on some made-up business or other, he would take one small item from the stove—a grate, a lifter, a damper or a door … anything that would travel easily—until soon the stove was looking pretty broken up, but still bright and clean. But Dave had a solution for that. Water. He doused it with water, and within a short time it was rusty, and impressively decrepit. Then one day Dave drove up to the fort in his wagon, and said he was cleaning up some junk around town—he was known as a "collector," remember—and had noticed some in behind the fort. He went to look with one of the officers; and there, amidst some broken-down rigging and remains of wagons and such, was a rusting shell of a stove. The officer said they'd be glad to get rid of it all, and would be very happy if Dave would take it away... and off went the stove in the wagon. A few weeks later, one of his friends on the force was visiting Dave in his home and noticed a beautiful new stove there, all cleaned up bright and shiny and working just fine. "Just got it," said Dave to the officer, who thought he recognized the stove but said nothing. They all knew Dave.

But he didn't mess with my grandfather, and their dealings were clear and clean. And for anyone who thought the Blackfoot were not quick to pick up the principles of the market, Dave himself had a story about the early days in town, before the railway was through to Calgary and almost all the supplies were still coming from Fort Benton by bull train. Groceries were always at a premium, and storekeepers would corner the market in the fall, with prices for sugar and bacon sometimes rising to fifty cents a pound in spring until a new shipment arrived. One November, after treaty payment, a young Blackfoot came to town to spend his money, and was told that some supplies were in scarce supply. He knew the folks well, and assumed they were saying this not because he was an Indian but because they were scheming storekeepers hoarding their goods until spring; but he was angry. He was also smart. Fighting fire with fire, he went around and bought out all the sugar he could purchase from every store in town, paying twenty-five cents per pound. He held it until spring, and sold it for fifty cents. He was Dave's hero.

Dave, however, was not a hero to some of the ranchers around, for he had squatted on land near Pincher Creek leased by the Walrond ranch some years earlier. The ranch manager was Duncan McEachern, who earlier had been one of the founders of the Cochrane ranch and in 1885 was appointed chief veterinary inspector for Canada, putting in place procedures to control the spread of livestock diseases that intermittently devastated the cattle herds in the foothills. Based back east in Montreal, McEachern was accustomed to having his orders obeyed; but he met his match in Dave Cochrane. On one of his regular visits to the foothills he told Dave, in no uncertain terms, to pick up and leave the property. Dave was not a man to leave empty-handed, and demanded payment for "improvements" he had made. When McEachern refused, with a dismissive snort of contempt, Dave lit his pipe and reminded him how easy it would be for a grass fire to start. Shortly after, he was paid—only half the amount he asked for, a sum arbitrated by three local men, but still a substantial payout; and the story was circulated, variously enhancing and impairing Dave's reputation in the community, depending on whom you asked. He continued ranching near what became the Blood reserve, and set the terms for his government buyout when the reserve was surveyed; but his confrontation with McEachern was the closest thing to a range war that the foothills experienced.

McEachern himself, however, did provide an occasion for a war of words with the editor of the *Macleod Gazette*, C.E.D. (or Charlie) Wood. In an eastern newspaper, McEachern had written a defence of the lease system and a celebration of ranching as the only viable livelihood in the foothills, dismissing farming as unsustainable in a region whose climate was generally unfriendly to crops. Wood was an outspoken critic of leaseholds, which at first prohibited and then discouraged farm settlement, and he became a loud advocate for settler rights. And Wood did not like McEachern, describing him in his newspaper as "a blustering and egotistical little man . . . whose bump of misrepresentation, to use a mild word, must be very nearly as strongly developed . . . as that of self-conceit, for he evidently finds it impossible to open his mouth without rushing into all sorts of extravagant and untrue statements. . . . The swelling of his head has rendered him oblivious to everything except his own self-importance." Welcome to the foothills, where few people kept their opinions to themselves.

. . .

A few years later, when my grandfather's bank was up and running, Charlie Wood published the following story in the *Gazette* under the heading "No Bank in Town" in a section devoted to lighthearted and good-humoured stories from various parts of the world. This one was from the western American frontier, set in a town like Fort Macleod.

> *The Colonel had the freighting of all the provisions over the trail from Silver City to Johnsonville, and also owned the only stage line, and one day he called the boys together at the White Wolf saloon and said:*
>
> *"Boys, what this town needs is a bank, and I'm thinking of starting one. I thought I would call you all together and see how you would take it. Joe Henderson, would you come in and draw a check, same as other folks do in the east?"*
>
> *"Not if the sight of a gun would answer just as well," replied Joe.*
>
> *"And how about you, Tom Smith?"*
>
> *"I feel like I'd kinder want to clean out the shop, colonel."*

"And you, Bill Johnson?"

"I wouldn't fool with no checks, as you call 'em."

"Well, the crowd seems to be ag'in me," sighed the colonel, "but I'd like to hear from Pete Green."

"How much money would there be in that 'ere bank, Kurnel Taylor?" asked Pete in reply.

"I'd start it with $5000."

"And who would handle it?"

"I will myself."

"And you'd be right thar ten minits after the bank opens for bizness?"

"Of course I will."

"Well, then, kurnel, there ain't no need of guessin what I'd do. I'd be right on hand with two guns, and them guns would be ready fur shootin, and I'd lay the bar'ls on the counter and say:

"'Good mornin, Kurnel Taylor.'

"'Good mornin, Pete Green.'

"'Is this bank open fur bizness?'

"'She are.'

"'Then hand me over them $5000 as quick as ye kin handle money, fur my fingers hev got the cramps and will be pullin on these triggers if ye wait to catch your breath!'"

The colonel treated the crowd and decided to keep out of the banking business.

My grandfather had seen this little story earlier in one of the newspapers from south of the border, but he must have been amused to see it in the *Gazette*, for there, on the front page, was the weekly advertisement for Cowdry Brothers Bank that had appeared every week since it opened.

His own local Kurnel, Colonel James Macleod, had been enthusiastic about the bank, but he became even more encouraging when my grandfather told him about his fiancée, Amy. There weren't many women in the settler community in those early days, and Macleod knew that his wife, Mary, would be delighted. "You have the same name as my mother," my grandfather said to her when they all went for dinner the following week. Mary assured him that Amy would have a warm welcome and good company in the territory. When she herself arrived, she told him, she had hired a woman she met on the boat coming up the Missouri River from Fort Benton as a housekeeper. Her name was Annie Saunders, and she lived with them all the time they were in Fort Macleod, helping with the children, and then, when James left the force, moved with them to Pincher Creek and set up for herself. Annie used to say that when she and Mary arrived they were the first white women in the foothills; and the humour wasn't lost on anyone who knew them. Annie was black. Known as "Auntie"—a name *she* chose to call herself, perhaps partly as a way of pre-empting any other names that new settlers might bring to town along with their prejudices—she later ran a laundry operation; welcomed guests (including children coming into Pincher Creek to school) to her boarding house (with "good accommodation for ladies"); and had a dining room that catered to everyone from the police boys after a baseball game, the Anglican church choir, costume parties with dancing through the night, and the Marquess of Lorne. One posh visitor noted that Auntie's establishment was "of a much higher character than Kamoose Taylor's," but nobody else was making comparisons. She was one of a kind, like

Kamoose and many others in a place full of characters and contradictions.

After their wedding in December, my grandfather settled with Amy into the new house he had built—he liked building things—and for Amy he had designed one with two storeys and a shingle roof, bought from a new mill close to town. They found a neighbour, Marie Cumming, to help with the housework, and with the children they hoped to have. "Sweet Marie" she was called by everyone in town; and she continued to assist the Cowdry family through my grandfather's time there, later marrying a North-West Mounted Police officer who had come to Macleod the same year he did. Amy and Jack's first-born, Mary, came along early in 1887; their son Fred was born the following year, but died within weeks; and then Augustus, or Gus, was born in 1890.

. . .

The buffalo had gone, cattle and cowboys—and horses—were roaming the plains, and the Blackfoot were settling by the rivers and on the benchlands of their old territory, taking up ranching and farming and entering each season with a new sense of surprise, though without the possibilities for hunting and gathering that had sustained them for generations. Meanwhile, Euro-American settlers were beginning to move along the trails and rails and into the scattered homesteads and small towns of the foothills. It was a new way of life for everyone; and they were making it up as they went along, making friendships and finding common cause as well as making trouble and finding fault.

Horse races brought together the Blackfoot and the rest more than almost anything else. The races at Fort Macleod were on a track laid out for the purpose at the edge of town: one mile for the fastest horses, a half mile for the cow ponies, and slow races for mules and plodding ponies, with good prize money. The Bloods and Peigan brought their horses to run against the others, and that mix of Indian and settler participation became the norm in the foothills, as it had been the early days around Pile of Bones. My grandfather told about a Dominion Day celebration in 1882 in Regina, the newly appointed capital of the North-West Territories, with First Nations, police and settlers participating together and First Nations riders taking the majority of win, place and show finishes in the half- and quarter-mile races. (A quarter mile was the rough distance down the main street in many towns in the old west; and what we call a "quarter horse" got its name from the races that were run there. The considerable width of these main streets, on the other hand, was designed to leave room for a mule team or an ox train to turn around.)

Horse races were usually straight in those days, rather than on a circuit; and although this reflected the British practice, it also copied the plains Indians, who held races that sometimes covered a distance as far as the eye could see on the open plains—which, interestingly, made them about the same length (four miles or so) as the racecourses that were common in England in the eighteenth and nineteenth centuries. Races of this distance were often run in the foothills in the early 1880s. George Murdock—the first mayor of Calgary and an articulate defender of common sense as justice of the peace, refusing to punish drinkers who broke the law prohibiting the consumption of liquor except for medicinal purposes—describes in his journal a race meet just after he arrived in the territory in 1883. "Attended races. One five mile race between the Police, One Blackfoot, One Sarcee, One Stoney (Assiniboine). Blackfoot won. I bet on Blackfoot."

Fort Macleod had put on the first fall fair in the foothills in 1886, the year after Jack and Nat arrived, with vegetable, flower and livestock exhibitions, along with horse races and a rodeo— and of course a parade along the dusty main street that ran through the small town, the staple of such gatherings for thousands of years around the world. Those parades quickly became an important part of all the town fairs, with Indian horses and riders and travois decked out in their finery to the delight of the crowd; and these increasingly became one of the main events of the week. And from early days the North-West Mounted Police set another precedent for collaboration by joining the parade ritual with their Musical Rides, later parading in London for Queen Victoria's Jubilee in 1897. The first Musical Ride was performed in Regina in 1887 (though Fort Macleod claims precedence, with a training ride there in 1876). Whatever the provenance of those Musical Rides, it is clear that not only were cowboys and Indians competing together in the rodeo, as they were on the range, but they were fellow travellers with the police on the parade circuit.

Other activities on horseback were also popular, including an unlikely game—polo. Indeed, one of the earliest polo games played in North America—some say the very first, though New York probably deserves that honour—was in the mid-1880s at Pincher Creek, with equipment ("real sticks and balls," according to the local newspaper) brought back from England by a local rancher. And in another unlikely setting, John Ware "rode to hounds," chasing coyotes and rabbits with a pack of dogs in a hunt modelled after the Quorn Hunt of Leicestershire by the English syndicate that bankrolled the ranch (called the Quorn ranch, not surprisingly) northwest of Macleod. There was no shortage of comedy, not all of it conscious, in the foothills.

. . .

There were significant differences between Canada and the United States on the western frontier, and American mythmakers were hard at work creating the storyline of an often violent American settler struggle against the elements, both human and environmental.

The different ideologies and instruments underwriting law and order, and especially the measured approach of the North-West Mounted Police and the relative absence of guns, fostered a distinctly less violent culture in the territory, with almost no vigilante intervention. In the foothills many cowboys, who south of the border became poster boys for firearms, didn't even own a gun. The Blackfoot traditions of peacemaking and peacekeeping, enforced by the elders and chiefs, also made a difference; and even though harder to calibrate, those traditions need to be appreciated if we are to recognize the unique character of these brief two decades in this time and place.

But it was land law, as well as the policies developed by the respective national governments to regulate land, which represented the most important difference between the United States and Canada. The nineteenth-century American aversion to monopolistic control, together with the ideology of the crop-rooted farmer as the pioneer and the grass-grazing rancher as the problem, persuaded the American government to resist granting large leaseholds to individual ranchers. The result, in addition to the fragmentation of the grassland commons and the breakup of fragile waterways into thirsty farm units, was an unregulated competition for land—between farmer and rancher, as well as between Indian and settler— that generated dangerous conflicts in the western states, and (since there was no security of tenure for the ranchers) some damaging overgrazing.

The Canadian government, in contrast (and after considerable lobbying in the early 1880s), issued grazing leases to large ranching enterprises—up to a hundred thousand acres at one cent per acre per year—for twenty-one years. In some cases, the ranchers didn't own any property at all; the Bar U, for instance, only secured deeded land in 1891, ten years after the ranch began operation. Not surprisingly, many of these leases went to individuals and groups with good contacts in Ottawa; but most were serious about ranching. If they weren't and didn't meet their "hoof and home" obligations, they had their leases cancelled.

Ranching *was* a favoured enterprise, even though many of the smaller ranchers didn't feel very special. Many of them had to work at other jobs, as small farmers in Canada still do; and they were vulnerable to forces that felt even more unpredictable than the weather, such as the practices and priorities of the railway for transporting their cattle to market. But even if ranchers didn't have large leaseholdings, they benefited from a land lease system that inhibited piecemeal farm settlement of the kind that was encouraged elsewhere on the prairies, and that had sustained the grasslands over generations in a way that would be the envy of many contemporary environmentalists.

The Viennese call a person who looks after a house for someone else a *Hausbesorger*, a "house-worrier." Ranchers were the open-range-worriers for the next generation. But however admirable, this raises a question. Whose land were they looking after? Rangeland in the United States was deemed "public land"; in Canada, it was "Crown land." The idea of Crown land—the Great Mother's land—may have offered the Blackfoot some comfort as being closer to their understanding of territory . . . and the concept may have contributed to the surprising sense that this time and place held promise for everyone. But it involved turning land that was Blackfoot by covenant with the Great Spirit into land that was in the constitutional safekeeping—and special giving—of the Great Mother's government. A sleight of hand; and as soon as they took stock of the treaty, it didn't fool the Blackfoot.

. . .

One thing that made some difference to the Blackfoot—especially the Bloods and the Peigan—was the richness of the rangeland on their reserves, which allowed them to build up and graze large herds of cattle and horses. For the ranchers, the open range of Crown land under lease gave them what was sardonically referred to by farmers and others as "free grass," albeit within a long-range strategy that required attention to environmental principles, which is to say to its carrying capacity in a region where drought was the norm. As the Blackfoot knew well, overgrazing the open range in summer meant there would be no grass for winter, and that meant there would soon be no cattle for the ranchers. (Even the buffalo knew better.) Which meant they would quickly be out of business.

Still, the land lease system privileged the big boys, since many cattlemen with small herds felt disabled by the large leases. But it wasn't only the large, long-term leases. It was the nature of herd ranching. Large ranchers were able to pay cowboys to round up their herds from the open range in the spring and move them about all summer, while those with smaller herds couldn't afford those labour costs, needing instead to keep the cattle close at hand and supplement winter grazing with hay and grain. And even if their cattle were ranging with the large herd, at round-up and branding time the cattle of smallholders ran the risk of being absorbed, willy-nilly, into the large herds.

Most of all, the open range created tension between the ranchers, both large and small, and the settlers, who wanted to break up the range into small parcels protected by the newly invented, relatively cheap barbed wire. It wasn't for nothing that when Lomax published his *Cowboy Songs and Other Frontier Ballads* he struck an elegiac note when he said, "The nester [the small farmer] has come, and come to stay. Gone is the buffalo, the Indian warwhoop, the free grass of the open plain."

The foothills in Canada were more or less fully opened for settlement following the signing of the treaties, but homesteaders were able to settle in the foothills only on Crown lands that were not held by ranchers under twenty-one-year leases; it wasn't until 1896 that the government cancelled all the big leases—notice of the change had been given in 1892—allowing ranchers to buy back 10 percent of the land they had originally leased and reapply for leases on the rest. This levelled the plains for small and medium-size spreads, though water rights continued to be contentious as farmers and ranchers and townsfolk, as well as the Blackfoot on the reserves, competed for scarce water resources on the semi-desert land. Settlers could put down wherever they liked but, in order to provide some protection for the ranchers, they couldn't block access to streams and springs for the cattle; and the reserves were strictly off-limits to settlement. Unregulated squatters, on the other hand, settled wherever they could, though seldom for long on reserve land, and continued to be described with generalized contempt.

Then came the barbed wire fences, easy to set up and hard for the cattle to get past. Fences and farmers would ultimately choke the open range, or at least severely compromise it. "Don't fence me in" became a catchy refrain for good reason. In the words of an Alberta cowboy, "Barb wire is what ruined this country. At first we could keep it cut pretty well, and use the posts for firewood, but it got so, after a while, they were putting up the damned stuff faster than a guy could cut it down. Every homesteader has his little bit fenced off, and there was that whole stretch between Standoff and Fort Kipp. The Cochrane ranch had three strands running for 25 miles, and fence riders straddling it all day. When I saw that I said to myself, I says, 'This country's done for'—and you see now I was right."

. . .

In gratitude for their support during the Riel uprising, Sir John A. Macdonald offered the "loyal chiefs" who had refused to join Riel a trip east by train to visit the capital. The chiefs of course included Crowfoot and Red Crow, who, to their chagrin, found themselves in the company of some of the Cree leaders, their long-time enemies. And there were other anomalies. Crowfoot had become a symbol of the proud and patriotic Indian to the eastern press and politicians, who lauded his loyalty during the Riel troubles; but in fact it was some of his fellow chiefs, such as Red Crow, who were steadfast in their hatred of the Cree and refused to join them, while Crowfoot wavered and almost went in with the Métis and the Cree.

That said, the visit through Regina and Winnipeg to Ottawa and back through the Six Nations Reserve in Brantford, Ontario, was a startling and in some ways inspiring one for all of them, and put them in the company of many other Aboriginal leaders, especially the Iroquois of the Six Nations. Red Crow and Crowfoot had travelled to Regina and Winnipeg the year before, towns that were already far larger than Fort Macleod and Calgary, which up until then were the biggest they had seen ... and this had made them aware that not all the white people in the world were in Blackfoot territory. Instead, as one of them commented, white people seemed as numerous as the blades of grass upon the prairie ... or a swarm of gnats, though they were too courteous to say that. During the trip in the fall of 1886, accompanied by their friends the Oblate missionary Father Albert Lacombe and interpreter Jean L'Heureux, they visited Ottawa and met with Prime Minister John A. Macdonald—called "One Spot" by the Bloods, one of whom commented: "I was deeply impressed with the ability and wisdom of One Spot, who is a great friend of the Big Mother ... there was only one chief to whom I would liken him, and that was our own chief,

Mékaisto [Red Crow], but *Mékaisto* is a greater chief than One Spot and all his wise men."

A couple of days later they travelled to Brantford for the unveiling of a monument to the eighteenth-century Mohawk chief Joseph Brant, an occasion that had been central to the trip from the beginning. Dressed in their finest regalia, they were in the official party, leading the parade directly after Mohawk chief William Wage, followed by carriages with the lieutenant-governor of Ontario, the mayor of Brantford and other guests. The statue was unveiled, as well as bronze plaques illustrating the life of Brant, and as the Six Nations Indians began a war dance the western leaders responded with the war whoops of the plains. At the banquet that evening, the head of the confederate Six Nations, Chief A.G. Smith (*De-ka-nen-ra-neh*), gave a speech in perfect English—witty and wise, and one of the best of the evening. That an Indian could surpass *their* "greatest chief," the lieutenant-governor, in *his* language, was something Red Crow never forgot; and a decade later on ceremonial occasions he still wore the badge signalling his invitation to the occasion as a guest of honour. Before the Blackfoot left the east, they also visited a lumber and shingle mill at Ohsweken, on the Six Nations reserve, which was owned and operated by the Iroquois. Red Crow was deeply impressed with the possibilities this suggested for his people. He knew that they were inferior to no one; and with education and training in the new technologies (including the relatively new language of English) he was convinced they could match anyone in any enterprise . . . as they had on the plains with horses, when their forebears turned their intelligence and imagination to mastering the new technology, and surpassed everyone else.

Red Crow needed all of his statecraft when he got back to the foothills and Blood territory from his trip, for all hell had broken loose. The deaths of six young men—four of them teenagers—before he left to go east were now confirmed to have been caused by Indians from the neighbouring Gros Ventre tribe. The Blood braves had gone south to recover horses stolen from one of their bands, and been ambushed by a Gros Ventre war party. Over the next weeks and months, the unrest seemed certain to produce a war that could have broken the Blackfoot nation. Only the winter weather stopped an outbreak of violence. Red Crow and Crop Eared Wolf took the lead in proposing the conditions for a treaty, though it was fiercely opposed by some members of his tribe. Small war parties from the Bloods went down and gathered sixteen Gros Ventre horses; and a few weeks later, Gros Ventre raiders came and took forty horses belonging to Red Crow and his family. This was a blow to his economic resources as well as to his leadership, and after discussions that involved both the American and Canadian governments, a treaty expedition set out, with Red Crow and several other Blood chiefs, three North-West Mounted Police officers, the Indian agent, and Jerry Potts as interpreter. At the border, they were met by an American cavalry escort and continued on to Fort Belknap in north central Montana, where the Gros Ventres and Assiniboines shared a reservation. The Bloods were received by both angry warriors and friendly chiefs; but after several outbursts the chiefs took the lead and a peace was secured, with Red Crow speaking to accept.

This was my country once. We used to hunt the prairies with the Gros Ventres and Assiniboines and I like visiting them.

I have come over to see them, to make a treaty, and what I say I mean. . . . I hope you will stop your young men going to war. I will do the same when I get home. I am glad I have got my horses back; I feel good. We have made a treaty and we will smoke the pipe at last. . . . Now the Indians must stop fighting with each other. I will not say we do not steal horses; all Indians steal horses and the whites are just as bad.

The peace lasted only a short while, but a kind of reciprocity had been reached, sternly enforced among his people by Red Crow not because the Gros Ventres had once been allies but because it made sense. Red Crow handled the crisis in his territory better than One Spot had the Métis uprising the year before.

. . .

For the Bloods, for Red Crow and for Crop Eared Wolf, a pact of peace (which is how they conceived Treaty Seven) had never meant giving up their heritage—their religion, their language, their customs, their land. The radical reduction of their traditional hunting territory into a reserve recognized by the treaty, and the attempts by the Indian agents to restrict their movement and manage their way of life, created resentment and resistance and ultimately the cultural holocaust institutionalized by the residential schools (which began here and there around this time, and took on a brutally widespread role in the twentieth century). But in the 1880s and '90s, and for the Bloods through the early part of the twentieth century—and for many to this day—sacred and secular ceremonies, the opening and reading and customary conveyance of medicine bundles with the first thunder in spring, band and tribal societies to be joined, language and livelihood and land to be maintained—these all still offered ways of remaining proud, and remaining Blackfoot.

Which was to say, remaining civilized; for the Blackfoot saw savagery in the newcomers' behaviour as surely as some of the settlers did in the Blackfoot's. Horses, once again, provided a mitigating influence; and the importance of horses to the Blackfoot, the police and the ranchers and the many settlers who loved horse races—or just loved horses, the way many of us now love cars—offered some common ground. Quoting a compliment extended to a nineteenth-century visitor on the Argentinian plains by an unlettered *gaucho*—"He is a foreigner, true, but very civilized"—the cowboy historian Richard Slatta reminds us that "to the *gaucho* this meant that the man could ride a horse well."

Which gives another edge to the old story of savage and civilized, and to the importance of horses; and an object lesson from south of the border. The importance of horses to the Aboriginal peoples was recognized throughout the Canadian west, but in the United States there were several examples of the damage that could be done by disregarding it. In one of the most famous moments in the long and sordid history of relations between Indians and whites on this continent, the Nez Perce Chief Joseph surrendered in 1877 (the year of Treaty Seven) to the United States's General Miles in his camp in the Bear Paw Mountains of Montana, less than thirty miles from Canada and (relative) freedom. In doing so, he turned himself and his people over to the mercy of the United States government and its agents. "From where the sun now stands I will fight no more forever," he said. I suspect that if a person knows only one line of an Indian speech, it will be this one. But Chief Joseph said more than this after the surrender, framing his comments with the loyalties and treacheries that he'd come to appreciate as part of the negotiations. He too believed in keeping your word. "I believe General Miles would have kept his word if he could have done so," Chief Joseph said later. "I do not blame him for what we have suffered since the surrender. I do not know who is to blame" for the forced relocation of his tribe first to malarial swampland in Kansas and then to a reservation in Oklahoma. They eventually returned to the northwest, but were devastated by the despair that Chief Joseph identified when he added, "We gave up all our horses— over eleven hundred—and all our saddles—over one hundred— and we have not heard from them since. Someone has got our horses." It was, from his perspective, impossible to remain civilized without horses.

The calibration of civilized behaviour is perhaps the oldest— and oddest—kind of social accounting in the world, and fraught with complications; so it is refreshing to have a comic rendering from the foothills around this time. My grandfather told a story about a fellow named Tennessee, whom Ned Maunsell had met in the North-West Mounted Police hospital when he was recovering from freezing his feet trying to negotiate that letter of credit. Tennessee had been arrested for selling a bottle of whisky, and was righteously indignant. "This country is not fit for a white man to live in," he said. Then, sounding like Huck Finn getting ready to "light out for the territory," he added, "As soon as I get out of here I'm going to live in another country. The country's getting too civilized for me."

A few days later, Tennessee asked Ned: "What is this here Europe I hear so much about? Is it getting settled yet?"

"It's well settled," replied Maunsell.

"By Americans?"

"No. Chiefly by French, Germans, Norwegians, Prussians, Italians, Spaniards, and a lot of others."

"Oh pshaw!" retorted Tennessee, "all foreigners. Well, I guess it will make a country some day."

10

CHINOOK COUNTRY

"It's your fault if you sleep cold: we only ask that you fold the blankets up in the morning and put them back on the shelf."
I.G. BAKER STORE TO RANCHERS IN TOWN FOR THE NIGHT

...

ALTHOUGH THEY HAD SEEN each other several times since their first meeting on the main street in Fort Macleod in 1885, my grandfather made a visit to Crop Eared Wolf at his home on the Blood reserve in Stand Off, south of Fort Macleod, in March of 1887. It was a surprise, in more ways than one, to both of them.

The winter had been brutally cold, thirty to forty below every morning for six weeks and it once went down to fifty-one below. (It was said in town that if you wanted a lawyer, you could always find one in Harry Taylor's hotel bar waiting for the next Chinook.) On March 10, my grandfather left Fort Macleod on the way to Lee's Creek, south of the Blood reserve at Stand Off. I don't know what he was wearing, but a local rancher's description of riding out in winter to check on the herd gives a sense of the dress code.

I have a good buffalo skin cap, made to my own order, which covers my ears and has a strip across the nose, then I have a woolen comforter round my neck, then a buffalo coat, buck- skin mitts with knitted mitts inside them on my hands . . . then buffalo trousers, and on my feet a pair of woolen socks, over them a pair of thick lined German socks and over these a pair of buffalo moccasins, hair side in and wrapped over these and the bottoms of my buffalo trousers to keep the wind from going up the legs, I wrap horse bandages.

There was an unusual amount of snow on the ground this particular winter, up to a foot and a half on the low-lying land; and there had been only one brief Chinook since before Christmas. But my grandfather was feeling good, turning thirty in a few weeks, and he and Amy were happily settled. When the weather was cold, travel was easy; and he started off expecting to reach Lee's Creek in a couple of days. He had heard about a proposed Mormon settlement there, and the first large group did indeed arrive by wagon train later that spring; and he may have had in mind some banking opportunities. But this trip was about something more personal. His oldest brother, William, had died in 1855, at the age of sixteen at his home in Cobourg, Ontario, in a hunting accident that would have been comic if it weren't so tragic; he was killed when his shotgun accidentally fired as he stood by a fence lighting a cigar, his gun against his side with its butt on the ground. Reaching down to brush off some embers that had fallen, he struck the hammerlock against the fence and the gun went off. My grandfather never knew him, since he had been born two years after William's death; but the tragedy—and that terrible year, when three of his siblings had died—marked his family in ways he had never really understood. They all took some comfort in the "mysterious dispensations" that the preachers talked about; but then each of them, father and mother, three sons and the one daughter still living, found their own ways of coming to terms, inevitably awkward terms, with their family's lives and deaths. One of the reasons Nat and Jack got on so well was that they respected each other's ways; for my grandfather's ways were often … well, let's just say unusual.

In this case, they involved Lee's Creek, which flowed down from the sacred Chief Mountain, the towering spirit of the foothills and Fort Macleod. It had been named after Lee Kaiser, a bullwhacker who accidentally shot himself in a hunting accident in 1872; and my grandfather had the idea that going there might be a way of paying respect to his brother, and to the dreadful wonder of his death. A curious way, perhaps; but my grandfather never seemed to do the routine. Not a pilgrimage; but not a picnic either, not this winter.

He had been down in that direction, south of Fort Macleod, several times the previous fall before winter set in, so he knew the trail. Earlier snowfalls had filled many of the coulees, but the weather had been dry for a week or two, and the snow covering the short grass on the higher ground was blown thin. The cattle had scraped and snuffled their way through, like hungry children raiding a refrigerator; but some had died from the bitter cold, their carcasses scattered across the winter range or piled in the coulees … and since many of them were carrying calves, the spring count did not look promising. From what he saw around him, he knew the bank would be in for a rough ride later, in this its first season. The ranchers would not be able to pay off their loans, and some of the merchants in town wouldn't either—like his friend Al Grady, who had opened a hardware store a couple of years before and expanded last fall—because they relied on the ranchers for their trade. But at least this would give him a chance to see what shape some of his customers' cattle and horses were in after the past terrible winter, and what to expect. Charlie Russell, the great painter of the American west, had done a watercolour that winter of a skeletal starving cow surrounded by several wolves in the Judith Basin in Montana, called *Waiting for a Chinook*, which had brought him his first national recognition. But there were unfortunately few corresponding images of starving Indians to catch the public attention during these years. Russell came to southern Alberta the following summer, his experiences with the ranchers and the Blackfoot there helping to shape his career. He would do a painting of his friend George Lane (of the Bar U ranch) being attacked by a pack of wolves in the foothills, one of which bit off the toe-cover on Lane's stirrup before he shot him; and while the story was often told—mostly by Lane himself—in the foothills, it is a measure of the role of visual images in storytelling that it was Russell's painting, *A Question of Survival*, that made the incident famous.

Travelling was easy for my grandfather that first day, and he expected to reach Lee's Creek the following afternoon. He made camp in a little coulee, fairly free of snow because it caught the wind, but with enough shelter for his horse, which he tethered in the cottonwoods down by the frozen creek. I still have the home-made sleeping bag he used during those years, with no zipper or buttons but a heavy sheet and blankets sewn into what we would now call a mummy bag, on top of which he would throw a wrap of heavy canvas and the horse blanket from under the saddle, still steaming and warm. The next morning, after a breakfast of johnnycakes and bacon that he cooked on a little fire fed by some cottonwood and serviceberry branches—instead of the old stand by, buffalo chips—he rolled up his bags, saddled his horse, and headed south. It was clear and cold; but in an hour or so he saw the unmistakable Chinook arch of cloud and a belt of blue in the western sky, and could feel the temperature rising. And then he began to notice the small splashes of water as he rode across another little creek up onto the benchlands above the Belly River.

Chinooks work like a refrigerator in reverse. When westerly winds carrying moist air from the Pacific hit the mountains, the air cools as its rises, dropping rain and then snow. If the conditions are right, the air, nicely dried, will slide right down the eastern slopes of the Rockies ten thousand feet to the plains below. Cold air heats up when it falls, because the air is denser and the pressure higher at lower altitudes; and dry air warms twice as fast as moist air. The warm air pushing out the cold creates the wind called a Chinook, raising the temperature dramatically. Chinooks were always welcome in the middle of winter, but they came with a warning. If they melted the ice, a traveller could be stranded on the wrong side of a river for days, maybe weeks. This one came with a vengeance, and within hours there was flooding everywhere . . . a reminder of the profound disinterest of the open prairie, or indeed any natural habitat, in your own particular welfare. At Fort Macleod, three of the new telegraph poles on the west shore of the Old Man's River and two on the east side were broken in two by enormous blocks of ice thrown into them by the flood waters; and all the southern rivers were impassable with the crushing ice floes sweeping by.

The cattle weren't paying attention to the rivers, at least at first. They sensed a change, a new lease on life. They wouldn't have to scuffle and scrape anymore. They looked up to the sky in a moment of faith, and stumbled on through the crud and the crust in a mellow mood. The temperature, which had been well below freezing that morning, was up into the fifties by now. The snow started to melt; and before long they could see the grass underneath the water that covered the land.

But this Chinook was breathtakingly short-lived. The cold weather came again, hard and fast, and within a very short while the water covering the grass was frozen so hard that the cattle couldn't break through. It was much worse now than it had been with the snow cover. All the cattle could do was look at the grass a few inches below the surface of the ice.

Late February to early March was known as the Uncertain Moon in the Blackfoot calendar, and it was the most dangerous time for snowblindness, with the intense glare of the sun, still low in the sky, on the snow. Snowblindness could be deadly, as Ned Maunsell almost found out some years earlier when he was found by some Bloods heading towards the mountains when he thought he was heading in the opposite direction towards Stand Off. My grandfather knew about it, but even Jerry Potts got caught a couple of times; and so did my grandfather this day, with the glaze of water on the snow dazzling his eyes. But he trusted his horse, and let him have his head. The horse, for his part, wondered what on earth was the matter with the old boy, but wasn't complaining because with his big ears and big nose and big eyes with big lashes to keep off the sun, he could hear and smell and soon see the horses of Crop Eared Wolf and his band, where he found a warm welcome for both himself and my grandfather.

Crop Eared Wolf greeted my grandfather, and praised the

sorrel—his horse—for getting him there. He took him into his house, and saw him through. His eyes eventually recovered, though he couldn't see for a couple of days, and he had a fierce headache, for both of which Crop Eared Wolf had remedies; and he had sent a rider to Amy to let her know that Sorreltop Jack was all right. When he was feeling a bit better, Crop Eared Wolf took him to his tipi, where a good fire had been laid in the hearth, and they smoked a pipe, which kept them in a conversation when words ran out. But then the Methodist missionary John Maclean came by, and thanks to his fluency in Blackfoot the three of them talked for hours together about their lives, about the troubles last fall when Maclean had found himself between opposing sides on the Blood reserve—he was friends with both the war chief White Calf and Crop Eared Wolf, who with his father was trying to avoid war—and about the challenges they were all facing now after a hard winter, though it seemed the Blood horses at least had come through well.

Maclean told my grandfather and Crop Eared Wolf about a reprimand he had received from Medicine Calf, White Calf's predecessor as war chief and one who initially opposed Treaty Seven. Maclean had put out new ropes to tether his horses one night... and woke up to find them gone. He told Medicine Calf—of whom he said to my grandfather on another occasion, "His word was true, and promises were never broken, and I was glad to number him among my friends"—and shortly afterwards he came to return his ropes, and to give him a dressing-down. "I thought you were a wise man," he said to the missionary. "Would you put new ropes on your horses and turn your animals out to graze in the white man's town? No, I would not do that. You would not expect to find your ropes again? No! And you tempt our young Indians. Do you think we have no bad men in our camps? You are not very wise if you expect our people to be perfect, and different from white men." In a journal note from around that time Maclean identified for himself several "noble men—orators—dignified statesmen" among the Blackfoot, listing Crowfoot, Red Crow, White Calf, Medicine Calf and Crop Eared Wolf.

Knowing that my grandfather had started a bank, Maclean said he was glad because he had just lent one of the Bloods some money to buy a wagon and another young man some cash and he wasn't sure how to handle the paperwork, because it was money he had from the Methodist headquarters in Toronto and he didn't like asking his friends to sign pieces of paper when he trusted their word. My grandfather said he would go with a handshake for something like that... but then he didn't have anyone to answer to except his brother. And then they listened to Crop Eared Wolf tell them about Chief Mountain, near where my grandfather was headed when the Chinook came.

Maclean had learned the Blackfoot language with the help of Jerry Potts and Joe Healy and Dave Mills, a black man with a Blood mother who came up from Fort Benton to Fort Whoop-Up as a bullwhacker driving the ox teams for I.G. Baker, and eventually settled by the Blood reserve. Healy and Mills had been called on to translate the text of the agreement made when the Blackfoot moved to their reserve on the Belly River, which involved signing a new treaty, giving up their rights to the old lands and taking possession of the new ones. Dave Mills was highly regarded by Red Crow, and regularly interpreted for the Indian agents, having a particularly literal instinct when it came to translating Blackfoot names into English. On one occasion, an Indian identified himself as *Pooksisi*... which Mills translated, quite correctly, as Small Asshole. It was changed in the agency records to Small Backside... and a year later changed again, when the Indian announced that he had been given a new name, Not Good. Translation can be complicated, as we have seen; and for all his idiosyncrasy, even Jerry Potts could be a stickler for sometimes unseemly accuracy. During the speeches that preceded the signing of Treaty Seven, each Indian was introduced to the commissioners, and their names given in English. One stepped forward and the interpreter at work on that occasion, apparently given to euphemisms, gave the speaker's name as Horse's Tail... at which Jerry Potts, who was nearby, yelled out, "You son of a bitch, you lie. I tell you it is Horse's Ass."

. . .

Banking may have been a trade for my grandfather, but with Crop Eared Wolf's welcome never far from his mind, he thought running one should be like running a hotel such as Harry Taylor's—he would be in the business of hospitality, credit hospitality, with its own rough and ready rules such as those Kamoose posted—except for "No Jawbone." That would have put my grandfather out of business. He believed in Jawbone credit, in a person's word and a handshake. Foolish familiarity would get you gone; but genial hospitality and good judgement would get you business, and keep business going.

My grandfather's approach clearly reflected the hospitality that was widespread in the foothills at the time, where everyone's latch-string was out—doors were never locked—and passing strangers were free to come in and help themselves to a meal or stay the night, as long as they left the place tidier than when they came. The I.G. Baker store in Fort Macleod routinely offered blankets off the shelves to ranchers who were in town for the night, saying (in the words of one of them), "It's your fault if you sleep cold; we only ask you to fold them up in the morning and put them back on the shelf." And John Maclean told about visiting one of the Blood tipis where he found a cowboy from one of the local ranches, seriously ill, being tended by the Indian family . . . just as my grandfather had been.

My grandfather obviously loved the risks involved in banking, for almost every loan was a risk in that time and place; and he loved the fact that the skills he put to use managing risk at the bank were also useful playing cards at Tony La Chappelle's saloon, and betting on racehorses . . . which he also loved to do, even winning some blankets from Crop Eared Wolf. In any event, the Cowdry brothers seem to have managed their risks, and the responsibilities to their depositors, remarkably well. Certainly others admired their style and appreciated their support; Jack was routinely involved in all the affairs of the community, and competitors such as the Bank of Commerce even appointed him as director for southern Alberta later in the 1890s. No other bank was as heavily involved in financing ranching operations in the foothills, even though that brought with it the ups and downs of the cattle business. Seasonal surprises, patterns and problems of family as well as commercial life, illness, all influenced business; and so did what could be the biggest surprise of all, the weather.

And it was the weather that winter of 1886–87 that put my grandfather's tolerance for risk to the test, for Jack and Nat Cowdry almost lost the bank. It was, as Jack had expected after his trip in March, a disastrous season for the ranchers, and the round-up that spring became known as the Big Die-Up throughout the north-west plains. Whether clustering in the coulees or huddling out in the open, animals died in staggering numbers, often piling on top of each other as they crowded close together for warmth. The country around Pincher Creek suffered the fewest losses—which is to say thousands of cattle, not tens of thousands—and the cattle ranging on the Blood reserve came through fairly well, but the numbers of Blackfoot cattle were still small in comparison with the bigger ranches in the district, several of which lost half their herds, and some more. One of the most experienced cattlemen in southern Alberta, Tom Lynch, had brought in two hundred and ninety "dogies"—scrubby orphan calves—the previous fall and rounded up only eight in the spring. To quote L.V. Kelly, praising the resilience of the ranchers in *The Range Men*,

> No business in the world can recuperate from losses that the cattle industry receives and recovers from. No known legitimate undertaking could meet the blows that the best ranches of this province come smilingly and hopefully through. No business, without insurance, could within three or four years be wealthier than it was before half its capital stock was utterly lost. What business, other than ranching, could have survived such damages as were experienced by the stockmen in 1886–87. . . .

Well, Cowdry Brothers Bank, for one. But it was a close call. On top of the catastrophic losses, beef prices fell in Canada and the United States (for there were many more cattle going *into* that winter than the year before, and even though losses were high so was the inventory of cattle). For the Cowdry brothers, it was not a good start. Nat and Jack's experience in Saskatchewan had helped them judge the needs of farmers and ranchers, but there was no telling about the weather. Still, they took on the losses with the same resignation that their customers and the community displayed; and very few folks went under in Fort Macleod, kept afloat by the credit the bank extended, along with some interest-free loans, which helped almost all of them make it through. For there was still optimism in the midst of the wreckage—you had to be an optimist in the territory, just ask the Blackfoot—and some of the optimism must have been nourished by the bank's backing, and the Cowdry brothers' belief in the future. They were treading water themselves, but they made it to the next season all right, counting on local businesses in Fort Macleod as well as the North-West Mounted Police and the government Indian agencies—less immediately vulnerable to the weather—to have money on deposit that they could put back to the ranchers, or some cash in reserve. And they all learned some lessons about maintaining supplies of feed for cattle that could not find grass beneath snow cover, or could not get to the coulees and benchlands where feed was sometimes available. Cropping hay and grain became more common, and Jack and Nat supported such ventures, though dryland farming was always marginal. Some ranchers brought in sheep to replace cattle. Few of the ranchers had turned to "stock farming" yet—finishing cattle for market on hay and grain rather than raising a herd on the open range; and Ned Maunsell, who had been farming crops for a couple of years to supply the small-parcel settlers as well as the North-West Mounted Police, gave it up and made cattle ranching his principal business that summer on the heels of that terrible winter. He was undoubtedly encouraged by the contrarians Nat and Jack, for he quickly became one of Cowdry Brothers' biggest customers. Keeping cattle on the open range in winter under minimal supervision was still part of life, and from that year on my grandfather rode out frequently in winter to get a feel for the situation ... though fortunately never again into the conditions he encountered on that trip to Lee's Creek and Crop Eared Wolf.

. . .

That late Chinook left many cattle to starve within sight of the winter grass that would have kept them alive, frozen after a brief taste. Grass under ice. It was as though all they had was food under glass. Or photographs of food. In a grim way, they were demonstrating the limits of what the new "virtual" world of photography and the telegraph and telephone had to offer.

Photography, which was fairly new at that time, brought the illusion of being there. Nobody was really fooled, but people were fascinated. The telephone would soon offer another dimension; but it was photography, perhaps because it came first, that made people nervous, and sometimes downright fearful. To take a picture is to take something, after all; and many people thought it might be something important, like their spirit. "We only want to capture the moment," explained the photographers, using another uncomfortable word.

Of course this is what good storytellers do too, capture the moment, even though in the case of historians they were usually not there at the time ... and indeed neither they nor their listeners ever are there, wherever "there" is, when any story is being told. This contradiction is familiar to all of us; and we are adept at taking virtual nourishment from stories and songs. Photography simply offered a new style of storytelling. In the nineteenth century, they used to talk about style and virtue in the same breath; and art critics would speak of the style, the soul, the *virtù*—the essential being—of Renaissance painting. In a nice turn that brings our new technologies into perspective, "virtual" comes from the same root as "virtue."

This may seem new, but it is in fact very old, for humans have needed imaginative and spiritual as well as real and material nourishment from the beginning of time, and seem to have always been well aware of the wonderful nonsense of language and story and song. Storytellers from the island of Majorca in the Mediterranean begin their tales by saying "It was, and it was not," and Khoikhoi storytellers in the southern African Kalahari Desert start with a single word—|garube—which means "the happening that is not happening." To remind us that this is not just a trick for the unsophisticated, the modernist painter René Magritte gives us an image of a tobacco pipe titled *Ceci n'est pas une pipe*—"This is not a pipe." On occasions like the Passover Seder, we are invited to believe that we *are* there, surrendering to the artifice of illusion even as we eat an actual meal. Belief is always surrounded by doubt, whether you are a storyteller or a banker. Put differently, belief takes place inside what T.S. Eliot called the "sacred wood," the occasion of ceremonial practice: bedtime for children, storytelling around the fire in the tipi, or giving your word to the banker or the Blackfoot. Jonathan Foer, who edited the *New American Haggadah*—the traditional guidebook for the stories, songs and ceremonies of the Jewish Seder—was once asked by his son, "Is Moses a real person?" "I don't know," he replied, "but we're related to him." Every culture has its version of this, in which wonder rests easy.

. . .

One of the friends from Ontario whom my grandfather kept in touch with all his life was the Canadian historian George Wrong. Jack was a couple of years older, and they had met in the late 1870s when George was on his way to becoming an Anglican minister and in due course head of the Department of History at the University of Toronto, where he served for over thirty years. (His successor was Chester Martin, who became the leading authority on the Dominion Lands Policy.) Wrong saw the central storytelling role of history, and the ways in which history is always close cousin to the stories and songs that constitute a national literature; and their conversations and correspondence nourished my grandfather's interest in the celebration of achievements such as Crop Eared Wolf had painted on his quirt. The warrior was well known for his artistic and historical craft, having recorded his exploits capturing horses across the plains and raiding other tribes as far away as the Yellowstone—exploits that secured his high status among his people and respect from many others—on a buffalo robe commissioned in 1882 by an Indian agent (later a rancher) named Charlie Geddes. The painted robe eventually found its way into the care of the North-West Mounted Police; and it provided the Canadian ethnographer Marius Barbeau with a defining story and an image for the coloured frontispiece of his landmark book, *Indian Days on the Western Prairies*. Later, the robe ended up at Royal Canadian Mounted Police (successor to the North-West Mounted Police) headquarters in Regina, to be used as a training text for recruits, not only for understanding troublemakers but also for recognizing Blackfoot history. In that sense, Crop Eared Wolf's robe—

celebrating his courage and craft in raids against tribal enemies—is a distinctly personal counterpoint to the war memorials that grace almost every town in Canada; as such it is also a sad reminder of Canada's failure to recognize the contributions of individual First Nations, Métis and Inuit warriors to Canada's military forces since Confederation. (The original robe is now back with the Crop Eared Wolf family, with a copy made by Blood artist Running Coyote in RCMP headquarters.)

Boasting and toasting. Praise singers (we call them publicists now) have often been paid for this, but for millennia historians have been our tribal toastmasters, boasting about the actors and agents, honourable or dishonourable, that they choose to highlight and toasting the results of their actions, constructive or destructive. Historians who are bored by their subject are boring. End of story.

There's a story an Irish North-West Mounted Police friend told my grandfather, and he passed on to my mother, about an ancient Gaelic debate in which the legendary Finn asked his companions about the finest music in the world. First his son Oisín proposed the call of the cuckoo singing from the highest hedge bush; then Oscar, their comrade-in-arms, suggested the ring of a spear on a shield; and soon the others in the group joined in: the belling of a stag across the water; the baying of a pack of dogs in the distance; the song of a lark in the morning; the laughter of a happy girl; the whisper of one making love. Then Finn himself was asked. "The music of what happens," answered the great chief. "That is the finest music in the world."

. . .

Wonder comes in various guises, which need to be factored into our understanding of Aboriginal life, as well as our own. Ironically, and despite what may be our scepticism about the wonders they were promoting, some of the missionaries in Blackfoot territory were ahead of their time in recognizing this. John Maclean, for example, described how he was sternly corrected, as one might correct a child, when he questioned why food and implements left for the use of the dead (placed on a platform in a tree or raised on a scaffold) were still there years after. "These are spirits and they live on the souls of these things," he was told. "We are material, and we live on the matter of these things."

John Maclean was a refreshingly independent spirit, and he had the respect of many Blackfoot friends, some of them among the angriest over what was happening to them. In 1889 he received a letter from the Methodist Committee in Toronto, which employed him, asking how it was that after nine years he had not converted a single person. (In fact, many of the missionaries of various denominations had very few conversions to record among the Bloods and the Peigan during these years ... but many friends.) I have not been able to find the letter Maclean wrote back, but a few years later he published a popular book in which he gave his answer. "We wish to make them white men," he wrote, "but they desire to become better Indians. They believe the native culture is best suited for themselves, and having developed under it, and enjoyed it so long, they care not to give it up for an untried system. There is a danger of educating them away from their real life." For Maclean, the "real life" of the "real people" was part and parcel of their imaginative life—their stories and songs and Sun Dances and medicine bundles that confirmed who they were, and where they belonged; their knowledge of the land, the weather and the plants and animals that told them how to live there; and the spirits of place and power that spoke to them.

The Kiowa writer Scott Momaday, author of the novel *House Made of Dawn,* once described how a traditional Indian view of nature involved bringing man and nature into alignment, first of all to achieve some kind of moral order and then to enable a person "not only to see what is really there, but also to see what is *really* there. Unless we understand this distinction," he added, "we will have difficulty understanding the Indian view of the natural world." Maclean understood that; and understood too that most of us know more than we realize about this, for the paradox is inherent in our own view of the world, shaped by the stories of science and religion and the arts that give meaning to our lives. "We're not sure" is the signature of good science, while "we are sure" is the signature of its storytelling. In the arts, it's often the other way around. Religion encourages us to forget the difference between being sure and not sure, if only for a moment. But that moment is at the heart of all storytelling, creating a covenant in wonder within a ceremony of belief that may be different for each tradition of storytelling, but eventually becomes as familiar as "once upon a time" or "let *x* be such and *y* be so" or "hallelujah." As the Australian anthropologist William Stanner wrote, about the customary forms of secular and sacred ceremony that constitute the "dreamings" of the Pitjantjatjara in Australia, "custom is the reality, beliefs but the shadows which custom makes on the wall." These are words that apply both to Blackfoot storytelling and to our own.

. . .

The first years of the bank were, to say the least, interesting ones, quite apart from that disastrous first winter. Fires were always a problem on the prairies, and fearsome stories of their spread haunted everyone who lived there. The railway had added a new threat with their "fire wagons," mitigated somewhat when they ploughed an eight-foot fireguard alongside the lines. But fires would continue to be a menace, especially with a wind that sometimes seemed to blow forever. So was liquor smuggling which had never really gone away, and everyone realized that it would probably be around until judgement day.

Jack and Nat had developed a good trade with many ranchers, mostly small and medium-size, though by the 1890s they also had business dealings with Pat Burns and George Lane and Archie Maclean and A.E. Cross, the big four who bankrolled the first Calgary Stampede; and with Ned Maunsell, who was building up a large herd and diversifying, buying up the old butcher business of I.G. Baker in 1892. Start-up costs for a ranch were substantial, but manageable with help from the Cowdrys. For a ranch of two thousand acres, the cost would be somewhere between fifteen and sixteen thousand dollars: $10,000 for the stock, including saddle horses; $2,500 for buildings, fencing and equipment; $3,000 for incidentals; and $165 for a lease and homestead of a hundred acres. Some of the bank's customers had herds of fewer than a hundred and fifty head, such as the spread owned by Dave Cochrane; but they had many customers with larger herds, up to six hundred head, including William and John Black's. The Black brothers were stalwart supporters of the town as well as the countryside, where they had settled in 1884, and few enterprises in the foothills succeeded without their mischievous participation, often in concert with a banker named Jack Cowdry. But their ranch was a serious venture, and Jack was delighted when they brought in a Devon bull from a famous breeder in England to beef up their herd. It was not only an ancient breed, from his father's home county, but its colour was chestnut. Another Sorreltop.

The Cowdry brothers had counted on the success of local businesses in Fort Macleod, slightly less immediately vulnerable to the weather, to have money on deposit to lend back to the ranchers; and in keeping that line clear, they protected their depositors and ensured the continued availability of funds to the community. And they had a strict agreement between themselves never to use bank funds to underwrite any of their own adventures (such as several rather doubtful mining enterprises in British Columbia that intrigued my grandfather). Henry Klassen, the most authoritative historian of Alberta business, said that "as bankers, the Cowdrys concentrated on public service." I'm not sure I'd go that far, but they certainly saw their success as the community's. They had to earn their good names, but earn them they did. They secured the trust of the national banks from whom they needed to borrow money if the bank were to grow; and during the 1890s their credit rating was remarkably high, especially for an unregulated bank.

In a familiar move, some of the ranchers—even those who had substantial spreads, like the Blacks—took other jobs to make ends meet. William Black hit the ground running when he first came to the territory, starting the ranch with his brother and at the same time joining in late 1885 with other folks in Fort Macleod to build a town hall. Since the modest property tax revenues all went to the North-West Territories government, he and his new-found friends formed a joint stock company to fund the building. The shares sold out before the prospectus was printed, and the town hall was built within a few months, functioning as a school, a courthouse and a very popular place for dances and concerts and public meetings. William worked for my grandfather in the bank for several years, and was a co-conspirator in their impudent newspaper *The Outlaw* before going to the Blood reserve to do the Indian agency accounts there.

His brother John started a business in town right opposite the Hudson's Bay Company, for which he had worked for several years, and his announcement of the opening of his store is a reminder that the sometimes rough-and-tumble folks in Fort Macleod were much more aware of things than we might expect. Recalling the distinction between "allies and friends" and "subjects" made by William Johnson in the early days of British North America and assumed by Canada on Confederation, and the casual misrepresentations of Treaty Seven and its Blackfoot signatories that were out and about around town, casting them as uncivilized and dependent wards, consider the advertisement for his new general supplies store that he put in the newspaper, with its cunningly contrary phrasing.

> *John Black, the gentleman adventurer into Fort Macleod and the Belly River, authorized by low prices and popular satisfaction to do business with the white subjects and red allies of her Gracious Majesty.*

White *subjects* and red *allies*. He had neatly turned things around, and in doing so turned the tables on some of the townsfolk ... and while no doubt this was lost on some of them, we can also be sure that their friends would have enlightened them.

11

HOMELAND AND FRONTIER

"The frontier ends when the pimps come to town."
PATRICIA NELSON LIMERICK
. . .

NAT HAD ALWAYS PLANNED to return to Ontario after they got the bank business going; but he stayed in Fort Macleod for a couple of years, and in 1887 he married and brought his Bermuda-born wife, Anna, there. During that time, both he and Jack also nourished other interests—my grandfather in horses and cattle, as well as local and territorial politics and public service; and Nat in history, both natural and national. He gave a talk to Fort Macleod's newly formed Literary, Scientific and Historical Society in November 1887; and he published a long article—unusually long for that newspaper—in the *Macleod Gazette* the following January on local plants and trees, drawing heavily on local (which is to say Blackfoot) knowledge. At the time, he had been there only a couple of years, but he seems to have spent a good amount of that time out and about the countryside... which, botany aside, would have given him and Jack a head start when it came to assessing projects for loans.

Then, with the birth of their son, Vincent, in 1888, and Anna's health uncertain, Nat took his family and went back east, giving Jack power of attorney over the bank and its business. It must have taken considerable faith in his brother for Nat to leave him in charge, since John was just thirty years old and not as experienced as the ancient thirty-eight-year-old Nat, and almost all Nat's money was bound up with the bank. But Nat trusted Jack, and both of them were straightforward—blunt, my mother said. And not easily rattled, which served the two of them well when they were having to make decisions at a distance, and quickly. Over the next seventeen years, they kept in close touch by telegraph and later telephone, and by frequent family visits.

After Nat left to go back to Ontario, he started a grain business and took a position in the local bank in Waterford, eventually managing it until it was taken over by the Bank of Commerce. He obviously played his part in that community too; and his interests in the natural sciences flourished. Much later, between 1919 and 1921, Nat spent time in China visiting Vincent, who was there to establish a medical school in Peking funded by the Rockefeller Foundation, bringing traditional Chinese medicine into conversation with Western techniques. During the relatively short time he was in China, Nat collected and classified and described over 2,200 plants from the northern coast and mountains in a monograph, published by the Peking Society of Natural History after his death in 1925 as the *Cowdry Collection of Chihli Flora*. His father Thomas's interest in natural science had clearly passed to him and his brother Ned and to his grandson Vincent; and to my grandfather too, but in the more practical way of understanding how things worked.

In some of his letters to his brother, Jack writes how much he misses him and how he is now working twice as hard on his own, expanding the bank—cautiously—to the small towns close by, such as Pincher Creek, and trying to take on a central role in the southern Alberta ranching and business and civic communities. My grandfather was not a dispensing angel, because he now had a wife and family to look after, and depositors to protect; but neither was he a carpetbagger, here today and gone thereafter. And he seems to have had remarkably affectionate relations with his customers. Fred Haultain's cousin's daughter, Henrietta (or Etta, as she was known), tells a story about a North-West Mounted Police officer finding himself in difficulties after buying some stock in a gold mining company that went broke, and then facing dismissal from the force for being drunk on duty after an all-night wake for a friend. Even in this unfortunate state the officer felt moved to say to friends in the barracks, "I feel very sorry for Cowdry," because he had taken out a loan to buy the stock against his future salary. It all turned out well— after an inquiry he was "retired" from the force with a small pension, perhaps partly because the commander of the detachment at the time, Sam Steele, was operating as what Henrietta called a "stock broker" for the Cariboo mining venture (in which my grandfather also put some money, along with the irrepressible Dave Cochrane). But it isn't usual, in my experience, for anyone to feel sorry for a banker.

Except perhaps for my own father, who took to banking himself. He had begun his working life as a logger and hard-rock miner in northern Ontario; but then he got a job as a teller in a bank, and by the time I was growing up he was manager of a branch of the Imperial Bank of Canada on Broadway at Cambie

Street in Vancouver. He made friends in the community, including the Chinese market gardeners and shopkeepers and the Sikh loggers and truck drivers who had been part of life in the city since early in the century. I remember one story of a Chinese customer of his to whom he had loaned a substantial amount of money and who then disappeared, leaving my father holding the bag—an empty bag. Local managers had much more authority to extend credit than they do now, when they are routinely overshadowed by head office; and this loan presented a serious threat to the local branch, and to my father's reputation. He didn't mention it to anyone (except my mother), but he was visited one day by a delegation from the Chinese community, who handed him a bag full of enough cash to cover the loan. They obviously felt sorry for Chamberlin. When my father asked, over the grateful cups of tea he had prepared for his visitors, what happened to the wayward customer, they said he had returned to China. Not, my father interpreted, of his own free will.

. . .

Life was not all business for my grandfather (or my father, for that matter), and maybe that contributed to Jack Cowdry's genial relations with his customers. He loved to get old and new friends together over a good meal to tell stories and listen to the music of what happened . . . and talk about what might happen next. He and Amy would throw parties at their house, with dinners like the one whose menu I found in a leather North-West Mounted Police order book he had that was filled with recipes. This one featured a summer feast of "tomato soup with bread in a napkin on the left; roast ducks with parsley garnish, gravy and apple sauce; scalloped potatoes, creamed celery and peas; and deep plum tart and sliced peaches for dessert, along with individual jellies with wine, whipped cream and macaroons." If asked about how all this gracious living, straight out of Victorian England or southern Ontario (there was little difference), fitted with being in Blackfoot territory, I'm sure Jack Cowdry would have said that Red Crow and Crop Eared Wolf often told him how important it was that he not give up the traditions of his people, because they would help him keep a sense of honour and humour and home . . . just as it was important, they would always add, that he not ask them to give up theirs. And he took that to apply not only to sacred ceremonies, sacrosanct as they were, but also to traditions of clothing and cooking and entertainment. This suited my grandfather just fine, for he was a bit of a dandy and liked dressing well and eating well and smoking cigars and drinking port of an evening and keeping up with the stories and songs and music and painting from his eastern Canadian and European heritage. He said holding on to such habits made him relish the ceremonies of the Blackfoot even more, which may have been an excuse, but he always brought it back to the Blackfoot men and their horses dressed up in their wonderfully beaded and woven rigging, while the men spent hours brushing and braiding the horses and as much time preening themselves, using tweezers to pull out any hairs on their face, for they prided themselves on their hereditary smooth faces, and their long, braided hair. As for my grandfather, my mother remembered that he always took trouble trimming his sorrel-coloured beard, which he sported all his life.

. . .

In the foothills during my grandfather's time, one form of specifically Blackfoot storytelling irritated the white custodians of civil society—specifically the police, and sometimes (but not always) the missionaries. They were relatively comfortable with Blackfoot stories about war, because that sort of boasting was familiar to them; they had grown up reading about Achilles and the Trojan war, and the pages of the *Macleod Gazette* were full of news about whatever war the British happened to be engaged in, from the Afghan war that had just ended in 1880 to the African Boer wars that began in the eighties and would end in 1902.

What bothered them was storytelling about stealing horses. They could see that horse stealing was a way of exalting the virtues of courage and cunning and conspicuous consumption (though the last of these a number of them might have deemed suitable for white folk but not for Indians), but they worried that it was also a way of exacerbating old conflicts, especially between tribes who had long been in competition with each other for territory and trade, and of engendering a proliferation of small but often deadly feuds. The authorities complained to the government, to each other and, in a completely futile gesture, to the Blackfoot chiefs about how ceremonial and social occasions like the traditional sacred summer Sun Dance gave warriors an opportunity to tell stories about old raids and their feats of bravery and achievement—including the number of horses they had gathered in from their enemies... exactly the sorts of stories the chiefs wanted to tell. "This," said Superintendent Sam Steele in 1889, "has a pernicious effect on the young men." Possibly it did—at least insofar as it inspired some of them to do what young people have done since the beginning of time: seek opportunities to match their elders' achievements by replicating their adventures.

But it also gave these young men a sense of pride that was hard to come by in those days, and a sense of purpose in finding new ways to demonstrate the heritage of a noble people—not once noble but still noble. Which is to say, it gave them a story to share.

But the risks of retaliation were beginning to tell; and the chiefs of the Blackfoot did their best to discourage, and by 1890 to prohibit, raids against the Crow and the Assiniboine and the other plains tribes south of the border (in which many of them had earned their own status), initially with about as much success as any elder talking to rebellious, rambunctious youngsters, but then going so far as to return stolen horses and turn over the horse thieves to the police ... though often misplacing evidence that they knew would be necessary to convict in court. Still, the stories kept coming, and kept the Blackfoot together, proud and positive even when they were feeling "downpressed" (as Rastafarians say, turning oppression upside down). That, after all, is what stories do. Oscar Wilde, the great Irish trickster, once suggested that "we should live our life as a form of fiction. To be a fact is to be a failure." Becoming addicted to facts is to become one of Mr. Gradgrind's students, making false choices between the familiar and the strange, the true and the untrue, the worthy and the worthless. To be fully human, we need to both surrender to a story and separate ourselves from it, to live in both grief-stricken reality and the grace of the imagination, to both wait for spring and wonder whether it will arrive, to believe the stories we are told, and not to believe them too. The Blackfoot knew this; and by holding on to their stories they reminded the settlers that they did too.

. . .

Since the beginning of time, storytelling has inspired people to do things … or to imagine doing them. One story that was soon to capture the imagination of many people in the United States and Canada was about "Lighting out for the Territory." It wasn't *The Adventures of Huckleberry Finn*, where "lighting out" is left to the last line of the book, but a novel written by Owen Wister called *The Virginian: A Horseman of the Plains*. It was, it is generally agreed, the first authentic western novel, and certainly the most popular; its hero was a fourteen-year-old orphan who displayed fierce pride and stubborn independence by heading west to make his way in the world. Its story, in the words of the American writer Teresa Jordan, "was absorbed into so many family stories that one would think the trails west were blazed by armies of homeless fourteen year olds." And it became a kind of history of the west, with both American and Canadian connections, shaped by a storyteller's imagination of how people were assumed to live in the western territories, their destiny and doggedness so interwoven that they become indistinguishable. It was dedicated to Theodore Roosevelt (who seems to have had a second career as a literary inspiration); and when it came out in 1902, it was a bestseller across the continent.

My mother, born in 1899, recalled having the book read to her when she was still a youngster … and being astonished when her father said he actually *knew* the Virginian. My mother didn't think anyone actually knew people in books, and said so. But then my grandfather asked what people she liked best in the world, and after dutifully listing him and all the other people in her family, she named half a dozen characters from her favourite books. And it turned out that a rancher whom my grandfather knew well, who had come to Canada from the United States in

1888 and taken over as foreman of the famous Bar U ranch from George Lane, was the *real* Virginian. His name was Everett Johnson (known as Ebbs since he was a boy, but called Ed by friends in later life) and he had gone out to Wyoming from his birthplace in Virginia, guiding Owen Wister on a trip he made to the west and inspiring the novel. In the copy he inscribed to Johnson, Wister wrote "to the hero, from the author," and that's as good as it gets from a writer. My mother thought that story was too good to be true; but her father said it was, as stories often are, the best of them confusing reality and the imagination... but by then she'd wandered off to join her aunts, who were teaching her how to crochet.

There was another part to the story that interested my grandfather, especially with his bank robbery in mind, though he didn't tell my mother until much later. I'll set it up by recalling the store and saloon keeper Tony La Chappelle, who saved Ned Maunsell's life on that ill-fated trip to get a cheque cashed. Tony, as I mentioned, knew every trail between Fort Macleod and Fort Benton in Montana, and the reason he did was that he had brought whisky into the foothills during the early days. And he still did, long after the trade had become illegal, securing it in "hole-in-the-wall" huts set deep into the cut banks along the rivers. Such holes in the wall were not unusual in the territory around Fort Macleod in those days, nor were stories like those you would find in a book such as *The Virginian*.

Ebbs Johnson had a couple of young cowboy friends back in Wyoming, where he had started his career at the famous "76" ranch in Powder River country. One was Robert Leroy Parker, though he gave his name as Butch Cassidy. The other was Harry Longabaugh; and the three of them remained close for years.

After Johnson left to come to the foothills, Longabaugh got himself into trouble stealing a horse and a saddle and a revolver and spent eighteen months in the brand new jailhouse in a town called Sundance, named after the sacred Blackfoot summer ceremony. When he got out, Johnson wanted to help him, so he brought him up to the Bar U northwest of Fort Macleod and gave him a job breaking horses. Unfortunately Harry wasn't very good at it; and no cowboy likes to ride a wring-tail (a nervous horse). So Johnson put him to work riding herd, which by all accounts he did fairly well. But Harry was restless, and after a year—during which he was best man at Johnson's wedding—he left the foothills and returned to his old habits and haunts in the United States, soon joining Butch Cassidy, finding a home with his Wild Bunch boys in the aptly named Hole-in-the-Wall Gang, and becoming known as the Sundance Kid. The Wild Bunch became the most famous outlaws, credited with the largest number of bank and train robberies, on the continent; but when my grandfather met him along the bar in Kamoose Taylor's hotel, he was simply good-natured Harry, an amiable cowboy. Or maybe my grandfather just knew how to handle bank robbers.

. . .

Just around this time, many people on both sides of the border were talking about the frontier, the Canadians looking south for a cue and the Americans just looking around, making a myth full of compelling contradictions. In 1893, from May to October, the midwestern city of Chicago hosted something called the Columbian Exposition, held (a year late) to commemorate the four-hundredth anniversary of Columbus's arrival in the Americas. During the fair, two notable storytellers took different stages and offered their different perspectives on the frontier. One was a historian named Frederick Jackson Turner, who came to deliver a paper at a historical congress to a mostly academic audience on what he called "The Significance of the Frontier in American History." The other was a showman called Buffalo Bill Cody, and his performance—twice a day opposite the fairground in a covered grandstand accommodating eighteen thousand people—was titled Buffalo Bill's Wild West and Congress of Rough Riders of the World. Together, they established markers for the understanding of the American west that continues to this day. Both Turner and Cody were quintessentially American in many ways; but being neighbours, they also offered a crucial perspective on the west in Canada at that time. In the United States, this moment was said to mark the closing of the frontier of so-called empty Indian land for the taking and primitive wilderness for the taming. In Canada, it marked a moment in which the national dream took over the native domain.

But for these couple of decades in the foothills, this was also a moment when western civic values, still in the making, had a chance to counter eastern establishment ambitions and merge First Nations and newcomer ideals, celebrating the different heritages of both Blackfoot and settler. The violence and vigilante justice, the Indian wars and range wars that made up much of the American narrative played little part in frontier testimonials in Canada.

In Turner's account to his scholarly audience at the Exposition, the frontier was definitely over ... though nobody told that to Butch Cassidy and the Sundance Kid, for whom the wild west continued well past the turn of the century. My grand-father, for his part, believed that the frontier as Turner and Buffalo Bill Cody understood it had never really existed in Canada, and certainly never among the settlers he knew ... but that was irrelevant to Turner's American storyline, in which he proposed that "the existence of an area of free land, its continu-ous recession, and the advance of American settlement west-ward, explain American development" ... and suggested that with a new census concluding that all land available for "fron-tier" settlement within the United States had been claimed, the frontier was gone. Closed. History. Boasting and toasting time for the settler storytellers. Behind this enormously influential account was the assumption that the so-called "free" land had been available for the "taking," an assumption that ignored not just the abstract idea of Indian sovereignty but the very real and unmistakeable Aboriginal use and occupancy of most of the ter-ritory—unmistakeable because, as Cody would insist, the Indians were *there* when the settlers arrived, attacking them at every turn to defend *their* territory ... though Cody would skip over that last part.

On his stage, Turner argued that American progress—or what he called "development"—began with the settlers, and required their retreat to the "prairie primitive" before they reca-pitulated the essential stages of civilization from the primary phase of subsistence hunting and commodities trading to homestead farming, and eventually to secondary industrial production and sophisticated cultural practices. In Turner's playbook, instead of the land that had been made available through various "homestead acts" in the 1880s—one of which had been the Dawes Act (also called the General Allotment

Act), which displaced millions of Indians—"education" was to be the new agent of progress now that the frontier days were done, and it would provide a new kind of freedom, virtual freedom, from the Old World chains of inherited power and privilege. Education was promoted as the way to move *beyond* the frontier, and *beyond* being Indian—and here the storyline crossed the border, not with regard to the settlers but to the Indians, with school becoming the instrument of advancement and assimilation ... though in Canada, shamefully, the financial advantages to the government of devolving responsibility for education to the commanding ambitions of the religious orders also figure in the story.

Not so many years earlier Chicago had been a fur-trading centre and had only recently grown into a metropolitan city— Fort Benton in Montana was already promoting itself as the Chicago of the Plains—so Turner's account had purchase with his audience. His image of the west before settlement was of a territory peopled, if that is even the word, by a few Indians, roaming over "idle" land that belonged to no one. The fact that this was contradicted by maps of the west circulating up until the nineteenth century, depicting a continent filled with people, did not distract Turner; for him, and for the census takers, the frontier had been a place occupied by fewer than two people per square mile— which is to say settler people, not what the Blackfoot language identified as *real* people. Now that there were more settlers (and fewer Indians) it was time to get on with civilization, Western civilization, and not so much forget about the frontier—it was too potent an image—but redefine it as a place of agricultural and industrial enterprise. Idle no more ... without the hard-edged, hopeful irony that this phrase has been invested with today.

The sheer idiocy of this erasing of indigenous peoples who had been there for hundreds and in many places thousands of years is astonishing in itself, but it is a measure of the power of storytelling that the myth of an uninhabited land without social structures or civil governance was believed by hundreds and thousands of people, even—or perhaps especially—those who also believed that the western frontier was teeming with Indians ready to pounce on unwary settlers. For the latter story was the one that Buffalo Bill peddled in his Wild West extravaganza, first mounted ten years earlier, though he always insisted it was not a "show" but a recreation of the real thing—the story of a frontier in which advancing settlers were the victims of Indians who attacked and scalped whites at every turn, domestic terrorists who needed to be eliminated with the use of deadly force, or imprisoned on reserves, in order to secure the frontier as a homeland. Conquering Indians was at the heart of Cody's story, and he told it well. Turner joined the chorus, using the language of "common danger" and "resistance to aggression," but his main storyline was about the conquest of nature by the civilizing energy and enterprise of the settler, and by the surveying of the land. Indians, it was assumed, would follow the lead of the conquering settler society.

An uncivilized and possibly empty frontier always had an appeal for newcomers; and if it wasn't in fact empty, then the people who were there must themselves be uncivilized—like nature, benign or malignant as circumstances revealed. It was a place to start, or to start again; and in a breathtaking, quintessentially storytelling contradiction, both a place to be free of the civilizing influences of Huck's Aunt Sally, and a place to bring civilization to the back forty (if you were in the farming mode) or to the back country (if you were an adventurer into a savage land, or had a missionary zeal of some sort). It was also a place to turn idle land, roamed over by primitive hunters and gatherers, into useful production, a place to test yourself with the challenges of adaption and innovation and to bring human ingenuity and Christian instruction into play. And for the metropolitan masters advertising pioneer settlement, it was a place where people with the "right stuff"—a phrase actually used by Canadian government officials in the mid-twentieth century to promote the surrender of Indian reserve land for soldier settlement—could make the desert bloom and develop resources for metropolitan needs... or for entertainment. In some circumstances it was both of these rolled up into a mythic bundle.

But for many of those who came to the foothills of Alberta, it was none of those things. It was a time and a place of contradictions, to be sure—but one imbued with hope, epitomized in the opening lines of the American frontier anthem "Home on the Range." It is perhaps the best-known cowboy song of all (composed by a travelling medical doctor from Kansas in the 1870s): "O give me a home, where the buffalo roam," it begins. *Home*, and *roam*: bound together in rhyme by their similar sounds, their senses pull in completely opposite directions. Wandering and settling down. It's hard to imagine a more fundamental contradiction affecting—and inspiring—the condition of settlers wandering onto the range of the buffalo. We underestimate both those who sang it back then and those of us who still sing it if we don't accept that our imaginations take this contradiction to heart every time we recite this rhyme, imagining the amazing grace of those stars in the prairie sky at night. We don't remember these lines because they tell one truth about ourselves, but because they tell two contradictory ones about our human condition and about the idea of "home": we are all both "bound to go" and "bound to stay" . . . And when we try to eliminate this contradiction, we are not only trying to straighten out a curve at the heart of being human, we are discounting a condition that is *not* as contradictory as it seems. It was a condition the Blackfoot understood fundamentally in their way of life before treaty, roaming freely throughout their homeland; and it is closer than we realize to the heritage of all people who have moved widely—and still do—within the tribal or national territory they call home . . . which is, of course, the experience of all Canadians.

There are, to be sure, other ways of looking at the opening and closing of the frontier than those presented by Turner and Buffalo Bill Cody. Paula Petrick, studying working women, including prostitutes, in Helena, Montana, talks of how in the early years of settler society women were their own employers and were able to hold on to the rewards of their business, as they did in the early years of the fur trade. In due course, as settlement, trade and commerce became citified, men came and took control of the women and their earnings... which, as the western historian Patricia Limerick suggests, makes for an interesting marker of the end of the frontier: the frontier ends when the pimps come to town. It is an open question whether Treaty Seven signalled their arrival. And perhaps too, whether the gender politics and male domination of a lot of settler society had a pernicious influence on the role of women in First Nations communities. Both notions underestimate the Blackfoot; but they do catch something of the conditions that developed over the decades leading up to 1905.

. . .

In 1891, a rodeo at the end of the Fort Macleod fair had marquee billing, and is often said to be the first "real rodeo" in Alberta, though riding and roping competitions had been around for a couple of decades. Two of the best bronc riders in the territory were competing: Johnny Franklin against Billy Stewart. My grandfather said that both Franklin and Stewart rode their pitching, bucking, wriggling, spinning horses to a standstill in such sensational style that the competition was declared a tie. A couple of years later, Calgary held its first rodeo, organized by George Lane to settle an argument about who was the best roper in the territory. Lane, who was no slouch, took four minutes before he was able to rope and tie his wayward steer. Then John Ware, riding a horse without a bridle, threw a loop as the steer came out of the chute, sprang off his horse, and had him tied in fifty-one seconds. The crowd, who knew and loved Ware first of all as a bronc rider in Johnny Franklin and Billy Stewart's class, went wild with delight.

This may seem like a typical frontier scenario; and rodeos may not be to everyone's liking these days. But they were part of life back then, another form of boasting about and toasting the skills of the cowboy. My grandfather told another story about Billy Stewart, who set up a gun fight at the Macleod Hotel in 1892 between a rancher and a cowboy. Well, sort of a gun fight... but in any event one that highlights a difference between the United States and Canada, then and now. The rancher was Lew Murray, a bronc buster and foreman of the Walrond ranch (where Dave Cochrane got reimbursed for his "improvements" when he lit a pipe in front of the manager, Duncan McEachern), and the cowboy's name was Leeper; they had had a fierce argument some time before, threatening to kill each other next time they met. Word went about; and several months later both were in Fort Macleod one day, unbeknownst to each other, drinking (fairly heavily, of course) at different hotels. Billy arranged for a couple of friends to slip their guns out of their holsters while they drank, take out the bullets and put the guns back. Then they told Murray the rancher that Leeper the cowboy was at the Macleod Hotel. Everyone watched as Murray entered the barroom, saw his sworn enemy, and walked towards him ... and when Leeper saw him coming he started walking too, just like in a movie that hadn't been made yet. As they walked, they both drew their guns and fired ... and fired ... and fired again ... but all they got was clickety-clack as they pulled the triggers. They were almost bumping into each other when they realized the guns were empty, so they flipped them in their hands to use as clubs ... by which point the whole barroom was convulsed with laughter, and after a few harsh words between them, settled both of them down to have another drink. That was the Canadian foothills frontier ... not without what Hugh Dempsey calls "its share of horse stealing, cattle rustling, bootlegging, theft, general mayhem and murder," but nothing like the frontier of American myth. And Dempsey would know something about all this. As well as being one of western Canada's most distinguished historians, he married into the Blood tribe, and his brother-in-law Fred as well as Fred's son Jim Gladstone became among the most renowned rodeo cowboys of the twentieth century, both of them as calf ropers and Jim as World Champion, later serving his Blackfoot community as a distinguished lawyer.

As for Johnny Franklin, he carried on to become one of the greatest bronc riders and horse breakers of his day. "Breaking" was the standard term used in those times, but it is often misunderstood by outsiders. No cowboy wanted a "broken" horse, without any spirit; or an unruly horse, except to show off. There were certainly those who used what we would call rough methods; but horses—being prey animals—are watchful creatures, and good horse breakers watch in return, trying to establish a bond rather than break one. In the foothills, a horse breaker who gratuitously abused a horse was generally fired, and sometimes charged by the police. Harry Longabaugh, the Sundance Kid, was arrested for cruelty to a horse, which may have led to his being laid off as a horse breaker at the Bar U. The charge was later dropped for lack of evidence, but he was never taken back to handle horses, and went instead into the hotel business in Calgary. Ways of accustoming a horse to having something on its back (unnatural for a horse, since its predators in the wild were large cats and dogs), often centred around tiring out the horse (which back in Johnny Franklin's day was the test of a bronc rider, who sometimes stayed on for fifteen or twenty minutes until the horse threw in the towel, as it were). Outside the rodeo arena it might mean starting him in a pond or river or on boggy ground, which slowed the horse down and made for a softer landing if the horse breaker (often a youngster) was thrown. One rancher described another way, following the practice of Mexican *vaqueros*, who would catch horses "by the front foot and by a twist throw them, and while they were down put on the hackamore (a bridle without a bit) and blindfold them, then let them up. A blinded horse will usually stand without too much fuss until the saddle is on," and then the hacakmore noseband was adjusted to make the horse easier to control.

Franklin later became a successful rancher; but his "bronc busting" skills remained his signature, and when the first Calgary Stampede was held in 1912 he was asked to judge the bronc-riding events.

12

WE KINDA FIXED EACH OTHER

"You know, everyone thinks we found this
broken-down horse and fixed him. But we
didn't. He fixed us; every one of us. And I
guess in a way, we kinda fixed each other too."
RED POLLARD, IN THE FILM OF *SEABISCUIT*
BY LAURA HILLENBRAND

...

AT THE TIME OF THE Columbian Exposition, with the academic Frederick Turner and the showman Buffalo Bill Cody on
their respective stages, Fort Macleod was trying to figure out its
future—as a frontier town, buying into the storyline that
inspired Turner and Cody in the United States; or as a homeland
supply centre, less colourful but with a much more compelling
scenario. My grandfather—with D.W. Davis (the former
Montana whisky trader and I.G. Baker manager in Fort Macleod,
who had been elected Alberta's first member of the Canadian
Parliament in 1887 when the district became a federal constitu-
ency), along with the mayor of Calgary and the manager of the
I.G. Baker store there—had secured a contract in 1889 to run a
railway from Edmonton through Calgary and Fort Macleod
down to the Montana border. It was a good idea, which they
thought would benefit everyone in the territory by expanding
trade beyond the monopolistic eastern markets, and it was not

part of the settlement scenario. But the Canadian Pacific Railway, with a monopoly of its own, thought otherwise, and Sorreltop Jack and his friends didn't have the kind of capital that railways require to get them rolling. And so, not wanting to go broke, they sold their option to the Canadian Pacific Railway.

The cooperation with Calgary in the venture was strategic, because railway access was crucial to Fort Macleod and it was trying to challenge that upstart. Fort Calgary had been built the year after Macleod, and it was first called Fort Brisebois, after the North-West Mounted Police commander in charge at the time; but when Colonel Macleod took over he renamed Brisebois "Fort Calgary" after his ancestral home on the Isle of Mull. It wasn't an arrogant gesture on his part—after all, he already had a town named after him; it was because nobody much liked Inspector Brisebois, who had commandeered the only cookstove in camp to heat his room during his first (very cold) winter there.

Given the original routing of the Canadian Pacific Railway through Fort Calgary, and the control that decision gave the national railway in deciding on the location of spur lines, Fort Macleod probably never had a chance to outshine that city. But in the opinion of most of its citizens, Macleod was becoming something better, with a reputation (grumpily acknowledged by even some impatient settlers and Indian "civilizers") as a place where the local Blackfoot had friends, felt more or less welcome, and found most of the things they wanted to purchase, as well as a ready supply of patsies for their horse races. And putting aside commerce and civic competition between Macleod and Calgary (and increasingly Lethbridge, which flourished with its coal mining), nothing could match the stunning countryside to the west of the town, beckoning from Main Street, and the great open range out there to support ranching.

. . .

The Blackfoot turn to farming in the territory had perhaps been made more congenial for them by their historical association with the agriculturally sophisticated Sioux tribes such as the Mandan in the Upper Missouri, and their own harvesting of root crops such as turnips. Many Bloods and Peigan had been planting potatoes since the early eighties, and although the weather was unfriendly to potato farming over the next decade they continued to try different crops. By that time, they were also supplying a good portion of the hay and some of the grain for the North-West Mounted Police horses and for many of the ranches in the district.

Crop Eared Wolf and his father, Red Crow, had been among the first to take up farming, storing their potatoes in a root cellar they dug, and distributing them to band members over the winters. Red Crow had been gathering and breeding horses for a long while, and by the time the Bloods settled on their reserve in 1883 he had a large herd, which made him a wealthy man by any standard, his stature measured by the fact that he paid a hundred horses to acquire (in an exchange sanctioned by traditional practice) a medicine pipe that was one of the most sacred items on the reserve. Crop Eared Wolf himself became one of the first Blood Indians to start raising cattle, trading fifteen horses for the same number of cows and a bull; and Red Crow had turned horses to the plough by 1889. In 1890, he built a large stable, putting up twenty tons of hay for the winter while his wife, Singing Before, bought a milk churn and a sewing machine for their home, bringing venerable Blackfoot skills to work with settler technologies. By the 1890s there were substantial herds of farm and ranch animals and rodeo and racing horses on the Blood reserve; and by the end of that decade, cattle ranching had taken its place among the Bloods, with band members owning over two thousand head. They took to ranching easily, for herding had always been an aspect of hunting the great herds of buffalo (as it has been for caribou hunters in the north, where indigenous people in some Arctic domains such as Norway have been herding reindeer for over a thousand years). The Blackfoot understood the management of herd animals, especially in their foothills homeland, better than many of the newcomers. And they continued to amass large horse herds, selling some of the stock to local ranches and the North-West Mounted Police.

As for farming, they certainly had success; but the unpredictable weather of their semi-arid territory on the western plains presented challenges, felt by everyone there. These could only be mitigated by new irrigation projects, some of them inspired and several of them led by the Mormons, who brought their Utah dryland farming experience to southern Alberta. Technological change was as powerful a force in foothills country as it was anywhere, and signalled as powerful a change as the coming of horses had been for the Blackfoot a century and a half earlier.

· · ·

"There is not a hedge or fence of any kind as far as the eye can reach," my grandfather wrote. "The plough is just put down wherever the ploughman may think fit. There are no trees except growing on some of the barrows and they look like islands in the plains." In the spring of 1885, he and his brother had driven their wagon across prairies untouched by a plow to the southern foothills of Alberta on their way to Fort Macleod. But this description of the land before the plough wasn't from anywhere near there. This was Salisbury Plain, another "frontier," which he had seen on a walk he took from Bath to Stonehenge during his trip to England in 1881. England too, like the North-West Territories and much of the world, was about to be changed almost beyond recognition. Soon, landscapes and livelihoods—and languages too, sometimes—would just be old memories, fading like the photographs that were being taken of these vanishing worlds— and in some cases vanishing peoples.

Later on that visit, my grandfather had gone to a production of Gilbert and Sullivan's comic opera *Patience*, in Richard D'Oyly Carte's new Savoy Theatre. The opera was a satire about Oscar Wilde—interestingly, the first issue of the *Macleod Gazette*, on July 1, 1882, also featured a satire on Wilde and aestheticism, inspired by this very production—but that wasn't the main attraction for him. It was the theatre itself, lit by twelve hundred arc lamps powered by six generators, the first public building in London to be illuminated by electricity. People were uncertain about it, and so was D'Oyly Carte. As befitting someone who traded in novelties, he said electric lights were an experiment "that may succeed or may fail."

Within a generation, life in London was transformed by new technologies. People were still talking, of course; conversation was high culture. And they were still writing letters, with a postal service that delivered mail every few hours. But the telephone and the typewriter were about to change all that. Other changes had been underway for some time, with the London Underground railway opening in 1863, four years before Confederation. All sorts of people were already getting their photograph taken; and by the end of the century, a few people were even getting their voices recorded on wax cylinders. And everyone was trying to find ways of understanding all this, using new images. A well-known scientist, Karl Pearson, wrote a bestselling book called *The Grammar of Science* in which he compared what we *really* know about the "real" world with the "clerk in the [very new] central London telephone exchange who cannot get nearer to his customers than his end of the wires. ... The real universe for him would be the aggregate of his constructs from the messages which were brought by the telephone wires in his office."

In those days, London and Fort Macleod seemed like different worlds: the metropolis and the hinterland. But both of them were experiencing changes unlike any that the world had seen since the coming of the horse or the invention of the printing press. And just as printing provided a new currency for thoughts and feelings, the late nineteenth century brought a new kind of illusion into the world, the illusion of being there when you weren't, of happenings that weren't happening right then and there, but seemed to be. This was both brand new and as ancient as storytelling. Virtual reality, much like the grass under ice that the cattle were faced with after that brief Chinook that caught my grandfather. Except that language—and the languages of the arts—has given humans the technology to nourish ourselves even in the most desperate weather and the most rapidly changing of worlds.

And with storytelling technology, oral or written, the Blackfoot were completely at home, combining carving and painting as well as dancing and drumming to sustain their heritage and their sense of home. The pictographic and petro-glyphic forms of ancient Aboriginal cultures, north and south—the Iroquoian condolence canes and wampum belts, the carvings of Haida totem poles and Kwakwaka'wakw masks, the knotted and coloured strings of Inca *quipu* and the painted robes and carved quirts of the Blackfoot—offer a reminder of how these uncertainties have been with us for a very long time, probably since language itself began.

Growing up, my grandfather had watched Upper Canada become Ontario, Canada become a Dominion, and the west become the land of opportunity. In the early 1880s, he had ridden on a Red River cart at Pile of Bones, a unique and stalwart and very noisy contraption (someone said it sounded like a horde of devils filing saws) that all but defined travel in the early days of the Canadian prairies—no iron was used, the frame was held together by wooden pegs, and the wheels bound with strips of *shaganappi* (fresh raw skin of buffalo or cattle, which shrank as it dried and formed a hard rim). Two years later, he took the Canadian Pacific Railway from Calgary to Regina. So he knew all about change. He had even listened, so he told my mother, to his family's friend Alexander Graham Bell make the first tele-phone calls from his summer home in Brantford; but like D'Oyly Carte and many other people confronted by something radically different, he thought the telephone was probably little more than a neat trick. With a few exceptions, people have never been very good at predicting the future. "I think there is a world market for about five computers," said Thomas Watson in the 1940s. At the time, he was chairman of IBM.

And shortly before he died in 1947, my grandfather flew on a Trans-Canada Airlines DC-3 from Vancouver to Calgary. It didn't have a pressurized cabin, so the passengers had to put on oxygen masks when they flew over the Rockies; as someone who loved a good pipe, he "smoked" the oxygen tube. Nostalgia comes in surprising forms, and so does new technology. He was very proud to have lived to travel in all these ways, and he said it helped him understand what the coming of the horse meant to the Blackfoot.

New transportation and communication technologies changed many things during Jack Cowdry's lifetime—for better, for worse and forever. The railway and (by 1901 in the foothills) the automobile; the typewriter, the telegram and the telephone; photography and film; wax recording cylinders and tape and disk recording, and then radio and television... these came quickly, and came everywhere, with computers now taking up the challenge of these changes. They brought people closer together; but in a paradox that we still haven't resolved, they also set them further apart. They changed people's sense of space and time; and they changed their sense of themselves and each other. Managing this has been the most important challenge of the past hundred and fifty years, and we are reminded every day how stories—and songs—are at the heart if it all. The technologies weren't always new, but when they were from different cultural traditions they sometimes required new ways of seeing and hearing. New imaginings. This was so with Crop Eared Wolf's quirt; and for my grandfather that quirt always represented the way in which different forms of storytelling, along with old and new technologies, offered common ground across cultures.

· · ·

On that visit to England, my grandfather wrote in a notebook about going to visit some galleries in London on "August 1. Bank Holiday." Bank holidays were new in England—this was only their tenth anniversary—and they were the first statutory secular holidays in Great Britain since the Middle Ages. Surprisingly, my grandfather already knew something about them. The man responsible for bringing bank holidays into being, Sir John Lubbock, was widely celebrated; indeed, even on that tenth anniversary they were still fondly known by the exhausted working people of Great Britain as Saint Lubbock's Days.

And Jack Cowdry knew about Lubbock from his naturalist father, Thomas. Lubbock had published an important book called *The Origin and Metamorphosis of Insects* in 1873, ten years after Thomas Cowdry had co-founded the Entomological Society of Canada; and by 1880 Lubbock's forthcoming study *Ants, Bees and Wasps* was being advertised in all the journals, and would become one of the most popular books in the natural sciences in the late nineteenth century. Lubbock was a neighbour and friend of Charles Darwin, who cited him in *The Origin of Species*, but he was known too for his unconventional curiosity—as when he successfully tamed a pet wasp, which he then took with him to the meeting of the British Association for the Advancement of Science in Brighton in 1872, and later, when he tried to teach his dog to read. These sorts of stories delighted my grandfather.

But Lubbock was remarkable for many other reasons too. He was the founder of the discipline of prehistoric archaeology, writing a book called *Prehistoric Times* in which he coined the terms "Paleolithic" and "Neolithic" (as precursors of the Bronze Age and the Iron Age); he was one of the early advocates of what we now call anthropology, with a book called *The Origin of Civilisation*; and of course he was a leading natural scientist. He had also become a Member of Parliament at the age of thirty-six, and did so believing he could make the world a better place, one step at a time—he often quoted John Henry Newman's "Lead, Kindly Light": "Keep Thou my feet; I do not ask to see / The distant scene; one step enough for me." True to these words, over the next thirty years Lubbock saw more important legislation through the British Houses of Parliament than anyone of his generation, securing improved conditions with not only more public holidays but also shorter working hours (which were well over eighty hours a week for shopkeepers and their assistants, and over ninety hours in some trades). He also promoted legislation to protect ancient monuments like Stonehenge; to expand public parks where games could be played and picnics enjoyed; and to establish lending libraries in villages. Lubbock believed in stories, and in the books in which we often find them; and his work as principal of the Working Men's College in London (which also included women—rare for the time) inspired him to publish what were known as Sir John Lubbock's Hundred Books, brought out in inexpensive editions and chosen from Middle Eastern and Asian as well as European cultures, including both the Qur'an (spelled Koran in the style of the day) and the Bible. When they came out in the early nineties, my grandfather said the only thing missing was a selection of Blackfoot stories.

Lubbock's "hundred" were not books of instruction but of entertainment and inspiration. And curiosity. Books of wonder, and wondering. Knowing things was only part of the story for Lubbock. The other was being comfortable with the unknown:

What we know is an absolutely infinitesimal fraction of what we do not know. There is no single substance in Nature the uses and properties of which are yet completely known to us. There is no animal or plant the whole life-history of which we have yet unravelled. We are surrounded by forces and influences of which we understand nothing, and which we are as yet but dimly commencing to perceive. We live in a world of mystery, which we darken rather than explain by the use of terms which can neither define nor explain.

"Many savage nations worship trees," he wrote, using language that makes us uncomfortable. But he continues in a manner that we can only admire: "And I really think my first feeling would be one of delight and interest rather than surprise, if some day when I am alone in a wood one of the trees were to speak to me."

All of this intrigued my grandfather. But what really caught his attention was Lubbock's line of business. Lubbock was a banker, all his life, having left school (like my grandfather) at age fourteen. Knowing all the rest about him—for Lubbock's story was widely told in the magazines and newspapers my grandfather read, and in letters from his father—his being a banker helped my grandfather believe that *he* could do something, however modest, to make his town, and the territory, a good place to live for everyone. A place where everyone's stories mattered, as long as they were told with craft and conscience.

John Lubbock had friends throughout the country, around the world and across the social, economic and political spectrum. But he remained almost completely independent of the institutional systems he worked and played in, whether financial or political, scientific or social, literary or legislative; and he loved to tell stories that exposed the limits of his understanding. One of my favourites goes like this.

One day, walking in a Norwich field, Lubbock met an old man standing next to a pile of stones, and struck up a conversation.

"Do you know how these stones were made?" Lubbock asked, expecting to instruct the simple soul.

"Why, sir, I 'spect they growed, same as 'taturs," answered the man.

"Well," rejoined Lubbock, a lifetime of association with the greatest natural and physical scientists at the ready, "but if they lay there for fifty years, they would not get any bigger."

"No, sir, of course they wouldn't," replied the countryman. "Same as 'taturs. Take 'taturs out of the ground and they stops growin'."

I like to think that, in their different ways, this wise old countryman and my grandfather's good friend Jerry Potts had something in common, a contradictory kind of intelligence and a genuinely scientific imagination illustrated by an anecdote about Potts. Responding to an impatient North-West Mounted Police officer who suggested on one exhausting trek across the plains that Jerry was lost because he couldn't find a stone marker, Potts replied, "The stone moved." And then he led him right to where they were going.

. . .

As the politics of regional autonomy in the North-West Territories rose higher on the political agenda of the nation, Fort Macleod came to embody a cultural and commercial character quite distinct from the rest of Canada. In the opinions of Fred Haultain and his friend the former whisky trader turned distinguished parliamentarian D.W. Davis, their hometown remained a place that credited the intelligence and imagination of all those, Indian and non-Indian, who were making the foothills flourish in the new dispensation. Though he started his career as a lawyer in Fort Macleod, Haultain was first elected to the North-West Territories legislative assembly in 1887 and won the next five elections by acclamation, becoming its first premier in 1897; but he always maintained close ties to the town, and for him and Davis it was a place where most people discounted any easy classification of folks according to race or colour or class, respecting the Blackfoot heritage that held together the first peoples of the foothills and dealing with dissent and disruption cautiously and according to the customs of the communities, interpreted by the chiefs and the North-West Mounted Police, often in concert. In other words, it was a good place—not perfect, but full of promise. However it would be a mistake to think that such noble thoughts were all that preoccupied the citizens of Fort Macleod. Other nobilities were on the minds of Blackfoot and banker alike. As Haultain's biographer noted, "names like Eagle Plume [a bay thoroughbred brought to the territory by the Quorn ranch into the keeping of John Ware] and Marcus [a dappled grey Percheron, one of the first in Alberta] were about as well known as those of Frank Oliver and Frederick Haultain, who were making platform pleas for self-government in the new northwest." This was not a simple time or place; it was a medley of complicated relationships and allegiances.

When my grandfather arrived, many of the men in the foothills were married to Indian women, some of them from important families in the Blackfoot community. D.W. Davis, for instance, married Red Crow's sister, Revenge Walker. The story goes that she married him so that her brother—who had been shot and knifed by his drunken brother—could get some medicine. In any event, her brother survived, the marriage produced four children, and Revenge Walker herself cut a dash on the social circuit. We have some wonderful descriptions of her—at Fort Whoop-Up in the early days, for instance, in "a dress of a very light coloured and well turned buckskin. It was made to conform to the shape of the body. It was trimmed with the usual buckskin fringe, but also had a double row of elk's teeth in a semi-circle beneath the neck and quite a number on the sleeves. Taken all in all, it was quite a spectacular looking dress, and one that would have attracted attention anywhere."

The community in those days brought everyone, young and old, together; and so when the earliest public school in Alberta was started in Fort Macleod in 1878, the students included the son of one of the North-West Mounted Police officers; the son and daughter of Jerry Potts; Jeff, John and Julie Davis, children of D.W. and Revenge Walker; and Bobby Gladstone, from the Blood tribe.

But marriage is never easy in any society, and as settlement increased so did the strains in some of those mixed families, with several of the Indian women leaving their marriages and returning to the Blackfoot circle, and some of the men taking up new wives from the settler community. The percentage of bad marriages was probably no greater than in any other community, but breakups were easier. That said, many of the men continued to support the children of those first marriages: Kamoose Taylor sent two of his sons by his first (Blackfoot) wife to the private Trinity College school in Port Hope, Ontario (where

Charlie Wood had taught before he came to Macleod); and when Revenge Walker returned to her people and D.W. married Lillie Grier, he sent his children by Revenge Walker to the same school; and one of them, Jeff, made a name for himself in South Africa during the Boer War in the last years of the nineteenth century, both for his magnificent riding—he was renowned for being able to ride fast and shoot accurately at the same time, a skill any Blackfoot with memories of a buffalo hunt would take for granted—and for refusing to surrender to the enemy during a losing skirmish, saying, "If they catch me they'll shoot me for a Cape boy," reminding his comrades of his colouring. He was celebrated in Fort Macleod as a great Blood warrior, as well as a national hero.

Sadly, some of these mixed family relationships later played into the negative stereotypes of Indian women and white men and "half-breeds," stereotypes that were becoming as common in Canada as they were in other parts of the empire, and that took hold of some of the newcomers in the foothills, especially those who had no continuing contact with the Blackfoot. It was not for nothing that at the annual New Year's Ball put on by the North-West Mounted Police, the most important social occasion of the year for the settlers and ranchers in the early days of Fort Macleod, Colonel Macleod always took the first dance with an Indian woman—a mark of respect from a man who knew, whatever the treaty said, that they were in Blackfoot territory.

And although it was often discredited by outsiders, the Blackfoot family structure was time-honoured, and equitable... certainly as equitable as the family structure in most of the rest of Canada. (And when it became an issue in the 1880s, the federal Department of Justice issued a directive that marriages according to tribal custom should be treated as legitimate.) Adoptions were common, an adopted child immediately becoming a full part of the family, and open to the same rights of inheritance. Traditionally, Blackfoot men had several wives, the number depending on wealth and status as well as responsibilities, for women took on a number of the tasks in a camp. As the historian Sarah Carter notes, "they enjoyed more options and autonomy than Canadian women of the nineteenth century married under English common law," and an anthropologist who worked with the Blackfoot noted that a Blackfoot woman of that time "could lead a war party; she could own property, receive and exercise medicine power, and give names. She was a necessary part of every ceremonial transfer; she was the custodian of the [sacred] bundles that her husband bought... the wife receives the power from the seller. Her husband could only gain possession from her."

. . .

A few of Fort Macleod's prominent figures (such as D.W. Davis) had political party loyalties, but the town, like the territorial government at the time, was surprisingly non-partisan. Still, politics was a favourite topic of conversation for both men and women, though in what was still a traditional Canadian custom it was men who usually took the public roles. In the case of Fort Macleod in those early days, all of them seemed to be a candidate for everything. During the town's first municipal elections in 1892, one wiseacre said that the only people who weren't running for council were those who were running to be its first mayor... which included my grandfather, age thirty-six, the same age as John Lubbock when he was elected to the British Parliament.

He won the election, took the town through incorporation, and became its first mayor in January 1893. The first council meeting was held in the Macleod Hotel, and the first year's business was mostly taken up with by-laws, one declaring that there should be no drunkenness in public places, no fighting or use of profanity, and no beating of horses or cows; another required an outdoor toilet for each house. The townsfolk also decided to drop the tag "Fort," as Calgary had done when it incorporated in 1884, and Fort Macleod became simply Macleod, in a gesture of civic independence from the frontier. (Later, in 1952, it changed back to Fort Macleod as a tribute to its beginnings, and to attract tourists ... a business enterprise that would have surprised, and probably dismayed, my grandfather.)

But I think there was another reason that he led the town in dropping its designation as Fort, a reason my grandfather kept to himself. He had never felt like he was in a garrison community, a "fort," protected from either the Indians or the environment; and he didn't want the name of the town to suggest anything like that. For him, there was no protection against life, and life in Macleod and the foothills included the Indians, who had faced a devastating loss with courage and conviction, the unpredictable weather, and each other. Macleod was an Indian town as much as it was a settler town, or a North-West Mounted Police town, or a ranch supply town. It was a town in Chinook country at the crossroads of the old Blackfoot Confederacy and the new confederation called Canada. "This territory and this town are not the frontier," he would say to anyone who would listen—especially over a meal at Taylor's Table in Harry's hotel, when they had no choice—"but a homeland we are trying to share with the Blackfoot, with whom we have signed a treaty. Macleod is a treaty town."

For him, nobody symbolized this better than his friend Crop Eared Wolf. Given their mutual love of horses, and especially after Treaty Seven, I think he and his friend would have liked a comment from the film *Seabiscuit*: "You know, everyone thinks we found this broken-down horse and fixed him. But we didn't. He fixed us; every one of us. And I guess in a way, we kinda fixed each other too."

. . .

Although the years from 1886 to 1893 included some uncertain times, the business of banking wasn't on any dramatic roller-coaster for the Cowdry brothers. Life was, though. Back in Ontario, Anna, Nat's wife of just three years, died in 1890, leaving Nat with their two-year-old son, Vincent, to raise. Jack and Nat's sister, Alley, stepped in to help raise Vincent, with assistance from a loyal housekeeper; but Nat's world broke apart for a while. Their father, Thomas, died in 1892 in Ontario; and although he had been ill for some time, it was another loss.

And then at the beginning of the year—in January 1893, a few days after my grandfather became Macleod's first mayor—his wife, Amy, gave birth to a little boy, whom they joyfully called Jack. Two months later, in March, Amy died at the age of thirty-one. A long obituary in the *Macleod Gazette* offers a heartfelt remembrance, reflecting how much she had given to the town in the seven short years she had been there; the pallbearers included James Macleod and Sam Steele and other close friends. My grandfather was shattered. And then six months later, in the fall, young Jack died from infantile cholera (a deadly form of diarrhea). Medical care was not enough to save either of them, or not

good enough. The doctor in charge was their friend and neighbour George Kennedy, who had much experience from years as
the North-West Mounted Police doctor, was dedicated to the
most up-to-date care, and was the one who put Macleod in the
lead in Alberta for hospital facilities. But knowledge of infectious disease was limited in those days, and women were especially vulnerable after childbirth, and children in their first year.
Kennedy was among the pallbearers.

In this time of devastating grief and loss, the friends my
grandfather had made since coming to the west helped him pull
through. And others shared his sorrow. The same week that
Amy died there was a notice in the *Gazette* that a son of Jerry
Potts had passed away; as with my grandfather, this was one of
several of his children to die young.

To no one's surprise, my grandfather did not run for another
term as mayor, though folks said he could have stayed for twenty
years if he had wanted. The next couple of years, with a five-year-
old-daughter and a three-year-old-son to raise—and a bank to
run—must have been a blur. In Nat's bible, I found three tele-
grams that he received from Jack that year, all of them telling
stories with the new technology as eloquently as any witness, in
any medium. One was to say Amy was "weaker but holding
strength well as possible." The next, three weeks later: "Amy
gone home. We will meet again." And in September, "Dear little
Jack died this afternoon."

Gone home. It is an image that everyone, including his
Blackfoot friends, understood; and that no one can fully describe.
It may be where we hang our hat, or where our heart is … which
may be the same place, or maybe not. It may be where we choose
to live, or are chosen to live. It may be here below, or up above;

real, or imagined; in our past, or in our future. It may be all of these things, or none of them. But whatever and wherever it is, it holds us close.

. . .

The death of Amy may have prompted my grandfather to do some things differently, or perhaps to do some different things. In the early fall of 1895, he decided to go elk hunting in the east Kootenays, near the headwaters of the Kootenay River in British Columbia. He knew the country a bit, and had closely followed the proposal of an Austrian entrepreneur named William Baillie-Grohman to redirect the water from the upper Kootenay River into the headwaters of the Columbia, at the point where they pass within several hundred yards of each other going in opposite directions, at a place called Canal Flats, in order to lower the water levels of Kootenay Lake in the west Kootenays and open up fertile valley land for farming. He was awarded a concession to do this, but the new Canadian Pacific Railway opposed it, worried that increased flow on the Columbia would threaten their bridges downriver near Golden and Revelstoke. Thwarted in his original plans, Baillie-Grohman negotiated a deal for more land in the west Kootenays, in return for which he undertook to build a canal and lock system between the two rivers at Canal Flats. And he did so, at enormous cost, and in defiance of the natural order—but that's what canals and dams are all about. A sternwheeler named *Gwendoline* passed through the canal in 1894—the first of only two boats to do so—and my grandfather was intrigued by the venture, and curious about that part of the country. He had heard about the Kootenai (*Ktunaxa*)

Indians from the Blackfoot, who had stories of both alliances and battles with them over the years (they too were well known for their fine horses); and they put him in touch with one of the chiefs, Abel Not-Bear, from Windermere, just north of Canal Flats on the Columbia River. After several messages back and forth, mostly carried by friends, the chief agreed to take him hunting in the mountains around Findley Creek, which heads up into the Purcell Range to the west of the Rockies and runs into the Kootenay just south of Canal Flats.

This was high-mountain hunting, which was new to my grandfather, though he had hunted with the Blackfoot on the eastern slopes of the Rockies. The chief was said to be an expert tracker, which interested my grandfather as much as whatever game they might find, though he was also hoping to catch sight of other game such as mountain sheep and goats as well as elk, happy enough if he saw them rather than shot them. He had a Winchester .30-.30 rifle, a new model on the market the previous year, which he bought to replace his old-style Winchester, the rifle used by most of the Blackfoot and the ranchers and the police.

The route for the railway through the Crowsnest Pass had been surveyed but the line not yet built, so he went by wagon trail across the pass and up the Kootenay Valley. Along the way, he saw the small sturgeon-nosed canoes that the Kootenai Indians used, made of pine bark on the bottom and birchbark near the gunwhales, sewed with cedar roots and sealed with pine resin; and he passed Fort Steele, where Sam Steele had established a North-West Mounted Police post a few years earlier. At Canal Flats he met—and liked—Chief Not-Bear, and they headed out right away with two pack horses and two riding horses. My grandfather was in his element and at ease on the ride up the river and into the mountains, which closed in quickly from the valley; and they made their first camp on the bench-land above the creek, surrounded by tall pines and cedars. They had a sack of oats out of which my grandfather took a small amount for each horse, and when they had gobbled it up he hob-bled them—taking a soft rope, unravelling its three strands and laying them parallel, tying both ends and looping the unravelled rope around one pastern, twisting it to set the length, slipping what was left of the length around the other pastern and knot-ting it by twisting the rope twice through the opening between the strands. Then he put a cowbell around the neck of one horse, an old mare, and set them all loose to wander up the trail and browse on the bushes. As they cooked supper on the little fire they had built, they heard the bugle of a bull elk in the distance, followed by an answering challenge from another direction… and Chief Not-Bear said that sooner or later a fight would be on to decide who would dominate the herd of cows that fall. Then he bugled back, and got a reply.

The next morning, they were up about five, my grandfather out to round up the horses while the chief rustled up some bacon and bread, and they were on the trail by seven, the chief watching for tracks. He knew the area like the back of his hand. Better, maybe, because he knew how it worked, how things connected, how they moved… which I certainly wouldn't be able to tell about my hands. They hadn't seen any elk on the way into the mountains but, hearing the bulls the night before, they knew they were about.

After a couple of hours along the trail and then up over a ridge, they came across some droppings, several days old. "This elk's not here," said the chief, getting down to walk and lead his horse. My grandfather, Amy on his mind as always in those years, thought that was a discouraging way to talk, and said so. "Of course he is," he grumbled. "Who else left that behind?" Not-Bear just grunted. But he was looking at everything, and smelling bushes. He pointed out where some grass had been stepped on and sprung back at a slightly different angle. "Not here," he said. And again, seeing a scuffle mark where an elk had scrambled up a small slope, "Not there." My grandfather thought he was saying this to irritate him; so being an obliging sort of person, he became irritated. "Goddam it, chief," he said, "the elk *is* here. Or are you telling me that this isn't an elk who did this?" Not-Bear just walked on, oblivious to his whining.

Now my grandfather knew that the chief was a legendary hunter. But despite himself he found he was thinking all sorts of not-nice things about him and about the Kootenai Indians— and their quirky habits, and their stubbornness, and their mischief-making—things he had heard from the Blackfoot. "Not here, my foot," he grumbled. Why not "they're over there" or "we're getting closer" or "another good sign"? Nothing but "not here."

Then Not-Bear started a story about how he was once out hunting in the mountains on the other side of the valley and saw a grizzly dancing in an opening on the far slope, holding a rack of elk antlers in his claws. After that, he described the elk they were tracking, the one that "wasn't there," and what he smelled like, and how he had hurt one leg some time ago, which was why he limped a little, and that he probably wouldn't be the winner in any fight with another bull because when they rushed at each other and their antlers meshed together, he would be thrown off balance to the ground and the other bull would gore him. So he'd probably stay out of the running for bull elk of the rut. But he might not, he added.

And they trudged along, my grandfather trying to pick up the tricks of Not-Bear's tracking but thinking he was probably missing almost everything . . . which, he said to himself, wasn't hard because it wasn't there. And then Not-Bear began telling more stories about this not-elk, and what he had done in his life, and why he was heading in this particular direction. My grandfather started to pay more attention. Sometimes the chief would veer off the trail, and head up the slope at a crazy angle, saying, "Now if I were him, I'd want to go up here about now" . . . and then, seeing some tracks or scat, repeat his mantra. "But he's not here."

And then he saw him. He was a beautiful bull, on the small side and with a limp as the chief had described, but with a wonderful set of antlers. They watched him for fifteen minutes; and my grandfather decided not to shoot him, but wished him luck. He told the chief that he himself was short, and lived among mostly tall men—the Blackfoot and the police and the ranchers— and he had discovered that he could do all kinds of things that tall people didn't expect him to be able to do, and this elk too might just become the ruler of the range. And he told him about his friend Crop Eared Wolf, who was also short, and had a limp from being shot in the leg on a raid against the Cree some years before—he made sure he mentioned the Cree because he knew the Blackfoot had also had some altercations with the Kootenai— but that had never stopped him from being a leader. The chief, who liked those stories, told him he knew something of that: he had been given his name—it wasn't his only Kootenai name, but it was the one he chose to use—because he always said what he had been saying when he was out hunting, and everyone made fun of him—but he became the best hunter in the tribe. He said the one thing a good hunter knows when he sees the track of an animal is that the animal isn't there. That's all he knows. Not-bear. And he has to go to work imagining the bear until it becomes real. Right there. Then he can say "hello bear." Or "hello elk."

But still not "hello Amy," thought my grandfather. Still, for some reason he was feeling much better. He understood something.

. . .

My grandfather preferred non-fiction to fiction, though he liked some of Charles Dickens; and his reading as a youngster seemed to be more inclined to the likes of Charles Kingsley's *The Water Babies* (published in 1863, when my grandfather was six) than G.A. Henty's nineteenth-century "boy's own" adventure *Out on the Pampas*, which came out (and he was given) when he was eleven.

For my grandfather, what endeared *The Water Babies* to him was its gorgeous nonsense, and he particularly admired (and would recite) one famous passage from the book when one of Kingsley's characters replies to a statement that there are no such things as water babies.

How do you know that? Have you been there to see? And if you had been there to see, and had seen none, that would not prove that there were none.... And no one has a right to say that no water-babies exist, till they have seen no water-babies existing; which is quite a different thing, mind, from not seeing water-babies.

Then he would give a familiar sermon about the North-West Territories. "The things that Louis Riel saw for the future of the territories, his visions, may not have been seen by others. The same for the visions that Red Crow and Crop Eared Wolf had, their dreams for their people. But that does not mean these things did not exist or could not exist."

. . .

My grandfather saw Crop Eared Wolf shortly after his return from the Kootenays, and told him about Chief Not-Bear and the hunting trip. They both liked the contradiction at the heart of the chief's tracking, how it brought the past and the present and the future all together in the hunter's imagination; and Crop Eared Wolf said the way the animal was both there and not there was just like the events and people in a story. And then one day he came to visit him with a gift, something which he had carved and painted, something that told a story.

He brought his ceremonial riding quirt—a wooden crop or whip about eighteen inches long and two inches wide in the shape of a thin cricket bat, with a braided leather tail about three feet long, and ornamental buffalo hide bound in at the end. It told—it still tells—the story of Crop Eared Wolf's life, or at least the audacious spirit he displayed when he was younger and proving himself, a spirit that sustained him when he got wounded and as he got older and lived through even more dangerous times after the buffalo had gone and the treaty had come. It was, my grandfather later said, like the weapon or the shield of a great warrior like Achilles. He knew Crop Eared Wolf had a reputation for stealing horses with craft and courage and in the most unlikely circumstances, and for breeding horses that were fast as well as ones that could turn on a biscuit and never break the crust, horses with grace and strength and skill. He told my grandfather, another time, that when he rode horses, or watched them running, he felt the spirit alive in him. Whose spirit, he didn't say. But he would say there was a moment when he felt one with both the earth and the sky. "Drinking the wind," said the Arabs fifteen hundred years ago. *Takh*, say Mongolians, using their word for spirit to describe a wild horse. *Ponokaomitai saam*—horse medicine—Crop Eared Wolf called it, the most powerful medicine among the Blackfoot.

Crop Eared Wolf had gone on his first raid in 1865, when he was twenty, in an advance scouting party with his foster father, Red Crow, who was just thirty-five. But since Crop Eared Wolf (like his father) was also a great peacemaker, the quirt has both a gun and a pipe on one of the flat sides, and below them two men carved and coloured in blue and red and rendered in traditional Blackfoot style. One symbolically represents Crop Eared Wolf; the other is an enemy . . . or a friend. There are eight marks in the shape of large staples on the narrow sides of the quirt, each coloured blue or red or yellow and signifying raids or other excursions, the number perhaps arbitrary but the enterprises certainly not.

At the top of the other flat side is a curved concave line in red, and three wavy lines perpendicular to it below, two of them blue and one yellow. They would have signified scouting expeditions, with several raiders waiting hidden at the top of a hill overlooking the enemy camp while the scout—Crop Eared Wolf—slipped down and after checking out the camp came back in a zigzag course to survey the countryside, and avoid detection. His comrades would have made a pile of buffalo chips or stones or small sticks, and the scout would scatter them on his return to indicate that a raid would be successful. His action would also represent an oath that he was telling the truth. Jawbone.

Finally, there are three finely rendered horses and a mule below the scouting figurations; they would have been stolen or "brought home," and they celebrated both the virtues of the horse thief and the value of horses and mules, as well as the imagination and skill of the person who gathered them up and rendered them on the quirt. The horses are coloured differently—two are shades of yellow-gold, one is red—and the mule at the bottom is blue. Two of the horses have reins running down to the ground, signifying that they were particularly prized and would have been attached by their reins at night to the ankle or wrist of the chief as he slept in his tipi. With that, and several dozen dogs outside, the horse thief would have had to have exceptional skill to steal them. The mule is interesting, for mules were relatively new to the west around that time; and they were valued, among other things, for leading horses across rivers in flood, when the horses would typically balk.

One highly respected Blackfoot ethnographer at the Glenbow Museum, the late Gerald Conaty, "read" the quirt for me and said, with disarming matter-of-factness, that Crop Eared Wolf must have had help stealing horses and a mule that were so highly valued and carefully watched. At first I thought he meant help from within the enemy camps—he and I came from the same academic tradition—but I realized he was referring, with the certainty of a scientist, to help from the spirits.

The Blood elder and tribal historian Frank Weasel Head also read the quirt for me, and he told the same story as Gerry Conaty...with one exception. He said it may have been—indeed he believed it was—the record of a dream, not a set of real events, and that the dream made these things—the raids and the horse and mule thefts—happen. Red Crow had had such a dream in the early 1850s—in his case, a dream of a herd of horses at a place called Big Butte—when he was leading a war party against the Crow, and that came to pass. This is certainly not new; it's the imagination creating the reality. It's a staple of storytelling in all cultures, and of hunters in many. I once worked with a Shuswap (*Secwepemc*) hunter named Mose Teneese in the east Kootenays who had dreams of what was going to happen or had just happened—bighorn sheep in an unlikely mountain meadow, or a grizzly who was feeding on a dead elk—with what seemed like impossible accuracy...until they all checked out. He said he had had these dreams since he was a child.

Was it a dream carved on the quirt, preceding and predicting the reality? Or the record of an extraordinary reality, still celebrated in Blackfoot territory? And what exactly is the difference anyway? The quirt (to use categories that are part of my literary training) is narrative, lyric and dramatic all at the same time. It is both a riddle, whose meaning needs to be interpreted, and a charm, making something happen. And all those uncertainties are what makes it so compelling. "Fled is that music," said John Keats, at the end of one of the most famous poems in the English language, "Ode to a Nightingale." "Do I wake or sleep?"

However we interpret it, and in language I used earlier with respect to Jerry Potts's unique style of interpretation, the quirt is a ceremony of belief as well as a chronicle of events; and the interpretation of it—requiring belief as well as knowledge—represented a crucial part of its power, then and now. There is a place near Fort Macleod where there are ancient paintings and carvings of animals and humans on the rocks, and many see the place as a kind of lecture theatre for a certain kind of storytelling, and a certain kind of history. It is called *Áísínai'pi,* or Writing-on-Stone Park; the Blackfoot word means "pictured." This quirt belongs in that company.

Crop Eared Wolf gave no reason for the gift of this quirt to my grandfather, except that was what he called it. A gift. It was a token of friendship, to be sure; but receiving it as a gift, my grandfather accepted that he had an obligation, a promise to keep. It was up to him to figure out what that was. When he asked Crop Eared Wolf, his friend said, "You will know." My grandfather said to my mother that he felt it had something to do with bringing things home, whatever that meant.

But whatever it was, it wasn't something my grandfather got for free. It set in play what Lewis Hyde, in his book *The Gift,* calls "the labour of gratitude," keeping the circle of giving unbroken. Indian giving—the original meaning of a phrase that has been grievously misrepresented, for it began as the description of a traditional practice. Giving back.

And the gift signalled something else, my grandfather thought, something about respecting the promise of the past in order to redeem the future. It marked a moment when he realized his friend knew that the future they believed in was in danger of being lost; and the gift was a reminder that together they not forget the promise. I hope this book will honour his gift as an agent of change.

13

THE LAW RECORDED NOWHERE BUT IN THE MEMORY OF THE PEOPLE

"There is praying all over the world.
Red Crow believes in his own praying."
RED CROW

...

TOO MUCH CIVIC HIGH-MINDEDNESS gets exhausting sometimes when you're still under forty, and mischief-making was beginning to look pretty attractive to Jack Cowdry right now. The town was flourishing, ranching had been on a roll the past couple of years and since no other bank in southern Alberta was as heavily involved in ranching, Cowdry Brothers was doing fine. But Jack was concerned about the impatience of the editor of the *Macleod Gazette*, Charlie Wood, for increased settlement in the foothills. He was worried that Wood, and others, including a few of the missionaries, were becoming too fond of saying that the Indians were not "progressing" fast enough—which meant that they weren't getting on with losing their Blackfoot identity and becoming white Christians, which some other people in the mixed-race and dubiously devout town of Fort Macleod weren't either. And he was increasingly worried that the party politics of the east, which had resulted in four govern-

ments in five years, three of them uneasy coalitions—a kind of
tribal warfare, sustained by compulsory contempt for the other
side, with religious differences (between Protestants and
Catholics) thrown in to stoke the fires of discontent—would
infect the west like the diseases that had ravaged the Blackfoot.

Since many of the ranchers he supported lived in Peigan territory to the west of Macleod, he went there often to visit. His
good friend James Macleod had died in 1894, but he kept in touch
with Macleod's wife, Mary, and Annie, their housekeeper, and
the Macleod children; and he had friends throughout that part of
the foothills. One of them was the Peigan chief Big Swan
(*Akamakal*). He had a reputation as a great hunter and warrior
and he along with his fellow chiefs Leans Over Butchering, Bull
Plume and Running Wolf painted their exploits on a single
buffalo robe completed in 1909 for the artist Edmund Morris,
son of Alexander Morris, commissioner for several of the early
prairie treaties (and an outspoken advocate of what he called,
echoing William Johnson, the importance of "securing the alliance of the Indian tribes and maintaining friendly relations with
them.") In 1877 Big Swan had been on the way to Montana for
one of the last buffalo hunts when Treaty Seven was called, but
he returned in time to sign. After the treaty, like many other
Blackfoot, he had taken up some new "adventures," as he called
them, planting potatoes so that within a few years he had a substantial farm in operation. He was probably counted among the
"successful Indians" by the editor of the *Gazette*, though not by
the missionaries there, one of whom reported that he had not
made a single convert in the past decade. Big Swan, like many in
that time of transition, was a cluster of contradictions: deeply
traditional in holding on to the annual Sun Dance ceremony,

and—drawing on his tribe's experience with newcomers to the territory—shrewdly aware of new opportunities. His people had been traders and travellers for centuries, and Big Swan was an entrepreneur as well as an imaginative leader. So he established a staging post, with a log house and stables, at Scott's Coulee, where he lived with his wives and family, welcoming travellers on the stagecoach between Calgary and the foothills around Pincher Creek and Fort Macleod, along a route that had been used for millennia (and may even have been ice-free during the last ice age over ten thousand years ago). While the coach changed horses, the passengers could buy some food and knick-knacks and take a rest—it was an early bus and truck stop, and was supported by the local banker.

The federal election was scheduled for that summer. For my grandfather it was time to ruffle some establishment feathers, and he came up with a plan to start a newspaper with a few friends. Its ambitions were clear: "to expose the shams and frauds and rampant hypocrisies that surround us on every side." Sometime in the winter of 1895–96, he went out to see Chief Big Swan about using his place at Scott's Coulee as a base for their newspaper, which they planned to call *The Outlaw*. Big Swan was delighted. They made plans to publish weekly, beginning the first issue in May, figuring out whom they would approach for good newspaper copy and how much they would write themselves—a lot, as it turned out; they met at least once each week at Big Swan's to put the issue together.

It ran for six glorious weeks, from May 19 to June 30, 1886. In that short time, it claimed to have outstripped the *Macleod Gazette* in sales, and was hilarious in its description of that paper even though it was in fact printed on the *Gazette* press. It also boasted that it had the largest circulation of *any* paper in the territory, noting that "its exclusive news franchises make it the most widely read and influential journal in the West." Its ambition to expose shams and frauds and rampant hypocrisies was made from a singular vantage point—the top of the fence, of course, on which the editors promised to remain,

> *not because we want to see which way the cat jumps before jumping ourselves, but for the reason that from the higher elevation it will be the easier for us to watch the struggling mobs below, and point out the foibles and vanities, the vices and tricks, that will make up the contest [the upcoming federal election] on which the people of Alberta have entered. "Spare none, praise none" will be one of our mottos for the next few weeks, and if politicians don't like its application, they had better get under the barn.*

The Outlaw would have been partly inspired, I think, by the great British tradition of satirical journalism going back to Jonathan Swift. But it had a distinctly foothills sense of satire and the liberating value of serious, scandalous fun.

The editors did not advertise themselves, though my grandfather and his colleague at the bank, William Black, were identified in the last issue: my grandfather as "first assistance to the chief editor," one Chollis Miller, who had been a close friend since before Amy's death—he was one of the pallbearers at her funeral. And Jack's Macleod neighbour, the town doctor George Kennedy, who had seen him through the death of both his newborn son and Amy, was also party to this scurrilous venture. William Black's job seems to have been to offer entertainment in the paper in the spirit of the "decadent nineties" that were being alternately celebrated and censured in England at the time, since he was routinely described as wearing lavender pants and writing poetry. He was joined by his brother John Black, the store-keeping "Adventurer and Agitator" who had advertised to "white subjects and red allies." My grandfather came in for all kinds of genial joking in its pages, including being called a "chump" for asking what the difference was between the Liberals and the Conservatives at a candidates' meeting; and in another issue he was described, in a piece on political affairs in Pincher Creek, as "Sorreltop Jack," a tribute not only to the colour of his hair and his love of horses but also, for those who knew the story of its coinage, to his friendship with Crop Eared Wolf. It also served to remind people that the name of the newspaper, *The Outlaw*, represented a nod to horses, for "outlaw" was (and still is) a term not only for someone who breaks the law but also for a more or less unmanageable horse that no cowboy would want to ride, and that any good bronc rider on the rodeo circuit would want to try.

They described Big Swan's staging post, the head office of the enterprise, as "Hotel de Log" in the first issue, declaring, "Big Swan, the genial proprietor, has thrown open the doors of his hospitable mansion" for performances by the local candidates. The motto of the newspaper was *Cultores Veritas, Fraudis Inimici*, which they translated as *With Malice Towards All and Charity to None*—though it might be rendered more literally as "followers of truth, enemies of deceit." Its politics were manifestly bipartisan and moderately incomprehensible, and the proprietors were as good as their word, lampooning everyone within the territory, and anyone who came by to interfere in its affairs. They expressed editorial contempt for both the Liberals and the Conservatives, and indulged in libelous commentary that would worry the editors of *Private Eye* or *Frank* today. They included expressions of respect and declarations of praise—made up, needless to say—from newspapers such as the *Globe* and the *Mail and Empire*, the eastern establishment organs of the Liberals and Conservatives respectively. From the *Macleod Gazette*, a special "tribute": "*The Outlaw* should have been named *The Outrage.*" There were challenges to a boxing match with my grandfather's neighbourly doctor, George Kennedy, by the local homestead inspector, named Thompson, who in the measured language of *The Outlaw* had called Kennedy "a white-livered chicken who can't tell Chief Mountain from a hole in the ground." And the "benign" face of the venerable missionary Father Albert Lacombe—they called him Perry, almost certainly a play on *pére*—is described in a painting (which also features Father of Confederation Charles Tupper and Liberal leader Wilfrid Laurier, elsewhere called "the poet Laurier") as having "a padlock of the Yale pattern, nickel finish" on his mouth. Lacombe had opposed the Sun Dance that year, which may have figured in the caricature, though the separate schools question was also alive and kicking. In another issue, there is a letter by Perry Lacombe to his dear children, the Métis, counselling the "repair" of the voters' lists to ensure the election of the Conservatives and promising that "Divine providence and the mandamants [a pretentious word for commandments] of the bishops will fix the rest." The Mormons are given a comic turn of their own, with suitable Biblical quotations. (The Mormons had settled at Lee's Creek on the southern border of the Blood reserve in Alberta in 1887, shortly after my grandfather's visit down that way, and changed the name to Cardston in tribute to Charles Ora Card, the son-in-law of Brigham Young. Card had been the leader of the wagon trek that brought them to Alberta, fleeing the United States because of persecution for polygamy, which was not yet prohibited in Canada.) There is an announcement of a magic lantern lecture on Political Purity, featuring the redoubtable D.W. Davis; the bronc rider Billy Stewart is described as "The Willow Creek orator"; a new journal, from the old whisky trading post called Slide Out, is celebrated with an article on "how to ship goods from Eaton's by Police team cleverly handled by John Cowdry, and his figures and forcible arguments are enough to convince the unprejudiced that he has the courage of his convictions." There is a spoof of Gilbert and Sullivan, called *H.M.S. Petticoat*, featuring the Conservative candidate, Thomas Cochrane, who received routinely scurrilous treatment from the newspaper; as did the Liberal candidate, Frank Oliver, whose career as a journalist with the *Edmonton Bulletin* must have given him some preparation for the satirical drubbing he was in for, with pieces such as an item of "Local News" about "Frank and Paddy"—unmistakably the same Frank Oliver, who had derided the west for its lack of "responsible government," and the Calgary lawyer Paddy Nolan—who

> came in "on time" this morning. They weren't quite sure where they'd come from, but said they were bound for Macleod. They were driving a high stepping team of mixed thoro'breds and when first observed were hitting the ground in high places. As we go to press, Frank is snoring in the hay loft, while the Irishman is hung out on the fence.

And a gloriously stereotypical Indian speech by Big Swan, titled "Medicine Talk," is reported, with its warning for Frank Oliver:

Oh Frank! Big Swan's heart is full. Last night, by the light of yonder moon, the redface strolled to the tree of our forefathers, and there amidst its mighty foliage appeared the first bud— the physique of paleface Adam.... Thou knowest, Frank, that The Outlaw *editors speak wisely and well, and for thine benefit, so listen. Unless thou stoppeth thine tongue and sayest nought ill of thine braves* The Outlaw, *whose arm will always be far fetching, will crush thee—yes, even unto the dust of the earth. Beware, paleface! Big Swan hath spoken!*

Throughout every issue, and through the mischief, one theme is clear. The 1896 federal election in distant Ottawa was almost comically—but would become cruelly—irrelevant to the communities of the foothills; and the partisan obsessions of the candidates were damaging to the compelling interests of the territory. Behind the banter in *The Outlaw* was a nervous concern that Indians and new settlers might both be buried by the government's increasing drive towards more settlement and trade, both of which were about to get an eastern booster in Ottawa in Clifford Sifton, a man dedicated to "settling the west." He had himself moved to Manitoba from Ontario, and would become the minister of the interior and superintendent general of Indian affairs in Laurier's soon-to-be-elected new Liberal government. He was an evangelical proponent of dramatically expanding immigration to the west—offering "free homesteading" to European farmers and "stalwart peasants in sheep-skin coats, born on the soil, with a stout wife and a half-dozen children"—and of centralizing the administration of everything—including Indians— in the eastern capital of Canada. His was the writing on the wall that would affect the Blackfoot for the next hundred years.

The Outlaw was just as sceptical about the Conservatives, for whom no love was lost among those who had watched the way in which the railway monopoly had taken hold in the west, and underlying its rhetoric was "a plague on both the Liberal and Conservative houses." But Frank Oliver was elected, and served for the next twenty-five years (succeeding Sifton in 1905 with responsibility for both settlement and Indians). From his early arguments for responsible government in the North-West Territories, his opinions continued to disintegrate in ways that put him about as far from my grandfather as Ottawa is from Fort Macleod; and his immigration policies became increasingly racist, replacing Sifton's class-based focus on farmers and peasants. My grandfather remained on cordial terms with him—until he showed his colours in 1910 with his new immigration proposals.

In its final issue, the loud little newspaper published its obituary: "DIED: At Scott's Coulee, Alberta, at 4:00 p.m. Tuesday June 30, 1896. *The Outlaw.* Deeply Regretted." Two weeks later Wilfrid Laurier became Canada's first francophone prime minister.

. . .

My grandfather always said that banking was a trade, and that a career in trades often runs in the family. All his brothers had gone into banking, though another thing they shared was a habit of doing several other things along the way. Just a year after the federal election, my grandfather's nephew Thomas came to work with him, bringing his experience with the Canadian Bank of Commerce in Simcoe, Ontario, where his father, Ned, was manager. Thomas proved immensely helpful, and after a few years was seconded part-time to Ned Maunsell to do his bookkeeping (a nice indication of relations between Maunsell and Cowdry, since this was when Maunsell took Cowdry Brothers to court about something or other and then applied a "discontinuance" to cancel the action). At about the same time, my grandfather's clerk William Black—the "Lavender Pants" of *The Outlaw*—moved to the Blood reserve as chief clerk for the Indian agency there.

In January my grandfather had been appointed a justice of the peace, joining 439 others in the North-West Territories in the enforcement of territorial ordinances and municipal by-laws, passing judgement for summary offences, and holding preliminary examinations in cases destined for the Supreme Court of the territories. It was a legal regime that had been formally established the year following the Riel uprising, recognizing his friend James Macleod's legacy of pragmatic mediation rather than doctrinaire argument. Though trained as a lawyer, Macleod was not obsessed with legal niceties beyond the presumption of innocence and the trump card of reasonable doubt. There was one infamous case that Macleod presided over (with Ned Maunsell in the jury—it was a small community). A Blood named Star Child was accused of murder, and widely presumed to be guilty. But the jury found him innocent, convinced that there was reasonable doubt. The verdict was widely condemned, and so was Macleod, but Star Child went free. His life had its ups and downs over the next while; but after several years on the other side of the law (including a stretch in jail and some adventures stealing horses), he eventually became one of the best scouts the North-West Mounted Police ever had.

So what exactly did it mean to be a justice of the peace in that time and place? Mostly, since the limits of orderliness were not always clear, it involved what one legal scholar describes as equitably applying the law and intelligently not applying it; and after his hunt with Chief Not-Bear, my grandfather would have approached each case recognizing that the first thing you know is that the accused is not guilty. Then you try to find out—that is, to imagine—what happened. And then exercise wise judgement. The chiefs of the bands and tribes of the Blackfoot often functioned like justices of the peace, and by this time my grandfather would have had enough friends among them to have learned some lessons, and probably to have taken their counsel.

Much is said about the way the Canadian legal system, translated (with few changes) from Britain at the time of Confederation and implemented by the new police force and a circuit court system, served the dominant interests of colonial expansion and the settlement of the west. It did that, to be sure. But in the foothills, and in many other prairie communities, it was mostly rendered and often contorted to serve the interests of the citizens of the territory, both First Nations and new nationals—which was to say, to keep the peace and avoid unrest. The principles and practices of this system relied on a British tradition of justice which recognized that the common law was based on local "customary law," understood not from written documents or decisions (so-called positive law, usually the law of state and sometimes referred to as the "black letter") but from observation and oral accounts that were brought together in a tradition of storytelling to become the municipal law of the land—a law that "can be recorded nowhere but in the memory of the people," as the English legal scholar Sir John Davies put it in the early seventeenth century. "Customary Law is the most perfect and most excellent, and without comparison the best, to make and preserve a Commonwealth," he added. It constitutes what one scholar, writing about the Greek historian Thucydides, described as "the truths that belonged to the people of the country ... [who are] best placed to know the truth about themselves. The truth about their city [or territory] belongs to them by the same right as the city [or territory] to which it pertains."

And so the legal regime in place in the foothills in my grandfather's time incorporated both customary and positive law, an inheritance of the principle that the common law be based first of all on the customs of the people rather than the dictates of the sovereign. It certainly suited my grandfather in his relatively brief time serving as justice of the peace. He realized from his association with the Blackfoot that there was a difference between peacekeeping and peacemaking, between maintaining balance, order and peaceful relations and restoring them. He never claimed to be all that good at either; but he did rely on his friend Crop Eared Wolf for some direction on where to draw the line.

. . .

Some years earlier his friend John Maclean had been invited, as a well-known Methodist missionary fluent in the Blackfoot language, to give the inaugural lecture for the newly formed Literary, Scientific and Historical Society. His title? Not Christian virtues, or pagan vices, but "Indian Literature." He believed that the Blackfoot stories and songs offered insight into their way of being in the world, a world out on the prairies that they understood better than the newcomers, and constituted their "real life" as surely as their actions. These were their national literatures as well as their spiritual texts, and included stories that belonged with those of the European traditions in which he had grown up and the Asian traditions in which he was surprisingly well versed, having turned to wider reading early in his life and becoming a comparative literary scholar as well as a correspondent with the leading anthropologists of the day. For the Blackfoot, he came to understand, some stories were more than textual codes to be deciphered; rather, they were genetic codes, determining destiny. In them, the Blackfoot realized themselves as "chosen," bound as a people into a place by ceremonies that fortified them in a world that was always more or less confused and conflicted, and filling them with obligations to each other, to the Creator, and to the wider world. Every culture has its own version of this, which is why the poet Samuel Taylor Coleridge called the Christian Bible a "science of realities"; the Blackfoot, the real people of the plains, would have understood what he was talking about. They would also have understood Coleridge's fierce resistance to the kinds of institutional pressures that were imposing themselves on the Blackfoot. "No power on earth," wrote Coleridge, "can oblige me to act against my conscience. No Magistrate, no Monarch, no Legislature."

The voices of conscientious objection for the Blackfoot were first and last spiritual voices, as they were for Coleridge; and they were collective voices, cherishing the institutions that defined *their* society. There was, and still is, an essential conservatism behind much Aboriginal dissent, a determination to protect values that transcend the sum of individual preoccupations and are enshrined in the institutions of both secular and sacred significance in their communities, their tribal lore and their tribal law. My grandfather could see that the Blackfoot were coming to a time of resolute resistance.

. . .

Many Blackfoot, when they saw newcomers arriving, must have said, "There goes the neighbourhood." Whatever they said—and their singing and dancing and drumming at the time would have expressed it precisely, albeit inscrutably to an outsider—they would have been convinced that only the continued presence of the Blackfoot would keep the foothills civilized. Maclean titled a passage in a journal in which he was drafting essays and stories "The White Savages: As the Indians see the white man."

Keeping the foothills civilized was everyone's obsession, and caused more conflict and confusion than almost anything else. For some, the terms had been laid down by Matthew Arnold in his widely read book *Culture and Anarchy*, which was first published as a series of essays in the year of Canada's confederation. Arnold had tried to redefine the categories of rich and poor (or, in the geography of England, south and north)—social and economic categories that he believed were mutilating his country. Instead, he proposed a set of dichotomies between order and chaos, civilians and barbarians, those with culture and those without, that shaped—or warped—nineteenth-century British colonial expansion and contemporary post-colonial reaction. No debate about cultural relativity and no discussion of national identity in the past hundred years has been able to ignore Arnold's formulation, or discount his celebration of ceremony and tradition.

The spectre of anarchy that haunted Arnold was both secular and spiritual, and was embodied in an excessive materialism—what he scornfully referred to in one of his chapter titles as "Doing As One Likes." He was dismayed at the subversive pluralism to which he felt his society had surrendered, which for him meant the disintegration of a sense of shared, permanent values, and a corresponding collapse of cultural standards. In the foothills, Arnold's dream of cultural identity had about as much relevance as Tennessee's dismissal of European diversity—"all foreigners," Tennessee said.

But while it was impossible to agree with Arnold's dream of a unified national culture in the foothills, precisely for that reason his apocalyptic vision of anarchy was immensely compelling to everyone in a time of worldwide demographic changes happening on a scale unknown since the last great period of cultural and territorial paranoia, the Middle Ages. And we misunderstand the encounter between natives and newcomers in the Americas if we think that the anxiety was all one-sided. Certainly, on the western plains, at precisely the same time as Arnold was pronouncing on culture and anarchy, the Aboriginal peoples were doing exactly the same thing, shaping their politics and their statecraft around a core belief in the importance of maintaining a continuity of cultural values in the face of the incursions and innovations taking place all around them. They believed, no less than Arnold did, that every culture must maintain an orderly balance between the stabilities of convention and the energies of change, or else anarchy will take hold. That was why they entered into treaty; and that was why they kept the promises they made, despite much pressure from those within the community to break their word even as the other side had broken theirs.

. . .

Aboriginal peoples had lived side by side with other peoples for centuries, making all sorts of arrangements to get through the season, or the territory, or the dispute, but maintaining their distinctive languages and customs. Our homogenized chronicle of Aboriginal victimization by Europeans since treaty time is understandable, and undeniable; but it masks the resistance, and the agency, of many of the Aboriginal communities. And it obscures the ways in which new technologies could be incorporated into old cultural practices without causing a loss in their core meaning and value, as the Blackfoot had done with horses, and as other plains tribes had done with the networks of trade and commerce that had been part of their world for the past couple of centuries.

The mistaken belief that change inevitably destroyed Aboriginal cultures may have been reinforced by the Blackfoot refusal to give up spiritual technologies such as the Sun Dance, though they also took to farming and ranching and to speaking English as well as their own language. James Macleod understood, and supported Red Crow's stern admonition, often repeated, that he and his people must be allowed to pray in their own way. "There is praying all over the world," Red Crow said at the time of a dispute over the Sun Dance. "Red Crow believes in his own praying. This next month [July, that year] is the time." That said, he converted to Catholicism in the course of his later life and married his youngest wife in a Catholic ceremony (using the new legal technology to ensure an inheritance for his baptized Catholic son Frank). And he was close friends with several of the Protestant missionaries. But he would not give up his traditional forms of praise and prayer. He would just accompany them with others.

Treaty Seven was supposed to establish new coordinates for maintaining Blackfoot cultural integrity against pluralistic anarchy; and the Blackfoot did their part, accepting the challenge of translating their covenantal relationship to the land—their belief that they were a chosen people—into the constitutional choice of a reserve, a small piece of the domain that had once been vast and varied. They did so with the conviction that this choice represented another covenant, this time with the Great Mother. She would be their protector, if they would be her people. The promises made under that covenant were at the heart of the treaties. Break them, and you have broken much more than a commercial "deal." You have broken faith. Failing to keep your word was for the Blackfoot the quintessentially uncivil, and uncivilized, act. It was also, to use a word with ancient spiritual associations, a form of pollution, poisoning the wells. And they were right. It would produce for them the very anarchy that Arnold was chronicling. As it would for many of the settlers in the foothills.

But keeping your word was inconvenient for administrators trying to manage the bipolar pathology of "separation" on the reserve and "assimilation" into white society (which morphed into "protection" and "advancement" early in the twentieth century), and bewildered by the impossible choices it offered. Some grim regulations were piled on to cover their confusion, but they had brutal consequences.

None were more devastating than those caused by the residential school system, set up to destroy the imaginative and spiritual integrity—what Arnold called the "culture"—of Aboriginal communities. The bleak vision of William Butler Yeats in 1919 (contemplating the disintegration of Europe, the bloody revolution in Russia and the civil war in Ireland) catches the character of what happened, though it doesn't come close to counting the cost.

Things fall apart; the centre cannot hold;
Mere anarchy is loosed upon the world,
The blood-dimmed tide is loosed, and everywhere
The ceremony of innocence is drowned.

With the residential schools, anarchy was indeed loosed upon the Aboriginal world, and the ceremony of innocence drowned. In a sense it had all started some time before the treaties, but the institutional conveniences that treaties introduced and the iron fist of the Indian Act (first passed in 1876, and establishing a uniform system of wardships rather than a network of alliances and friendships) made it easier to undertake the program of cultural genocide that it truly was. The story is told with clarity and compassion in the Report of the Truth and Reconciliation Commission, and although I listened to months of testimony during the Royal Commission on Aboriginal Peoples in the 1990s, I am once again, as we all must be, brought face to face with the horror of this institutionalized holocaust.

It begins in the Americas with the earliest encounters between Aboriginal peoples and settlers over five hundred years ago, and once again a poem tells the story. Written by one John Rastell about twenty years after Columbus made his first landing, it reads as follows:

And what a great and meritoryouse dede
It were to have the people instructed

To lyve more Vertuously
And to lerne to knowe of man the maner
And also to knowe of god theyre maker
Which as yet lyve all bestly.

Oh, that such a strangely simple-minded sentiment could unleash such a deadly plague as the residential schools. But it did, not directly of course but over time in various guises around the Americas, and with startling ruthlessness in Canada. This poem presented the orthodox missionary problem, and proposed what became its orthodox solution. "To live more virtuously" requires people to live less beastly, which is to say less like Aboriginal savages and more like civilized citizens. And "to know of man the manner and of God their maker" was to receive instruction in the blessings of civilization—that is to say, of Culture with a capital "C"—and of Christianity, also with a capital "C," and thereby to become compelled and converted by their truths and beauties and goodnesses. The only question that literally bedevilled the early compellers and converters was which should come first—civilization or Christianity; and the history of the cultural and spiritual coercion—a.k.a. "education"—of Aboriginal peoples in the Americas shuttled between these alternatives.

Until, in a stroke of demonic institutional genius, the Canadian colonial and then Dominion government decided to combine the two, and at first sanction and then wholly support church-run schools in which students were removed from the influence of hearth and home, sheared like sheep, forbidden from speaking their language, and forced to behave in the ways of settler society . . . except that it wasn't always the settlers' ways they learned, but the ways of some strange society of sociopaths.

Arnold is not off the hook, for he spoke of the importance of "getting to know, on all the matters which most concern us, the best which has been thought and said in the world," and of the need to create a society in which the "coarsely tempered natures" of the "barbarians and philistines" would be imbued with the "sweetness and light" of a truly cultivated, civilized community. In saying this, he played into the hands of those who knew a barbarian or a philistine when they saw one—and he or she was invariably an Indian. And when Arnold proposed a secular canon of cultural touchstones, he was thinking of a specifically European index of stories and songs, setting the stage for another kind of brutality. For along with the horrendous pain and suffering the residential schools caused Indian children separated from their families, they also did one thing that was designed to make the damage permanent. They changed the stories, and the storylines, that had held First Nations communities together for generations and had been hard won by their ancestors and hard-wired into their consciousnesses. To change the story was to change the languages and the lives and the livelihoods and the lands ... and to replace them with ones they couldn't believe. That is a deadly legacy.

The residential school system was started in the middle of the nineteenth century, often in the form of what were called "industrial schools" that taught some valuable new crafts and skills to the young Indian boys and girls but in doing so relentlessly discounted the knowledge and the experience of the faithkeepers and scholars and scientists and storytellers in their communities and the culture their parents held dear—a defence against the very same anarchy Arnold talked about. It was to one of these schools—St. Joseph's Industrial School built by the Roman Catholics in 1883 in Dunbow, south of Calgary—that Red Crow sent his son Shot Close, convinced by his visit to the Six Nations Reserve in Ontario of the importance of education and training. There were schools on the Blood reserve, but Red Crow was not impressed with the results, and he felt that a break from the distraction of family and friends would be good for his son, by whom he set great store. He knew this would mean long periods away from home, but he saw it as a kindred sacrifice to that of the warriors of old, giving up much for new knowledge and experience. When he arrived at the school, Shot Close was given the name Frank Red Crow, number 166. His hair was cut short, he was dressed in a grey uniform, his traditions were routinely discredited and he had to speak English . . . but at least, unlike many less fortunate children, he kept his Blackfoot language and later returned to become a chief in his Blood tribe.

The name "industrial school" also reveals another purpose behind the schools: to imbue in the students those habits of industry and thrift that were *the* Victorian virtues, and which in the myopic gaze of the newcomers did not seem evident in their parents. Thrift had been pretty well looked after by the treaties, you might think; but Indians still loved dressing up, and parades, and spending money in town. Just like everyone else. However, their joy on such occasions seemed to be particularly irritating to the crusaders for industry and thrift.

Not everyone was caught up in this system of Indian "improvement" during my grandfather's time in the foothills, for it was just gathering steam, and schools had not been established everywhere, certainly not enough of them to make them compulsory, as they would become by the 1920s. And the Blackfoot, for their part, refused to accept the alternatives of assimilation or separation—refused to be either drowned in the sea or marooned on an island—and countered some of the effects of the changes that followed the treaty, and the loss of the territory that followed the disappearance of the buffalo, by maintaining a sure sense of their place, literal and figurative, in the foothills; and of that place as a homeland, however diminished. The stories, old and new, that sustained the Blackfoot became part of the ceremony of belief around which they lived their lives, an imaginative centre. New neighbours, like my grandfather, recognized this because it mirrored their own convictions about community and culture. But even the most sympathetic had trouble comprehending all that was happening to the Blackfoot, especially after residential schooling, when some of the youngsters moved to the cities and their sense of dislocation and dispossession became different from anything their parents had experienced, and bewildering to both.

. . .

"We live in a place / that is not our own, and much more, not ourselves, / And hard it is in spite of blazoned days," wrote the American poet Wallace Stevens a half century later about the human condition. That's the bad news. The good news is, in the words of Stevens that follow, "From this the poem springs." As did Blackfoot songs and stories, reconfigured to make their new place home again, looking backward and forward at the same time. Such stories fight a mental fight against all institutions and ideologies that bewilder and benight rather than empower and illuminate us. These are not systems, but *shitstems*, the singer Peter Tosh said, with Rastafarian wit and wisdom. Shitstems of thought and feeling that compel us to accept the terms of their temporary categories, hypnotizing us into the delusion that their elements are permanent, their priorities immutable, the choices they present to us both urgent and irrevocable. When we submit to them, we move closer and closer to what Thoreau once described as a life of quiet desperation, in which we are always under pressure to react to what is happening outside ourselves, or elsewhere. That's if we are lucky. If we are unlucky we become violent, ready to burn down Babylon; or we go mad; or we surrender to the first thing that offers us survival of any sort, or any sort of power. It is only through the pressure of the imagination that anyone can resist the overwhelming pressure of reality. The Blackfoot knew this better than anyone, and it saved many of them.

"How can we sing our Creator's song in a strange land?" some Blackfoot youth asked their elders when they came back from school, quoting Psalm 137's lament for the exile of the Jewish people by the waters of Babylon. Just watch and listen, said their leaders, singing their war songs and dancing their scalp dances like Old Testament prophets even as they made peace with the newcomers and fenced their land, raised cattle and potatoes, and bred their beloved horses to win races and herd cattle, and showed their spirit in the rodeo, and then rode in parades with traditional trappings. Parades and pageantry, like stories and songs, have provided ways in which communities define their identity for thousands of years, all over the world. This was sometimes mistaken as being simply for show, and it was that. But it was also the "essential gaudiness" of the imagination—the extravagance celebrated in all cultures even when it is frowned upon by the agents of utility and morality—pushing back against the everyday. In that sense it was something that all human beings in all societies cherish, whatever their circumstances, and express in ways that convey important elements of meaning and value in their lives.

It had its counterpart in settler society, with its formal dances and social dinners and church rituals and cowboy displays of skill and style. And such displays, such extravagances, often do provide common ground between native and newcomer, for the simple reason that they give pleasure. Pleasure has been a moral test for a long time around the world. Louis Riel knew that, when he wrote that "evening prayer gives more pleasure in heaven than all the military music played by the North-West Mounted Police outside my cell window." In the old rationalist crossroads of Europe, the Roman poet and philosopher Lucretius based his theory of the *Nature of Things* (*De Rerum Natura*) on the relationship between pleasure on the one hand and truth, beauty and goodness on the other. Francis Bacon, at the beginning of the seventeenth century, insisted that "all knowledge and wonder (which is the soul of knowledge) is an impression of pleasure in itself." In the eighteenth century, the philosopher David Hume insisted on the equal importance of feelings and thoughts in civilized society, especially feelings of pleasure. That may sound revolutionary; but it is ancient, and Aboriginal. And among many other things, it is at the heart of parades—making everyone feel good. This delight in display, bringing out your very best and putting it on show, was something my grandfather and Crop Eared Wolf would often talk about, the importance of show for its own sake. For my grandfather, it was pleasure for pleasure's sake in defiance of the utilitarian urgencies and moral strictures of Victorian life. For Crop Eared Wolf, it was being Blackfoot.

. . .

Perhaps because of his ability to balance the books, perhaps because of his rebellious turn, perhaps because *The Outlaw* had been very popular and people liked to have fun, but mostly because the town had a crisis on its hands with a water and sewer system that everyone felt had been responsible for a dangerous spread of diseases, Jack Cowdry ran for mayor again in 1898, and was easily elected. He was encouraged to do so by his friend George Kennedy, who as well as being the senior general practitioner in town was also its health inspector. (Water wagons hauling water from the river had for some years provided a regular supply to the town, along with wells, but it was past time to bring things up to date.)

Heavily influencing my grandfather's decision to take on the mayor's job again was another factor. He was becoming fed up with the ignorant, negative attitude of some of the newcomers in the 1890s towards the Blackfoot, and their ambition to keep Indians out of town on the grounds that they were ... well, they were *Indian*. Because, as new settlers moved into town and the countryside around, the attitude towards the Blackfoot started to change, and there were more grumblings about Indians crowding the streets and stores.

This was also an attitude fuelled by a federal immigration and settlement policy that identified the best sort of people by their occupation; and later, under Frank Oliver, their ethnicity. The occupation of an Indian, in this accounting, was simply being an Indian—an idle Indian. But in Fort Macleod the merchants at least had a different view: they certainly didn't mind Indians in town. As far as they were concerned, their occupation was being good customers, and shopkeepers continued to welcome them and give treats to their kids, many of whom they'd watched grow up. And most of the established merchants did so not just because the town depended on the Indians for business, but because they genuinely felt that they were part of the community, as worthy of respect as anyone else—and more than some, I'm sure they would have added. When Jerry Potts, who was Métis, died two years earlier, the town had come together to honour him, with a large funeral and full military honours. "His memory will long be green in the hearts of those who knew him best, and 'faithful and true' is the character he leaves behind— the best monument of a valuable life," proclaimed the *Macleod Gazette*. My grandfather—treasuring the photograph that Jerry had recently given him of himself with his wife, Long Time Laying Down, the daughter of the Blood chief One Spot, whom he had married in the late 1880s after his two Peigan wives died—was not sure anything like that would happen now, just two years later, in the town he loved so well.

For there were displays of what was beginning to plague many western towns, setting Indians into a kind of civil competition with newcomers. Charlie Wood, who had peddled the stereotype of primitive savages and civilized Christians in the *Gazette* (rebuked time and again by Fred Haultain and Jack Cowdry), was adept at misrepresenting the showiness of the Blackfoot on parade or at market for a refusal to become civilized... even as he celebrated their civilized spending of money in town, their civilized participation in community activities, and even had some grudging praise for their gloriously uncivilized and infuriatingly successful participation in horse races and rodeos. Also, he had to admit that the horse parades were becoming very popular, just like the Mounted Police Musical Rides.

My grandfather believed that the Blackfoot were what made Macleod different from Calgary and Lethbridge and Edmonton and Regina. This was not because he had many Blackfoot friends; indeed, I think it was exactly the opposite. He had many Blackfoot friends because he believed this. The Blackfoot were the future of the foothills—as reliable, and sometimes as reliably exasperating, as the winds that blew all the time across the prairies. They sometimes irritated people when they came in the hundreds by cart or on horseback and took over the town on treaty payment days, but like the wind they also brought blessing and beauty and business to the town and all its people.

Maybe it had something to do with that quirt—I would bet the bank that it had a lot to do with that quirt—but my grandfather wanted to bring the town's ambitions into line with Blood and Peigan aspirations. He also wanted to be sure that his friends were always welcome in town. He never wrote much about all this; my mother said he told her it was what he did that mattered. But I suspect he said a lot on this subject at the time, especially around Taylor's Table. We just weren't around to hear it … though we see traces in *The Outlaw*. Another upstart newspaper, less mischievous and more municipal, began publication in 1899. It was called *The Advance* and it raised the issue bluntly, encouraging old-time consideration

> *for the Indians themselves [rather than merely for their money] and not [being] tight-fisted in the matter of expending a few dollars for the people whose trade they seek to cater to.… Macleod was a thriving town years before [when] the merchants were in the habit of brewing large quantities of strong tea, which would be placed in some convenient spot in the store*

where the Indians could get at it readily. A barrel of biscuits would be left uncovered close beside the tea. . . . Money would also be subscribed and this would be spent in furnishing . . . sport in the way of horse racing and other kinds. . . . Our businessmen held the confidence of the Indian populace and if they have of late years lost their grip, they must blame themselves for it.

For my grandfather, that advice needed to be directed to everyone in town . . . and he decided to see what he could do about it as mayor once again, full of ambition for a town that he knew could not compete with Calgary for metropolitan appeal but was a much better model for the west he was trying to nourish, and was calling home.

14

WHEN MY GRANDMOTHER DIED

"Take a long look at the world around you."
NORTHROP FRYE

. . .

IT WAS IN AL GRADY'S hardware store that Mayor Cowdry fell for the schoolteacher Miss Thompson. They had met several times a year or so earlier—her name was Augusta, though everyone knew her as Gussie—and she had come from Ingersoll, Ontario, to teach at the local school. Shortly after she arrived, she was taken in hand by Lillie Grier, who had been the first teacher at the new school organized in town the year my grandfather arrived, and who married D.W. Davis the year after my grandfather opened the bank. With Lillie as her mentor, and Grady—who was on the school board—as her friend, Gussie would have gotten to know the town well, and Jack had seen her at several dances and a horse race; but he tumbled into love while watching her choose some glazed redware flowerpots for the school's spring fair.

After that, they moved quickly, almost as though they knew they didn't have much time. During the summer they were back and forth from Ingersoll, Jack telling stories to her family and Gussie giggling, and they got married in December of that same year, 1898.

By early in the new year—my grandfather's second year as mayor—Gussie was pregnant; but the pregnancy was not easy, and after several months of feeling more than usually poorly, and on the advice of George Kennedy—who had seen my grandfather through his earlier losses, and maybe doubted himself a bit this time—they decided that Gussie should go back to Ingersoll to have the baby. Neither of them wanted that so they waited a while, and she was soon feeling much better; but as the time got closer Jack got worried, and they both thought the comfort and care of her Ingersoll family might be a good thing. So he went back with her on the train, stayed a few weeks, and then returned to Macleod in late August.

In mid-October, he got the good news that my mother was born, and healthy. He was getting ready to go to Ingersoll to see her when a telegram arrived saying that Gussie was seriously ill. She died just after he got there.

Men have had no monopoly on courage in the history of the world; and it isn't for nothing that in the Book of Common Prayer that was part of my mother's Anglican upbringing there is a service for women who have given birth to a child, asking for "safe deliverance and preservation in the great danger of childbirth." It was indeed a great danger, next to which the rough-and-tumble of even American frontier life was a picnic. There is much—though not yet enough—written about the role women played in the late-nineteenth-century western territories, the women who came as settlers to the North-West Territories, and the women of the Blackfoot Confederacy and other First

Nations, and the Métis women; but it is too seldom recognized that often their bravest contribution was bearing children. At the time my mother was born, for some time afterwards, and indeed in many parts of the world to this day, childbirth has defied available health care, with infection, bleeding and convulsions the most perilous threat for women, and digestive and lung disorders and epidemics of virulent diseases often taking the children and young adults (while pneumonia took the same toll on adult women and men as it does on the aged today). One in ten children would die before the age of one in Canada in the late nineteenth century, better than in many European countries at the time but devastating nonetheless. The figures in the North-West Territories were, surprisingly, better than in Ontario and Quebec, but that wouldn't have been much comfort to my grandfather; and anyhow it wasn't realized at the time. And no count was kept of the mothers.

· · ·

After the funeral, my grandfather returned to Fort Macleod, arriving back on December 6, a day before what would have been his and Gussie's first wedding anniversary. Pole-axed by grief, he went around town with a box of Cuban cigars that he had ordered to celebrate my mother's birth; and he resigned as mayor. Then he had to face a grim reality. He had two children—Mary and Gus, age twelve and nine—in Fort Macleod, and my mother, age two weeks, in Ingersoll. With a heavy heart, he agreed that his baby daughter, my mother, would stay for the time being in Ingersoll with Gussie's parents and her three aunts: Bertha, Edith—whose name my mother was given—and Elizabeth, or

Lizzie, who was always called Diddy by my mother. Diddy, bless her, gave up her own engagement to raise my mother as her daughter . . . and to tell her about Gussie, whom my mother was to know only from the stories told by Diddy and by her mother's family, and later by her father.

· · ·

Back in Fort Macleod, my grandfather's resignation brought much sympathy and some consternation. A good mayor had never been more needed, and the editor of the *Gazette* was anxious to take charge and turn Macleod over to the new settler reactionaries. The national economy was going up and down, as economies do, during the 1890s, with the costs of the railway stretching capacity, and familiar conflicts over language, education and religion causing unease not only across the west but also back east. Federal party politics had been fairly ramshackle until Wilfrid Laurier came to power. But the period unleashed a cohort of belligerent bureaucrats in the Indian service both at headquarters back in Ottawa and in the field, some of whom did their best to brutalize many First Nations communities.

John Maclean tells of Blood war chief White Calf's contemptuous diatribe one day against him and his people, upholding their warrior virtues of resistance and valour (which Maclean agreed were admirable) in response to the barbarities they were enduring. John Maclean was a Methodist missionary of great character and commitment, as were others such as John McDougall; not perfect, either of them, but dedicated to the people of the plains. And then there were the likes of their colleague Alfred Andrews in Lethbridge, who suggested in those terrible years following Treaty Seven when the buffalo had gone that "the Indians seek things in garbage heaps not because they are starving, but because they are curious and not over particular." He was fiercely denounced by Maclean and McDougall and another Methodist, James Robertson, so perhaps three to one is not a bad average for missionaries at that time; but it is a reminder of the ignorance and stupidity, seasoned with malice, that was around and about in all quarters. And is still around and about.

But underlying everything was the blunt and brutal fact that during these times both the spirit and the letter of the treaties were being dishonoured throughout the west: rations were intermittently reduced on instructions from Ottawa, and sometimes completely withheld by Indian agents who treated rations— promised under treaty—like gold stars for good behaviour, or as incentives for the Indians to get out of the way of the railway and move onto their reserves. McDougall, familiar with conditions throughout the prairies, denounced "the almost despotic power of the ration house." Things were a bit better for the Blackfoot, since their choice of reserves, however constrained, had been made by them with both the railway and their traditional territories in mind. But there were confrontations with agents who did not like the idea that Indians had rights as well as responsibilities, and who certainly did not see themselves as treaty people too. A "pass system" designed to keep Indians on the reserves had been introduced on the prairies in 1885, partly as a crowd management program—an early form of police kettling, or of placing displaced persons in refugee camps—and partly in response to the uprising of the Métis under Louis Riel. It was deeply offensive in principle, as well as intermittently irritating in practice. But it was also illegal, a fact that was recognized by the North-West Mounted

Police—at least throughout Blackfoot territory, though inconsistently in the rest of the North-West Territories—with Macleod's stern instructions about the rule of law ringing in their ears. It was, however, convenient for autocratic Indian agents, anxious to exercise their authority (and what some of them understood as their righteous responsibility) to "protect" Indians from backsliding or wayfaring. The Irish among the police—and there were plenty—recognized the pass system as nothing more or less than an attempt to criminalize vagrancy, which they knew all about from relatives who had migrated to England, where being Irish often meant being arrested for loitering . . . which is to say, for being Irish. There were occasional injunctions from senior officials condemning the system; and at the end of the 1890s, a letter from David Laird, newly appointed Indian Commissioner for the North-West Territories, laid it out bluntly to the Indian agent on the Blood reserve. "The pass system as it stands cannot be enforced by law." Still, it continued to be used, and abused, and represents one of several regimes that menaced and marginalized First Nations peoples across the prairies. (More recently it has found another life, as illegal—and as convenient—as its foster parent, in the system of "carding" that makes racial profiling police business.)

Some of the agents tried to break down the authority of the chiefs, convinced that the traditional structures of order and good governance in the tribal communities—where consensus was carefully balanced by the varying levels of authority of chiefs in the band and the tribe—represented one of the major obstacles to the "civilizing" of the individuals and fostered resistance to whatever objective the agent might have at that particular moment. And they would use dissent and discontent within the

band or tribe as evidence of immature politics rather than demo-
cratic openness.

In many ways nothing did more damage across the country
than this attitude on the part of the Indian agents, often working
under direction from both politicians and bureaucrats in Ottawa.
In the foothills, the Mounted Police generally sought to maintain the authority of the chiefs, which inevitably produced some
awkward moments, but sustained a structure of governance that
in that time worked well (though the police in Blackfoot territory
were no more homogeneous than the Indian agents, except in
their overwhelmingly British and Irish ethnicity). And some of
the agents did defend the rights of the Indians, opposing among
other things the infamous pass system. One of them, William
Pocklington—who worked closely with Red Crow and Crop
Eared Wolf on a number of difficult occasions—resisted an
attempt by an impatient Mounted Police superintendent Sam
Steele to tidy up the territory and keep the Bloods in their place,
responding bluntly that "the Indians are not confined to the
reserve by any law or regulation . . . and [they] know they have the
right to go and come as they please." Steele got slightly better at
working with the chiefs during his ten years in charge, which
made the job of his officers easier. In 1898 he was transferred to
the Yukon, where he was in his element, managing a volatile
situation with greedy gold miners.

Motivating these actions were familiar ambitions. The first
was practical: exercising despotic power with arbitrary ruthlessness made life easier, and maybe even more fun, for the agents.
The second was what we might call theoretical, and it was the
deadliest, for it was part of a deep-seated determination
described by John Maclean when he said, "We wish to make

them white men, but they desire to become better Indians." This was social engineering on a national scale ... or national scales, since it involved First Nations whose lives and livelihoods were as different as the woodlands and the lakes and the mountain valleys and the coastal waterways and the tundra and the prairies they had called home for centuries, often millennia. It was a gimcrack notion that had immense appeal as a way of tidying up the territories for "development"—which is to say, for the agricultural and industrial enterprises, and the urbanization, that were associated with civilization. And before we feel too superior to this, we need to recognize that this idea has infected much of our international enterprise to "help" and "improve" many struggling societies around the world, destroying indigenous cultural traditions and viable harvesting practices by identifying them as insignia of "underdevelopment," to be replaced by models of "development" that are not only inappropriate but often economically, socially, culturally, environmentally and spiritually toxic. Canada can take cynical satisfaction in establishing something of a model for this.

Now is the time for us to show a better way; and we can begin by recovering the spirit, and retranslating the letter, of the prairie treaties.

· · ·

My mother's grandparents, the Thompsons, had been farmers near Ingersoll before they moved to town, and my mother said they had lots of visits from the Oxford County farmers they knew, bringing them corn and other vegetables in season and eggs and chickens and cheeses throughout the year and turkeys

and hams every Christmas. Her father—my grandfather Jack—
came from Macleod to visit her several times a year, always bringing chocolates, she told me. Once, she remembered, they were in
a box with a picture of a young girl called Evangeline on the cover.
He said Evangeline once lived on the east coast of Canada and
went on a long journey looking for someone she loved. Another
time, her father brought chocolates from a man he called Candy
Rogers, who he said had started making them in Victoria on the
west coast in 1885, the year he went to Fort Macleod.

My mother said that one thing she noticed about her father
was that he was shorter than the farmers she knew; but he had a
beard just like they did, and his hair was the colour of the horse
that pulled the wagon that brought the milk every other day.
Diddy told her the colour was sorrel. He always wore wonderful
hats when he came to visit, a different one each time, and as soon
as he arrived he would take it off and place it upside down on the
side table. She asked him why he did that, and he said it was so
the brim wouldn't flatten out like a johnnycake ... which was a
kind of pancake, but tasted better. Then he would ask her to hold
St. Bruno, his tin of sweet-smelling tobacco, while he filled his
pipe and lit it with a single match and started telling stories. He
would always start with a story about the long pipes of the
Blackfoot Indians who lived near Fort Macleod, telling her how
they smoked them in their tipis, and when favourite guests came
they would share a pipe. And to show her he gave her a puff on
his pipe when the aunts weren't looking. She said it smelled
better than it tasted.

Every few months he would send her clothes from the Eaton's
catalogue: on her birthday when she was eight she got a green
Ulster coat, double-breasted, with a high storm collar trimmed

with fancy braid; and at Christmas that year, a pair of single-strap slippers made of chocolate-coloured kid leather. She had fond memories of her life as a little girl in Ingersoll with Diddy and the aunts, especially tea time, when the crocheted doilies would be brought out to put under cups and saucers with pretty designs, and a spoon would be put in the cup before pouring in tea to draw off the heat so the cup didn't crack. They lavished their stern, sentimental Victorian attention on her, and engaged a tutor to come and teach her about the world as far away as, well, Woodstock, down the road a full ten miles. She remembered how everyone knew a neighbour's opinions by the newspaper that was delivered to their front door—either the conservative *Mail and Empire*, trumpeting Tory politics, or the liberal *Globe*, favoured by the unsavoury Grits. "Civilized towns and countries work best that way," said Diddy. "Nonsense," her father said when they talked about such things on one of his visits, "because there isn't much difference between political parties anyway ... except that they always favour different friends," and added that he wished the new government of the North-West Territories wouldn't have any political parties at all. And then he told them about *The Outlaw*, which made fun of both the Liberals *and* the Conservatives. My mother was hustled off to bed by her aunts about then; but she heard them talking about it for weeks afterwards, as they rehearsed their arguments for his next visit. They liked her father. And so did she.

During those early years all my mother really knew about him was from his stories, and from Uncle Nat, who came to visit every month or so. And from her own imagination, which Diddy and her aunts told her was what brought stories to life. She wasn't sure where her imagination was, but they said it was what they relied on for their sense of his life out west. That and the novel called *The Virginian*, which they had bought when it came out in 1902. By the time I knew my mother, both her imagination and her storytelling were well exercised; and I grew up in a world that shuttled between Ingersoll and Fort Macleod and Vancouver, where I was born.

On one visit when my mother was nine, her father brought her a gold nugget and some flint made into an arrowhead from the mountains to the west, and a piece of rock called ochre that he had picked up just a few miles from Fort Macleod, with which she wrote her name in orange in the front of the journal he gave her. He told her how he had got the nugget from a stream in the mountains to the west of Macleod by taking a pan and swirling the stream water around in it until everything had swished out except the heaviest bits of sand—and if you were lucky some of those were gold, and sometimes big pieces of gold like this nugget. He said the people who lived in the mountains had traded flint to the plains Indians to make the spears and arrows they had used to hunt the buffalo in the old days; and the Blackfoot had found ochre in the hills close by and used it to paint on the rocks near Fort Macleod hundreds and thousands of years ago, and sometimes to paint their horses or themselves. A year later around Easter, he brought her a jade pendant shaped like a tear and attached to a gold chain, which she wore around her neck every day for years afterwards. He told her it had been Gussie's favourite piece of jewelry.

The new Cowdry Brothers Bank is on the left halfway down the street, just past the telegraph pole doubling as a barbershop sign. Other shops include Charles Reach's greengrocer and dry goods store and Chow Sam's restaurant on the left opposite Singkee's laundry.

John Ware's pleasant ranch, northwest of Macleod with John on horseback and his wife Mildred (known to all as Mother Ware) standing on the verandah. He was a celebrated figure in the foothills: the fact that he was black being far less important than his stature as a respected cattleman and one of the best rodeo cowboys in the foothills.

In 1900 the Cowdry brothers put up the first brick building in Macleod—and their third bank since they began business in a wooden shanty. Starting construction that spring gave my grandfather something to take his mind off the death of Gussie.

In August 1897 John Black put an advertisement in the *Macleod Gazette* welcoming "the white subjects and red allies of her Gracious Majesty" to his new store: his mischief-making was loved by settlers and Indians alike.

The Outlaw.

Cultores Veritatis, Fraudis Inimici—With Malice Towards All and Charity to None.

Vol. 1.   SCOTT'S COULEE, ALBERTA, MAY 19TH, 1896.   No. 1.

THE OUTLAW

Is published every Tuesday at Big Swan Block, Scott's Coulee, by the Scott's Coulee Publishing Co., Ltd. Subscription, 10cts. per copy.

A limited number of advertisements will be accepted, space not to exceed one inch. One dollar each insertion. All communications must be addressed : Business Manager OUTLAW, P. O. Box No. 50, Macleod. N B.—Advts. that are changed more than once a week will be charged double.

The OUTLAW has the largest circulation of any paper in Southern Alberta, and is consequently the best advertising medium in the country. Its exclusive news franchises make it the most widely read and influential journal in the West.

SALUTATORY.

The appearance of the OUTLAW in the journalistic field of Alberta at this moment, needs no apology, and but little explanation. The newspapers of this district are bound hand and foot to their respective parties, two of them being owned by the parliamentary candidates, and of the other three, true charity prompts us to remark "least said, soonest mended." The consequence of this deplorable state of affairs is that party views are represented while the people are sold. There is no organ to voice the feelings of the great mass of voters whose franchises are so merrily passed from one political heeler to another, and there is no medium by which the honest, independent citizen can bring his views before the public and have insured to them that recognition which honesty and independence ever merit. To meet this long felt want, to be the *vox populi* of Southern Alberta, and to expose the shams and frauds and rampant hypocrisies that surround us on every side is the philanthropic object of the OUTLAW.

To do this, we are, as between Grit and Tory, "on the fence," not because we want to see which way the cat jumps before jumping ourselves, but for the reason that from the coign of vantage of the higher elevation it will be the easier for us to watch the struggling mobs below and point out the foibles and vanities, the vices and tricks that will make up the contest on which the people of Alberta have entered. "Spare none, praise none" will be one of our mottoes for the next few weeks, and if politicians don't like its application, they had better get under the barn.

We invite communications, but owing to the exigencies of a limited space, they must be brief, and we hope correspondents will see to it that they are to the point. With

a circulation in this village already in excess of the combined circulation of all other Alberta papers, and with new subscriptions pouring in from Macleod, Pincher Creek, Lethbridge and Cardston, it is hoped and confidently expected that the proprietors will be justified in doubling or trebling the size of the OUTLAW possibly by the time the next issue is ready for publication. And so we make our bow.

THE MACLEOD GAZETTE AND MR. COCHRANE.

Our readers are respectfully invited to watch the journalistic tumble which our unstable contemporary will take during the next week or two. For the past year its columns have been filled with abuse and ridicule of Mr. Thomas Cochrane, and now, because enough representative delegates were purchased to secure that brilliant politician the nomination of a Conservative convention, it will have to switch round, wheel into line, and support him as the best representative the people can send to Ottawa. The Gazette has executed some fairly sharp curves during its career, and may fairly be deemed a past master in the art, but we confess to a feeling of amused curiosity as to how it will turn this particular corner. If we are disposed to hazard a conjecture, we should expect to find it dwelling as little as possible on the candidate and rallying the faithful round the old flag, the old party and the old policy. We shall hear all about how the Conservatives have developed the North-West, built the CPR, encouraged irrigation and railway enterprises, and about how the Liberals have opposed every measure designed to advance the interests of the North-West, but about the candidate—nary a word. It won't do, however, friend Gazette. Men count for something nowadays, and as Mr. Cochrane has chosen to try and hoist himself on the people—as he is now a public man and subject to the search light of public criticism, he must take his medicine just the same as if he were not the grandson of the Earl of Dundonald.

MACLEOD CONVENTION.

A crowded meeting of the Macleod Liberal-Conservative Association was held last week in the Court House, to elect delegates to the Conservative Convention for Alberta. The meeting was in fact packed ram-jam full to the doors—whether it was a Conservative meeting is "another story." It is no secret that the meeting was the occasion of a trial of strength between what one might call the "Harris gang" and—everybody else, and in the result, the honors were easy. For though the "gang" were outnumbered, still they evened matters up substantially by the introduction of some smart tactics.

In the words of an energetic member of the band, who was in the running himself ; "we jobbed 'em, sir ; and if that job hadn't done, we'd have got another one." The job consisted of sliding in the name of Mr. Curran Grier, who it appears was not even a member of the Association, as a candidate for the delegation, thereby occasioning much confusion to Mr. D. J. Grier, who was on the ticket of "everybody else." The "job" was certainly a neat one and resulted in Mr. Charles Farley Harris getting in at the bottom of the delegates in place of Mr. D. J. Grier, a good, solid true-blue Conservative ; and who, but for the fourteen votes that were disallowed on account of there being no initials to the name of Grier, would in all probability have headed the poll. A striking feature of the performance was the Spartan-like conduct of a number of half-breeds, who were full to the brim of Harris and cheap rye. There was no palpable reason for the first element. The second was produced from bottles. The combination acted like nitro-glycerine, and it was deemed expedient to prevent any further quantities of the rye being absorbed until after the poll, when a sufficient amount of Harris would have been extracted to fill a vacuum. Accordingly the back door was locked, and the sheep were properly corralled. So Harris got what he wanted ; and the breeds got what they wanted ; and Cochrane's got what he wanted. I have finished.

The announcement that Mr. Frank Oliver, the nominee of the Alberta Liberals, accompanied by Messrs. A F. Grady, Jim Brown and 'Boggy' Rhodes will arrive here to-day week, has created considerable excitement in our small community. Every preparation for the most enthusiastic demonstration ever given in our village, is being actively urged. Big Swan, the genial proprietor of Hotel de Log, has thrown open the doors of his hospitable mansion for the occasion, and every inducement will be offered to procure the attendance of Billy Stewart, the Willow Creek orator.

Whoop-Up Sentinel : Mr. Bob Evans, of Lethbridge, was unable to secure the Liberal-Conservative nomination in Cardwell, so will shortly be thrown on his own resources. "Bob" is a truly typical backwoods tavern keeper, nothing more, and should endeavor to curtail his vanity within bounds, attend to his veterinary duties (if any) and leave well enough alone.

We quite agree with our esteemed contemporary. Not only has Mr. Evans been unnecessarily interfering in political matters in Ontario, but he had the audacity to threaten the OUTLAW staff that unless they voted for Mr. Cochrane, he would have the government printing discontinued.—EDITOR.

One of a sequence of photographs of the construction of the Sun Dance lodge by the Bloods in 1893: the pole is in place and the people are coming together in praise. The Sun Dance was the most important spiritual ceremony of the year, and, like religious occasions around the world, it brought the people together in secular as well as sacred communion.

Renowned Peigan chief Big Swan, who had signed Treaty Seven, turned to farming after the buffalo had gone, and opened a staging post at his home in Scott's Coulee for coach travellers between Calgary and the Manitoba border. He collaborated with my grandfather and the other reprobates responsible for *The Outlaw*, contributing one spectacular spoof of the wise Indian speaking to the unenlightened white man.

This picture of my grandmother was taken in Ingersoll in 1898, a few months before her marriage to my grandfather—and just over a year before her death giving birth to my mother.

My mother was eleven when this picture was taken in Ingersoll, before she moved to Vancouver to live with her father. She is wearing her mother's jade pendant and probably wondering what school will be like because she has never been to one.

John Maclean was the Methodist missionary to the Bloods during the 1880s and a friend to Red Crow and Crop Eared Wolf. He was schooled in the Blackfoot language by Jerry Potts and Joe Healy. From early days he saw Blackfoot spiritual traditions as companionable with Christian beliefs. His admiration for the Bloods during this time of brutal challenges was unqualified, and he had a sharp tongue for those who disrespected the Blackfoot.

The great Blood rodeo cowboy Tom Three Persons, here having just won the bronc riding competition—the premier event—at the first Calgary Stampede in 1912, being looked up to as a hero by a young boy.

The classic rodeo picture from this era, with Tom riding an outlaw called Cyclone, who had never before been ridden by anyone though many, many cowboys had tried. Tom rode him to a standstill, the test at the time before modern eight-second rides; making an Indian the first "Canadian" to win the competition.

The Blood Indians, like the rest of the Blackfoot tribes in 1912, were camped on the Stampede grounds, proudly displaying their painted tipis, their horses and riders turned out in traditional regalia, celebrating the persistence and pride of the Indian horse cultures of the northern plains.

Here is the picture that would have brought joy to Crop Eared Wolf's big heart: the Indians leading the parade at the start of the first Stampede week. Crop Eared Wolf was too ill to attend, but he had been a determined advocate of Blackfoot participation in ceremonial events, working to make the parade a showpiece for Indian culture and presence at the heart of the foothills communities.

This remarkable photograph taken at the Stampede catches the promise of Chinook country that is at the heart of this book, the Packard Model 30 touring car signalling a new era for its passengers, seated together. The driver is the Provincial Treasurer Malcolm Mackenzie; sitting beside him in the front seat is the Peigan head chief Leans Over Butcher (*Stokinota*); behind are Bull Plume and their friend Ned Maunsell; three Peigan fellow travellers are in the back seat. They are on parade together, the rancher and the politician outnumbered by the Blackfoot, heading into the twentieth century.

15

YELLOW BUFFALO STONE WOMAN PUT UP THE SUN DANCE BY FORCE, AND CROP EARED WOLF BECAME CHIEF OF THE BLOODS

"We wish to make them white men,
but they desire to become better Indians."
JOHN MACLEAN, METHODIST MISSIONARY

. . .

FOR THE BLACKFOOT, IT ALL came to a head in 1900, and at the centre of it was the one ceremony that had become a flashpoint for the Blackfoot and the Indian agents: the Sun Dance, held in summer when the saskatoon—sometimes called sarvis—berries were ripe. It was the great sacred gathering of the year; but it also had a secular component, as sacred gatherings often do, bringing the tribal communities together—consolidating the status of the confederacy, sustaining its material well-being and celebrating spiritual presences and the power of prayer as well as the knowledge of medicine and ritual vested in particular individuals. And it confirmed the Blackfoot understanding of the seasons and of home, just like pow-wows and green corn ceremonies and thanksgivings and "national" observances such as Canada Day do. This made some of the Indian agents and a few of the police officers angry, because they thought that the Sun Dance encouraged the "progressive" Indians to go "back to the blanket" when instead they needed to get on with becoming civilized, give up their primitive sense of home and go out and become (as the Methodist John Maclean put it, but with hard-edged irony) "good white folks." And as Sam Steele noted grumpily, it was also a forum for boasting and toasting about the old days and the old ways, reimagining and rediscovering the past. Like a lot of good history, he should have added.

The Sun Dance represented a range of ceremonial practices among almost all the plains buffalo-hunting tribes, though many referred to it by other names such as the sun-making dance, the lodge-making dance, the thirsting dance, and the sacrifice lodge. Preparations for the Sun Dance began long before its celebration; in the case of the Blackfoot, a woman would have vowed to give the dance (in order to secure the benefit of its sacred medicine) and then told the chief, who spread the word to all the bands, who would then come together when the buffalo were gathered in large numbers. As a social as well as a spiritual occasion, the Sun Dance was a time for political discussions and family reunions and the recounting of successful raids, with gift giving, the transfer of songs and medicine bundles, and the trading of goods. Bull buffalo tongues, given into the care of the presiding medicine woman, were a crucial part of the ceremonies in buffalo days, replaced in my grandfather's time by the tongues of beef cattle. There were meetings of sacred societies; and for a time the Sun Dance included a ritual of self-imposed sacrificial flesh-wounding by some men to keep vows made earlier, usually before going to war or on forays to gather horses from enemy camps. John Maclean made a connection between the Sun Dance and Sunday that did justice to both, highlighting the complicated heritage that Christianity represented, bringing sun worship into the company of son worship and the suffering of Christ on the Cross into communion with the Sun Dance self-mutilations. Maclean preferred to celebrate the sacredness of suffering without advocating its actual performance, and in one of his journals he records gratefully that in 1886 only one participant at the annual Sun Dance tortured himself with skewers through his chest, and two cut off fingers—an improvement, he wrote, from the previous year, when the count was three and seven. By the end of the decade, that practice had ended.

The rituals of Christianity may be virtual, but they are in some traditions no less graphic; and the belief in transubstantiation gives the body and the blood of Christ a terrible but transformative reality. And here the connection with horses comes back into focus. Horses, being the archetypal prey animal, are stoic; whinging and whining are for predators, like dogs and cats who howl and yowl at the smallest inconvenience, and like some humans. When you are a horse, you keep quiet. A sign of weakness is a sentence of death. And you are always watching for surprises, as horses do. The Blackfoot took that into their own culture, and it shaped their conduct in war as well as the custom of ceremonies such as the Sun Dance.

The cutting of the central pole of the Sun Dance lodge initiated a series of ritual actitivites, including the placing of the pole in the ground with willow branches tied in its forks and supporting poles attached to construct the ceremonial lodge. The movement of the gathered bands to the selected location was traditionally in the nature of a "dress parade" when (in the words of one observer) "the Indians wore their finest clothes, decorated their horses with the best trappings, and the men rode with their weapons and shields exposed to view."

The last war party raid—at least the last to get attention from the authorities—was in 1889 against the Assiniboine, in which one scalp was taken. Crop Eared Wolf led a protest against the subsequent attempted arrest of the raiders at a Sun Dance that year, precipitating a scuffle in which the guns and clothing of the police were ripped from them. Red Crow managed to calm things down, and in doing so highlighted the sanctity of the ceremony itself. In this, he was supported by James Macleod, who said that intruding on a Sun Dance was like trying to arrest people in a church. Even so, conflicts with the government and church authorities over its celebration continued, especially during the 1890s when a particularly belligerent Indian agent among the Bloods became determined to stop the Sun Dance, punishing those who were planning one with reduction of rations and treaty payments. He had no real authority to stop it, since the Indian Act only prohibited giveaway ceremonies such as the west coast potlatch (no credit to the Indian Act, I should add).

The agent tried to have one of the chiefs, a leading ceremonialist, deposed for incompetence, stating that "any head man who so persistently refuses to obey the wishes of the Department cannot be said to be competent." The Anglican bishop Cyprian Pinkham (called Chief Holy Rest by the Bloods) intervened; Governor General Lord Minto took up the issue, advising that the Sun Dance should not be prohibited; and the police were mostly onside. But the agent was stubbornly opposed. Whole buffalo or cattle tongues were (and still are) an important part of the ritual; and the Indians would begin saving them in spring, with at least a hundred often required. But the Indian agent maliciously impaired the ritual, first by cutting the tongues in two and then by withholding them entirely from the rations, effectively putting a stop to the Sun Dance for several years.

The summer of 1900 threatened to turn the conflict into a crisis. In the winter, Yellow Buffalo Stone Woman had promised to sponsor a Sun Dance that summer to restore her sick husband to health. Red Crow took a major role in resisting the efforts of the agent to stop it by supporting the preparations, seeking the help of the superintendent of the police and, when he heard that the agent was refusing to provide the necessary beef tongues, offering to slaughter some of his own herd. But that turned out to be unnecessary when the North-West Mounted Police arranged for their police scouts from the Blood tribe to take their treaty meat allotment in whole tongues. The Sun Dance that year was the biggest in a decade, and was never again denied to the Bloods. The year was remembered in the winter count as when "Yellow Buffalo Stone Woman put up the Sun Dance by force." And it signalled the Blackfoot determination not to have it said, in a quotation from the Old Testament book of Lamentations, that "our dance is turned into mourning."

Even with all his achievements in leading his people towards material self-sufficiency, securing the place of that spiritual ceremony in the life of the Blackfoot was perhaps Red Crow's greatest triumph. And it was his last. Two months later, he died, having indicated that he wished his adopted son Crop Eared Wolf to succeed him.

. . .

The ceremony of the Sun Dance, along with a wide range of stories and songs that constitute the Blackfoot sacred and secular heritage—the distinction is not a tidy one—offers them comfort and courage in a world of conflict and confusion... which the world always is, even (despite New Age romanticism) the Aboriginal world. "As it is written in the Psalms of David," said the late Rastafarian elder Mortimo Planno, recalling biblical covenants and echoing Louis Riel, "To Every Song is a Sign and I always Sing the Songs of the Signs of the Time." The music of what happens. This was his way—a Rasta theologian's way—of insisting that the past portrayed in stories (such as those in the Old Testament, for him, and in the ceremonial narratives and lyrics of the Sun Dance, for the Blackfoot) is *present*, just like the Passover during the Seder, and in this case constitutes the "real life" (in John Maclean's words) of the real people. The Blackfoot understood what it was like to make a new place home, because that was the challenge they had been served, with the buffalo gone from the plains and reserve life come upon them. The literary critic Northrop Frye began *The Educated Imagination*, his classic account of the relationship between literature and life, by asking us to suppose that we are shipwrecked on a South Sea island. "The first thing you do," he suggested,

> is to take a long look at the world around you, a world of sky and sea and earth and stars and trees and hills. You see this world as objective, as something set over against you and not yourself or related to you in any way.... So you soon realize that there's a difference between the world you're living in and the world you want to live in. The world you want to live in is ... not an environment but a home; it's not the world you see

but the world you build out of what you see. You go to work to
build a shelter or plant a garden ... transform[ing] the island
into something with a human shape.

That's the story of Robinson Crusoe. It is also, unnervingly
for those who rankle at suggestions of dominion over the environment, the story of what it is to be a thinking and feeling
person in the world. It was the settler story, writ large. And
although it may not seem obvious, it has been the story of indigenous peoples all over the world from time immemorial as they
turned their sciences and their arts and their spiritual and material technologies to the business of making the land or the sea
their home. And it continued to be the story of the Blackfoot—
and all the First Nations—when they signed treaties and agreed
to settle on reserves.

The most disabling thing that happened to many First
Nations in Canada was having someone else take that long look
at the world around them and decide what kind of world they
should build out of what they saw. The damage this has done has
been overwhelming. It has imprisoned Aboriginal peoples in
someone else's imagining, no matter how benign—warping
their own imaginations, and weakening their sense of the new
reality they find themselves in. The Blackfoot resisted this at
every turn, and the Sun Dance—as well as testaments like the
quirt—played an important role in this resistance.

To have that done, to have someone else's imagination shape
your reality, is to be "ad-ministered" by someone else, which is
what the federal administration of Indian affairs has been all
about for a hundred and fifty years. It is like being told by someone else that you are a "distinct society," when you know that

already; and it is an attitude that the Royal Commission on Aboriginal Peoples unconsciously continued—the preposition *on* infuriating many First Nations peoples at the time—though the commission did many good things and illuminated some dark corners of Canadian history. Frye's description is ethnocentric not because he thought that he, or indeed any human being, was at the centre of things—nobody who read the English poet William Blake as carefully and imaginatively as he did could think that—but because he knew that was all he knew about such things, and that such a centre was where you had to imagine yourself if you were going to make your new house a home, and avoid the anarchy of a life without a culture. His description is not a real plan, but a dream vision. And insofar as the Blackfoot have been able to thrive through the trauma of the past century, it is because they kept their dreams alive, and stayed close to many, indeed most, of the things that mattered to them, imagining *and* making their new reality—the reserve—into a home, a place with a human—which is to say a Blackfoot—character.

Until, for many of them, the experience of the residential schools destroyed those dreams, disabling their relationships with things of value in their lives, and corrupting their reality by discrediting their imagination. Some of the schools were cess-pits of criminal behaviour; but many of them were devastating simply because—or not so simply because—they were in the control of men and women who liked to be in control. By the 1890s, there were several such places around the Blackfoot community run by missionaries with a cluster of ambitions, all of them more or less coercive, and consequently corrupting, even when they offered valuable technical instruction, as some of the industrial schools certainly did.

Here is anthropologist William Stanner again, following on his celebration of "custom as the reality." The reference is once again Australian, but it illuminates the condition in which many survivors of residential schools have found themselves... what he calls "a kind of vertigo in living."

> They had no stable base of life; every personal affiliation was lamed; every group structure was put out of kilter; no social network had a point of fixture left... yoked by new regulations, into settlements and institutions as substitute homes. The word "vertigo" is of course metaphor, but I do not think it misleading. In New Guinea some of the cargocultists used to speak of "head-he-go-round-men" and "belly-don't-know-men." They were referring to a kind of spinning nausea into which they were flung by a world which seemed to have gone off its bearings.

That sense of losing the centre is what the Blackfoot thought the treaties were intended to prevent, by establishing a shared understanding of the untranslatable as well as the translatable senses of "home," and of the boundaries necessary to regulate settler authority and protect Blackfoot tradition in homelands that were also frontiers. In many cases, sadly, the treaties and the regulations they sponsored, as well as the misunderstandings and misrepresentations (including the outright lies) they encouraged, did the opposite, setting the world off its bearings for First Nations. In doing so, they also set Canada off its bearings.

· · ·

Crop Eared Wolf consoled my grandfather on Gussie's loss in the fall of 1899, and my grandfather comforted Crop Eared Wolf when his father, Red Crow, died the following year, and congratulated him as the new head chief of the Bloods. My grandfather never remarried, and for the rest of his life he grieved the loss of Amy and Gussie, and of those of his children who never made it past their first year. But he also believed in getting up and keeping going. Crop Eared Wolf's friendship helped. And they both kept their mutual love of mischief alive a few years later when a survey was being done to appraise some reserve acreage bordering the Mormon settlement in Cardston that the government wanted the Bloods to surrender for sale.

My grandfather had done a fair bit of banking in the community of Cardston by then, opening an office there so he had a comfortable association with the Mormon community—more comfortable than for Crop Eared Wolf, who was engaged in a dispute with them over their "occupation" of land bordering the Blood reserve that he believed was Blackfoot. He had become enraged when word came to him that the government surveyors were on Blood land to prepare a case for the "surrender" of part of the reserve for sale to the Mormons, and was about to send a letter to David Laird, who was by then the commissioner of Indian affairs . . . but my grandfather said no, wait a bit . . . and the next week, a bit more . . . and a week later, a bit more—he had learned a trick or two from Chief Not-Bear on that hunting trip—until Crop Eared Wolf got completely exasperated. But just then, my grandfather (who knew something about surveying from his uncle and Ned Maunsell's brother George) came down to Crop Eared Wolf's home in Stand Off to say that the survey was all done—which was the last thing Crop Eared Wolf

wanted to hear—and that they should go and see . . . and to bring
a shovel and a big potato sack. Now Crop Eared Wolf trusted my
grandfather, and was sure he wouldn't have done anything
wrong deliberately. But he thought that he himself had done
wrong in taking his advice . . . until they got there, and he found
out what my grandfather had in mind. The survey stakes stood
about a foot above the ground, numbered in red crayon, with
"hub" stakes (for positioning the transit) driven flush to the
ground at each angle in the line or at a convenient point in
between. Beginning at the boundary where the surveyors had
started, Crop Eared Wolf rode and my grandfather walked
along and carefully picked up every stake they came to and could
pull or dig out, which was nearly every one, and put it in the sack
that Crop Eared Wolf had tied to his saddle. It took them half
the day, made more interesting by the stories Crop Eared Wolf
told about "surveying" the terrain as a scout on raids, using a
looking-glass to signal from one hill to another, but they eventually came to the other boundary line, and had all the survey
stakes safely in the sack. "Now," said my grandfather, "let's go
and take this to the Indian agent's office (where his old friend
and former clerk William Black was working) and tell them we
were riding down at the southern boundary and came across
these stakes, and I said they were government survey stakes and
you couldn't figure out what they were doing there and I said
they must have misplaced them on your reserve land and we
should bring them back in case they were wondering where they
got to." The agent wasn't there; William "Lavender Pants" Black
(with memories of *The Outlaw* fresh in his mind) couldn't
speak, he was laughing so hard; and nobody ever said a word
about what had happened, because the surveyors had not asked

permission to come on the land, and they had been outsmarted by the Blackfoot and the banker. The story has never been told before because everybody had a reason to keep it quiet—including Crop Eared Wolf, for some members of his tribe were keen on selling land they weren't using.

. . .

In the meantime, my grandfather got on with looking after his children, Mary and Gus. There are receipts in his diary for the purchase of a doll's house and a tricycle, and a little later a side-saddle and tack and a regular saddle and bridle from Harry Litle, who had come to town the first year my grandfather was mayor. My mother was still in Ingersoll, and he went there more and more often as the years went by, and as she got older he brought her more and more presents, and more and more stories.

As for Crop Eared Wolf, he had his hands full with the matter of his people's land. Drought came and went, as surely as the seasons, and irrigation proposals for the Bow and the Elbow Rivers prompted calls to seek the surrender of some of the northern Blackfoot (Siksika) land. This was eventually secured with Siksika assent, providing significant financial resources to the tribe—they became the wealthiest in Canada—but of course diminishing their land. Meanwhile, the Bloods maintained their stalwart resistance to land surrenders, and the Peigan were right behind them. Their mostly good relations with the ranchers—who valued their land for grazing leases and relied on the hay they produced—certainly helped, but the leadership of Red Crow and Crop Eared Wolf and (after his death in 1913) his son Shot Both Sides was crucial.

. . .

Along with the ranchers, many in the foothills community felt
their lives, and those of their families, were enriched and illuminated by living with and learning from the Blackfoot. Farm
instructors and medical officers often brought their own expertise and intelligence together with Blackfoot experience and
wisdom to serve the communities. One of them, Dr. Oliver
Edwards, was appointed medical officer on the Blood reserve.
He had begun his career in the Indian service as medical officer
at Indian Head, near Fort Qu'Appelle, in 1882, the same year my
grandfather arrived thereabouts. So they had known each other
in Saskatchewan, and also had a mutual friend in William
Osler—my grandfather had spent a couple of summers in the
company of the Oslers when he and William (later Sir William,
of medical fame) were young, once (so the Cowdry family story
goes) saving Willie from drowning in a local lake—and they
were delighted to renew their acquaintance when Oliver Edwards
and his wife, Henrietta, arrived in Stand Off in 1902.

Henrietta, better known as Hettie, became the more
renowned of the two. A formidable presence, she was co-founder
of the National Council of Women and the Victorian Order of
Nurses with Lady Aberdeen, wife of the then governor general.
But more infamously at the time, she was one of the "Famous
Five" Albertan women who fought to have women recognized as
"qualified persons" in one of the (shamefully) landmark cases in
Canadian legal history. It was officially designated as *Edwards v.
Canada*, but much better known as the "Persons Case"; and it
arose from a provision that only "qualified persons" were eligi-
ble to be appointed to the Senate, a phrase widely accepted (by

men) as referring only to them. Taking advantage of a provision in the Supreme Court of Canada Act that said that five persons acting together as a group could petition the court for an interpretation of any part of the constitution, the "Famous Five" took the case to the Supreme Court—which ruled against them. But Hettie and her sisters were not so easily put off, and went to the Privy Council in England, at the time the court of last appeal for Canadians—which decided in their favour in 1929. Women were persons.

Though she would almost certainly have been remarkable anywhere, it is safe to surmise that some of Hettie's determination was encouraged by her close contact with the women of the Blood community around Stand Off. She was an inveterate collector of Indian artifacts, but unusual in that she took the trouble to identify their provenance and purpose, as well as the stories and beliefs associated with them. She commissioned paintings from the First Nations communities, as well as becoming a painter herself before she turned seriously to photography—her Christmas card to family in England in 1900 featured a picture titled "Chief Joe Healy and Brave," which she signed "from one who lives among the Indians." She had close associations with many Blood women, and was honoured with the name "Otter Woman," after the animal sacred to the Blackfoot, entwining her own Christian spiritual convictions with her support for the community. With tuberculosis common in the hospital and maternal mortality high on the reserve, she lobbied (sadly unsuccessfully) for a separate maternity home for the women; and she wrote several texts on the legal status of women that addressed some of the particular inequities facing First Nations women. But perhaps her most notable contribution, as so often in life, was personal; she had many women friends in the Blood community, and she accepted their different spiritual practices comfortably so long as they did not interfere with her own, her relations with them prompting some very un-Christian comments from a few of the ranching women. On the occasion of her daughter's wedding in 1907, Hettie engaged several of the Blood women to help her and her housekeeper with the arrangements, but sent them all home to bed afterwards while she washed the dishes and cleaned up herself . . . "while those savages slept," said one of her lovely guests.

One other medical officer with the Blackfoot during the early years of the twentieth century is worth mentioning, especially in a book like this, dedicated to people who are not included in the standard storyline. Writing about the residential school program, which the government first allowed and then encouraged to take hold for most of the next century, he observed:

> *Indians themselves favour the day school, [which] serves as a little social and cultural centre on the reserve and its influence is conveyed by the children from the school to their parents and relatives in the home. My chief objection to the residential schools is its disruptive effect upon the family. The children become estranged from their parents and this factor is a source of grief to the latter. I have had Indians come to me asking for a day school on their reserve who told me with tears in their eyes how their children returning from residential school ridiculed and despised their fathers and mothers. . . . We are all more or less envious of the centurion in the Bible and enjoy ordering people around. Ecclesiastics are not free from this failing, and derive satisfaction from*

congregating people into institutions and thus exercising
full control over them.

This was not a casual observation. It was written in 1945 by
Dr. Harold McGill, who had just retired as deputy superintendent-
general (deputy minister) of Indian affairs, succeeding Duncan
Campbell Scott. In fact, Harold McGill had not retired. He had
been fired, not so much for opinions like that—though they certainly irritated his political masters, many of them dedicated to
the favourable economics and careless arm's-length operation of
the residential school system—but for opposing the surrender of
eighteen thousand acres of reserve land belonging to the
Blueberry and Doig Bands (*Dunne-za*, or Beaver, First Nations)
near Fort St. John, up in the Peace River district, which infuriated the politicians (and many of the bureaucrats) because they
wanted the land for soldier settlement after the Second World
War. Much later, I was involved in a breach-of-trust court case—
called *Apsassin*, after one of the elders—that the bands brought
against the federal government in the 1980s with regard to that
surrender (which was eventually forced on the bands). With trial
and appeal court judgements against them, they took the case to
the Supreme Court, which decided in their favour: Canada had
broken its word. I quote these remarks here not just because they
shed some small light on the opposition to the residential schools
that existed within the Department of Indian Affairs, but
because McGill was medical officer on the Sarcee reserve in the
Blackfoot Confederacy from 1912 until 1914, when war broke out
and he enlisted. Something of his fierce, if not always successful,
streak of resistance on behalf of the Indians of the country,
which exasperated his civil service and political colleagues, may

have been nourished by his time working with the Blackfoot. Crop Eared Wolf may have known him—he was ill at the time, and not travelling much, so I don't know for sure; but he would have certainly liked his resistance to the Dunne-za land surrender. And the legacy Crop Eared Wolf left of irritating (to the bureaucrats and politicians) independence may have influenced the young doctor to the benefit of others in future years.

The story of the residential schools is a wretched one; and it is no comfort to anyone who suffered there to be told that someone in a position of authority was thinking this way. I know from several years in the archives, and from conversations with those who were around back then, that Harold McGill fought many fights on behalf of the Indians of his time, and won a few; but he was in a position to fight harder to end the residential schools, and he should have done so. I think he felt that too, because that excerpt was from a Toronto newspaper article he wrote after his "early retirement" to draw attention to the issue and force the government's hand, following an earlier letter from him about the inadequate medical services on reserves, with particular attention to the ravages of tuberculosis and trachoma.

. . .

Jack was busy in town. His nephew Thomas was playing an increasingly important role in the bank's success and would take on the management of a couple of the small branches in nearby towns, joined for a short while by his brother Harry. In 1900 my grandfather gave him power of attorney for when he was away, which was quite often; and as a testament to the success the bank was enjoying, Jack supervised the construction of the first brick building in Macleod for the bank to move into, ushering in (as he hoped it would) a run of new buildings in town, and a time of relative prosperity. (Maybe this inspired Nat to do something similar in the town where he had settled, for two years later there is a picture of him as part of a construction crew standing in front of the new brick town hall in Waterford, Ontario.) In the spring of 1903 disaster struck a town close to Fort Macleod when half the mountain came down on the coal-mining village of Frank in the Crowsnest Pass. The town recovered, after a fashion; but it shook everyone in the foothills, a reminder that nature ultimately holds the cards. It still counts as the deadliest rockslide in Canadian history, killing scores of citizens and covering part of the town, the CPR line and the coal mine itself.

. . .

The Blackfoot loved the rodeo, and so did my grandfather. Their skills on the rodeo circuit, roping as well as riding, came from their heritage of horsemanship, their everyday life with horses on and off the reserve, and their work on local ranches in the foothills; and over the years many of the greatest figures in rodeo in both Canada and the United States were from Blackfoot and other plains Indian communities.

The Calgary Stampede was not the first rodeo to be called a "stampede." That honour is claimed by the little town of Raymond, about fifty miles southeast of Fort Macleod, where they have held a rodeo every July first since 1902—unless Canada Day falls on a Sunday when, in deference to the Mormon community that founded the town, the rodeo takes place the day before. They called that first rodeo the Raymond

Stampede, and it is sometimes referred to as Alberta's first rodeo, though as we have seen, rodeos had been held for several decades during round-ups and along with local fairs and agricultural exhibitions.

My grandfather went to that Stampede, where bronc riding and steer roping were the signature events. It attracted a crowd large enough that Raymond set up a proper rodeo arena with a bucking chute and covered grandstand the following year. Ray Knight, whom the town was named after, took the lead in establishing the event, won the roping competition that first year, and went on to become one of the most prominent rodeo performers and stock producers of the early twentieth century. The town had been named by his father, Jesse Knight, a wealthy Mormon who in 1901 had followed the earlier migration of Mormon settlers in 1887 from Utah Territory up to the North-West Territories.

But Jesse Knight was no follower. Before his migration, he had been a very successful mining entrepreneur, notable in that age of "robber barons" for being honest in his dealings with everyone and conscientious in his treatment of his workers, providing them with schools and meeting houses. He bought land for a cattle ranch some distance from Cardston near what became the town of Raymond. Later, using the skills in dryland farming that the Mormons brought to Canada, he established an irrigated sugar beet farm there. My grandfather liked Knight and would sometimes quote him. Knight liked to be quoted, it seems, and had a gift for grand statements. My grandfather's favourite, full of both biblical and banking wisdom, was "The earth is the Lord's bank, and no man has the right to take money out of the bank and use it extravagantly on himself."

My grandfather went to Raymond for the rodeo; and he said he must have been meant to go because there he saw a familiar face: the pick-up man's, risking his life to protect the bronc riders if and when they were thrown. He was the same would-be robber who had come into his bank a few years earlier and left a chastened boy... and thanks to Sorreltop Jack, not quite empty-handed. My grandfather didn't go up to him because the young man had seemingly turned a corner and might not want to be reminded; but he thought the fellow recognized him, with a self-conscious grin.

16

FOR SALE:
COWDRY BROTHERS BANK
AND
FOR SURRENDER:
LAND ON THE BLOOD RESERVE

"The Carriers of No."
LESLIE PINDER

. . .

IN DECEMBER 1904, ANOTHER family tragedy. Thomas, my grandfather's nephew, died suddenly of scarlet fever in Fort Macleod at the age of twenty-seven, just four months before the birth of his first child.

Maybe that was the reason the brothers decided to sell the bank. Or maybe it was the moves underway towards a version of provincial status in the territory, moves that seemed designed to develop the industrial economy of the east by exploiting the natural resources of the west. The rhetoric of western alienation was at high volume during these years, setting the stage for a storyline that has continued throughout the twentieth century and to this day. It was fostered by the prospect of continuing federal control of natural resources and public lands in the western provinces, and railway freight rates that skewed western development towards west-east trade rather than north-south local transportation; but also by the eastern governance of many organizations, from trade and labour congresses to the churches. Much energy was given over to east-west antagonism, bolstered by the fiction of refreshing western freedom and depressing eastern convention, but what was lost in the importation of a Liberal–Conservative party dynamic to the west was a sense of solidarity with First Nations against what might (with only a little hyperbole) be called eastern totalitarianism.

My grandfather's question, quoted in *The Outlaw*, was still on his mind: What was the difference between the two parties, and who said it mattered in the west? He and others were almost certain that unless something like Fred Haultain's idea of a responsible, representative and *non-partisan* government in a single territory was introduced (whether it was called Buffalo or not), the possibility of withstanding the well-practised economic and political power of the big, bad "east"—as well as establishing a framework for self-respect and self-sufficiency and self-government for First Nations communities on the prairies—would be severely impaired, if not destroyed. That conversation was underway, though it was drowned out by the dramatically orchestrated noise of impending provincial power. Clouds were gathering over the town and country my grandfather loved; and Jack and Nat (who was consulted at every turn back in Ontario, and heard a fair bit of cursing from Jack over what was happening) started to think it might be time to close the book on the bank. The national institutions, including the national banks, were buying up local businesses and either bringing them into line with national priorities or building on a frontier ideology in which Indians were mere distractions. Alberta ranching and Saskatchewan farming interests were both demanding separate roles in the new federation, and a single province was looking more and more unlikely. And no one was thinking seriously about the First Nations except as wards who were always on the verge of being betrayed.

Whatever the reasons, and I suspect they were many and varied, Jack and Nat decided to sell Cowdry Brothers Bank to the Canadian Bank of Commerce in 1905. They had excellent relations with the Commerce—my grandfather was one of their directors in the territory—and the Commerce (along with a couple of the other national banks) had provided good lines of credit for Cowdry Brothers through the years. The deal went through at a price of $105,904.88, with the Bank of Commerce taking over nearly half a million dollars in loans, and my grandfather personally guaranteeing a little over fifty thousand dollars for six months . . . at the end of which he was only a couple of hundred dollars short. Everyone had paid up on unexpectedly short notice, even in that uncertain time, to make sure my grandfather was not out of pocket. As L.V. Kelly, the author of *The Range Men*, put it in his history of the ranchers and Indians in the territory, that was "an astonishingly pleasing average for any banker." Or anybody at all. My grandfather, for his part, was both very pleased and not surprised. "They just kept their word," he said.

What was not so pleasing was how some things changed for the community when the Canadian Bank of Commerce bought the bank. The Agricultural Society of Macleod asked the new "national" bank if it would support horse racing at the annual fair, as Cowdry Brothers had done from the beginning in 1886. The big bank said no.

. . .

My grandfather took his portion of the proceeds of the sale of the bank and put it into a ranching venture with Ned Maunsell, who had a lot of experience both with cattle ranching and with Jack Cowdry. The Cochrane ranch, which had been staggering along for a number of years, had decided to sell off both its cattle and its land holdings. The ranch, which was one of the first in the territory—it had been established in 1881—owned 67,000 acres in the area around Cardston which the Mormons were anxious to purchase; and a deal was soon reached for the Cochrane ranch to sell the land and ranch buildings to the Mormons for six dollars an acre, with the cattle—about twelve thousand head—to be removed as soon as possible. Enter Ned and Jack, with an offer for the herd. The cattle—a.k.a. chattels—needed to be counted to confirm the price; so in due course the count was completed and a cheque for nearly a quarter of a million dollars signed on the seat of Ned Maunsell's saddle. Family gossip has it that Jack went in on the deal because the Cochrane brand was "C"—just right for Cowdry; and that has his hallmark sense of humour. But he also wanted to turn his twenty years of banking back into a local business; and for him *the* local business was ranching.

That said, there were some things to be sorted out ... among them the fiery personality of Ned Maunsell. He already had about six thousand cattle in his herd and seems to have seen this as his chance to be *the* big rancher in southern Alberta, rivalling George Lane and Pat Burns. Pat Burns was a very good friend of my grandfather's, and thrived on competition; but my grandfather had no such ambitions. By this time he did know the cattle business, however, having been banker for most of the ranchers in the foothills, including Burns, through thick and thin and round-ups and die-ups for the past twenty years. And he had spent lots of time listening to Crop Eared Wolf. The only things he didn't understand about ranching, he used to say, were the cows and the weather. The horses he could figure out.

With the days of the open range numbered, one urgent issue had to do with leasing more grazing land for such a large herd. Leases were hard to get, given the changes in leasing arrangements in the 1890s, and Ned Maunsell had already had some unpleasant run-ins with the government about cancelled or amended leases. So my grandfather went to Ottawa to see Frank Oliver, who had just been appointed minister of the interior and superintendent-general of Indian affairs. Maunsell had singled out Oliver for some of his less courteous invective, so it would have been hopeless for Maunsell to go and see him, or even to come along. But Oliver liked and trusted my grandfather, and he helped him acquire the 60,381-acre Galway Cattle Company lease, a rare treasure since it was one of the few that was still irrevocable for twenty-one years. Oliver was pleased too, because the Galway Cattle Company had nothing to do with cattle; it was a front for a well-known Laurier Liberal. Selling it to my grandfather—described in Pierre Berton's *The Promised Land: Settling the West, 1896–1914,* as a *bona fide* cattleman, which would have delighted him—resolved what had become a political embarrassment for Oliver and for the party. The cost was something over $22,000, which was substantial... but so were twelve thousand head of cattle.

With his name on the line, my grandfather also secured five other leases, with a total acreage of nearly 126,000 acres. These five were subject to cancellation on two years' notice if required for settlement, but they were valuable for now, and might well be renewable. Also, my grandfather—and Ned too—had very good relations with the Peigan, close to where the new leases were, and he was optimistic they would be able to lease some reserve land for grazing if they needed to.

He returned from Ottawa with the leases and the legal documents all completed (by R.B. Bennett, the same Calgary lawyer —and future prime minister—who had just sold the late John Ware's horses and then had to hire some to round up his cattle). But R.B. Bennett got it right this time—he was dealing with the banker, after all—and my grandfather was registered as the lessee on all the leases. This is where the two partners, Cowdry and Maunsell, had a bit of a conflict. Maunsell asked that the leases all be put in his name. My grandfather refused point-blank, having been told by Frank Oliver that he wouldn't let the big lease go through for anyone else, and if my grandfather didn't take it he was quite happy to have the leaseholders eat dirt. My grandfather had given his word to Oliver about his partnership with Maunsell (whose dislike of Oliver was matched by Oliver's dislike of him) in the purchase of the Cochrane herd; and my grandfather wouldn't go back on his word. "This caused friction," wrote Maunsell later—I think it was more likely an unholy row—but he must have known that he could throw a buffalo more easily than my grandfather when it came to something like that. Jawbone.

In many ways my grandfather and Ned Maunsell were like chalk and cheese; but they had worked together for many years, in good times and bad, and were old friends. So they worked it out, with Maunsell quickly shifting the blame to Oliver. And ranching in the foothills was never the poorer for having two people with different temperaments and talents in partnership, even though it might cause sparks to fly from time to time. My grandfather had learned a lot from Crop Eared Wolf.

So my grandfather sold his house in Macleod and moved with the kids to a ranch near Pincher Creek on the long-term leased land. He stayed in very close touch with the town of Macleod, which was just down the road a ways, and was there often. He also kept up other interests, helping out a friend in Calgary who was starting a business there. The leasing arrangements worked well, and Ned was a good cattleman, the equal of any in the territory when it came to stewardship of the grazing lands, and that (along with their friendships on the reserve) served them both well when it later came to leasing land for the winter from the Peigan.

. . .

But the year had other setbacks, a couple of which touched my grandfather deeply. His friend Archie Maclean, rancher and cattle trader (and later one of the "big four" who bankrolled the first Calgary Stampede), suffered the death of his wife of just two years in childbirth. My grandfather did what he could to comfort him . . . but he knew as well as anyone just how hopeless that could be, at least at the moment. And a fire in the town of Macleod on December 7, 1906—the anniversary of my grandfather's marriage to Gussie eight years earlier—destroyed most of the wood frame buildings on the main street. Many of my grandfather's closest friends were affected, though the brick bank he had built was left standing; and he was there to help the next morning . . . which was the anniversary of his marriage to Amy.

As so often in the ranching business, and especially in the foothills, the weather was about to take charge. And Ned

Maunsell was about to recognize that he and my grandfather were evenly yoked when it came to dealing with adversity, just like two old oxen. The winter of 1906–07 was as bad as 1886–87, and took over the tag as the Big Die-Up. Cowdry and Maunsell lost over half their herd—the numbers are inevitably a bit sketchy, but Maunsell put the losses at $120,000. They had seen this before, from both sides of the corral—banker and rancher—and both times they got through it. It was a tough way for the boys to start a new business, but so had it been for the new Cowdry Brothers Bank and the nearly new Maunsell Brothers ranch twenty years earlier.

Other ranchers also took heavy losses, some catastrophic. Discouraged by the closing of the open range with the withdrawal of large, long-term leases, many turned into stock farmers rather than herd ranchers as they "beefed out" their herd, spaying cows and selling off breeding stock to stay in business; but that in turn created an oversupply that brought down the price of beef. Some, like George Lane at the Bar U, diversified, maintaining as much of a commitment to open-range ranching as was possible while developing crop and cow-calf operations and a very successful breeding program with Percheron horses. And Pat Burns moved to integrate ranching with food marketing, understanding the need to find common cause with the farming communities. Both Lane and Burns continued to believe that the best livestock was the least pampered, but they were practical about the continued availability of winter range; and all the ranchers had an independence of spirit that served them well in bad times, though sometimes not so well when times were good. They shared a reputation for honesty and hard work and a sense of humour, and for putting in hours that would make most of us melt.

For their part, Cowdry and Maunsell Brothers took their
losses, bringing Jack's credit and Ned's craft together to
manage the next season, with my grandfather working from
his base in Pincher Creek and arranging to sell some of the
Cowdry Maunsell cattle to Pat Burns the next fall at a better
price. I have correspondence in which Burns writes a note to
my grandfather saying, "You can draw on my account at any
time for the amount we talked about," without saying what
that amount was. I know it was a large amount, since my
grandfather was delivering a substantial herd of cattle to him;
but it is a nice indication of the trust that existed between
them that Burns didn't need to confirm the amount, and a
reminder that being as good as your word was still the way of
the world in the foothills. One of my oldest friends is Pat
Burns's great-grandnephew, John Burns, who grew up on the
old Bow Valley Farm in Midnapore, the head ranch for the
Burns holdings (south of Calgary city limits at that time, and
bound on the north by the Stampede grounds, on the east by
the Bow River, on the south by what is now 146th Street, and
on the west by the Macleod Trail). I visited there often in the
1950s and early '60s, and we would ride all day and never leave
the property. Some things change; but others don't. John
Burns is like Pat Burns when it comes to hard work, and to
honest dealings; and I like to think some of my understanding
of those early days comes from our friendship.

. . .

The years after 1900 were challenging ones for the Bloods, as
they were for all the Blackfoot tribes. The Bloods, having won

the Sun Dance war, now faced a new threat with the rush of settlement encouraged by the federal government, which increased homestead entries from just over 7,400 in 1900 to nearly 31,000 five years later. And to top it off, or bottom it out, there was the appointment of an Indian agent on the Blood reserve who was determined to secure a surrender of some of their land. When he met with opposition and a blunt refusal from Crop Eared Wolf, who rallied the tribe against the proposal, he became determined to destroy him.

Bad idea. And a hopeless one. The agent's name was Robert Wilson, and he knew the territory well. He had begun his time in the foothills with the North-West Mounted Police before becoming a trader and then signing up with the Department of Indian Affairs, posted first to the Peigan and then to the Blood reserve. He was knowledgeable about Blackfoot life, to the point that he fancied himself something of an ethnographer, in touch with the anthropologist and naturalist George Bird Grinnell, who visited him regularly on the reserve; and he was a photographer of considerable talent and tenacity, one of the very few to have received permission to photograph some of the ceremonies. He also had entrepreneurial agricultural ambitions first for the Peigan and then for the Bloods (when he became their agent in 1903), designed to create the conditions of self-sufficiency which leaders like Crowfoot and Red Crow envisaged. But they were *his* designs, not those of the Blackfoot—his "wards," as he would later describe them—and they masked an impatience that was brutally uncontrolled.

Sadly, even the most well-intentioned politicians and officials, if they forget William Johnson's counsel about allies and friends, can let their ambitions corrupt their actions. The most renowned figure in Indian affairs in the United States in the first half of the twentieth century was John Collier, architect of the Indian Reorganization Act, which restored tribal governments (after half a century of deliberate legislative demolition), and gave the tribes control over their lands and resources to sustain their local economies. But Collier had two loves—Indians, and soil conservation on the dryland plains—and when it came to deciding between them . . . well, father knew best; and the Indians fared worst. There was an issue with overgrazing (after years of negligence by non-Indian leaseholders) on the Navajo reserve; and Collier instructed that an audit be taken of all the livestock on the reserve. He determined the animals should be counted in sheep-units, sheep being deemed the most economically "useful" animal on the range, while horses—symbolizing wealth and prestige to the Navajo, as well as beauty and strength—were reckoned to be more or less "worthless." According to Collier's calculations, horses eat as much grass as five sheep; so the Navajo were ordered to sell or destroy large numbers of their five-sheep-unit horses. The Navajo were appalled at the Gradgrindish language almost as much as at the administrative order . . . and they said no, recognizing that doing so would make the future more challenging for them. But their horses counted for much more than sheep-units.

Collier should have known better. He had lived in the southwest among the Pueblo, was deeply committed to self-determination for Indian peoples and respect for the diversity of their cultures, and certainly understood the power of words. Robert Wilson's undertaking with the Bloods was much more belligerent even than Collier's, and the word he used—"surrender"—was associated with a military attack rather than an accounting measurement. But both declared, "My way, or the doorway." And, apart from outright warfare, that has been the curse of relations between natives and newcomers since first contact.

And Collier did not have Crop Eared Wolf to deal with. A couple of years before Agent Wilson took on the responsibility for the Blood reserve, the Mormons in Cardston had asked for more land to be opened for settlement. There was little question where that land might come from, since the Cardston community bordered the Blood reserve, and those trespassing survey stakes were obviously intended to map out the sale. Before he died, Red Crow had already been disputing with Cardston about what he perceived as encroachment on the reserve, a dispute in which he was awkwardly implicated because some in the Blood tribe blamed him for not paying attention to decisions made when the reserve was surveyed back in 1883. Knowing that the issue, and the grasping ambitions of settlers, would not go away easily—and they still haven't—Red Crow had secured a solemn promise from Crop Eared Wolf that as chief he would not sell any of the land on the reserve, a promise that was kept by his son and by his son's successors. Thus Crop Eared Wolf and his son Shot Both Sides (who served as chief from 1913 until 1956), along with the so-called "minor" chiefs of the Blood bands—the term is misleading, for they play an important role in tribal decisions—became what the Aboriginal rights lawyer Leslie Pinder once called "the Carriers of No." This is an honourable tradition among First Nations in Canada; and many of us remember another noble "carrier of no," Oji-Cree chief Elijah Harper, who stopped the federal Meech Lake Accord, negotiated without the consent of the First Nations, by holding up his eagle feather and withholding the unanimous consent of the Manitoba Legislature that was required if the accord was to go ahead as a constitutional amendment in 1990.

Keen on increased settlement, the government put considerable pressure on the Bloods to surrender some of their land to the Mormons, and eventually forced a tribal vote in 1907 on the sale of 2,400 acres near the southern border of their reserve. Crop Eared Wolf went to every family in the tribe arguing against the sale—an angry enthusiast reported that he "scared some, coaxed others, and still others he persuaded to abstain"; and when the vote was taken, to the surprise and dismay of the agent and the government, who had predicted a landslide in favour, the surrender was rejected by a margin of over three to one.

Agent Wilson was furious; and for the next four years, with compulsive energy, he tried to humiliate Crop Eared Wolf and terminate his tenure as chief. Exercising his role as "warden" of his "wards," he also tried to prohibit the Indians from participation in local fairs and rodeos and other events—even though by this time the Blackfoot parades had become a star attraction—on the grounds that it interfered with their harvesting of hay to secure revenue to pay for reserve expenses. Writing to the secretary of Indian affairs in Ottawa in the spring of 1908, he complained that Indian parades, with their paint and feathers, represented "a revival of barbarism under the direction, and with the substantial encouragement, of municipalities or similar organizations of wealth and influence.... At Macleod the Indian show was practically the whole thing, the ordinary fair of the white people being quite insignificant." Sounds as if the local white people knew where they wanted to be. Certainly my grandfather, ambling among the crowd of admirers, was delighted. Later that season, Wilson tried to stop the Bloods participating in the Dominion Day pageant in Calgary by refusing them permission—commenting that "the Indian Pageant business [has] been so much overdone in late years in neighbouring towns as to become a distinct detriment to the progress of the Blood Indians." Fortunately, his refusal made no difference. Among those who pushed back was the respected Methodist missionary John McDougall, who wrote bluntly, "the Indians being the original dwellers on this country should take a leading part."

Wilson had set his store by agricultural production on and off the reserve, and his reaction to these setbacks was pathologically vindictive against Crop Eared Wolf. He thought he was smart, and certainly he was devious; but he was no match for Crop Eared Wolf, and soon the wheels started to come off the warden's wagon train. He cut off rations for those who participated in the fairs; in response to which, the fair committees butchered steers for the Indians. And he refused to approve the chief's annual treaty payment. But Crop Eared Wolf was not sitting this out. Unwilling just to react to Wilson's actions, he went on the offensive, making the rounds of the hay camps to persuade the Bloods not to work on contracts with one particular cattle company favoured by Wilson, saying that if they withdrew their labour—a time-honoured strategy for those who control little else—it would be easier for him to get Wilson discharged, and then they would get a new agent. But even then, the old warrior was not through. Wilson had tried to get him deposed as "incompetent"; Crop Eared Wolf turned this back on him, and was almost certainly behind a letter from the secretary of the

Department in Ottawa chastising Wilson for "neglect of duty" for not reporting on the number of cattle owned by that same favoured company on the reserve—a very serious charge for what was a fairly routine lapse. And taking up new legal technology, as his people had taken up horses and guns and farming and ranching, he filed a formal complaint of harassment through a Macleod lawyer (Colin Macleod, an expert litigator trained in the Maritimes, who later advised Big Swan on a fraudulent surrender); and as an extra measure Crop Eared Wolf complained about the actions of the agent to the commissioner. It was a mistake to push him and his people around.

Wilson was gone by 1911, returning to ranching and trading—and, interestingly, to pamphleteering, where he demonstrated his talent for both contentiousness and contradiction. Nothing wrong with either, in my book, but in this case they called attention to something that undermined not only his argument but the foundations of Indian administration—there's that word again. The impassioned report he wrote in 1921 was titled "Our Betrayed Wards: A Story of Chicanery, Infidelity and the Prostitution of Trust," and it told about the damage done to the Blood cattle industry by decisions taken to lease land as part of the Greater Production Program introduced during the First World War. Like the Soldier Settlement Program, which resulted in the surrender of those eighteen thousand acres of rich agricultural (and, it turns out, oil- and gas-producing) Dunne-za reserve land in Peace River country up near Fort St. John, these programs often proceeded at the expense of First Nations; and Wilson's intervention was admirable . . . albeit rather surprising given his earlier attempts to force a surrender for sale. But let's assume he realized the error of his ways, however late in the day.

Even so, the title betrayed him, for it signalled an attitude towards First Nations that has infected so many in the past century and a half, nourished by the ideology of both the Indian Act and the Department of Indian Affairs. It is the word *wards*, with its condescending baggage under cover of concern. Not that the concern was absent; many agents and officials in the Department of Indian Affairs were rightfully concerned about the conditions and the prospects facing First Nations, and tried to do something to help. But they too often did so within a hierarchy of adult and child, or sophisticated and simple, or civilized and barbaric which obliterated any serious recognition of the dignity and sophistication of Aboriginal peoples, or of the intelligence and imagination they displayed and the pride they carried into the cultural climate change that was upon them after the treaty and the departure of the buffalo and the arrival of the white settlers. To recall William Johnson's warning early in the eighteenth century: if you call the Indians "subjects," you'd better have an army at your back. To Wilson, someone should have said: If you call the Bloods, or any of the Blackfoot, "wards," you'd better run for cover.

17

WHITE SUBJECTS AND RED ALLIES

*"I'll just ride both them horses myself. That's the
only way to find out which bucks hardest."*
JOHNNY FRANKLIN

...

FOR HUNDREDS OF YEARS, many newcomers seem to have
thought that it was all over for the natives. It began early, and
not always with regret. In 1639 Marie Guyart, Mère de
l'Incarnation, arrived in Quebec and co-founded the Ursuline
Convent, of which she became Superior. "When we arrived in
this country," she remarked, "the Indians were so numerous
that it seemed as if they were going to grow into a vast population; but after they were baptized God called them to Himself
either by disease or by the hands of the Iroquois. It was perhaps
his wise design to permit their death lest their hearts should
turn to wickedness."

A couple of centuries later, General William Sherman of
the United States would suggest that "the only good Indian is a
dead Indian"—a particularly brutal statement from someone
whose middle name was Tecumseh, recalling the great
Shawnee chief (who supported the British in the War of 1812).

In any case there is little enough difference between these two responses. "Work, or starve" has been one crude expression of it: the "starvation" may be physical or cultural, of course; and "work" has meant something different to each settler generation. Cultivate the land; speak English (or French or Spanish); become an individual, like the white man; develop habits of industry and thrift; seek waged employment . . . the basic message has remained constant, and yet is always changing with the attitudes towards self-interest and mutual interest that each age espouses. One thing, however, has not changed; but it must change. Indigenous peoples must be free to act out of their own self-interest, which can then become part of the mutual interest of the wider community so that their interest is shared by "us," and ours by "them" . . . and so that together we take up the responsibilities of being treaty peoples, first and latest.

For this to happen, we need to acknowledge that the attitudes of Marie Guyart and William Sherman are often couched in more politically convenient terms. During the 1830s in the United States, President Andrew Jackson, fresh from sending the Five Civilized Tribes (Cherokee, Chickasaw, Choctaw, Creek and Seminole) along the Trail of Tears from the southeastern states to Indian Territory west of the Mississippi, said that "treaties with the Indians are an absurdity not to be reconciled with the principles of government." A hundred and thirty odd years later in Canada, the architects of the federal government's 1969 White Paper advocated the abolition of the special relationship between Aboriginal people and the Crown (without any serious consultation with Aboriginal people), obviously thinking the same way as Andrew Jackson; and his Canadian counterpart, Prime Minister Pierre Trudeau, spoke in this vein just after

Canada's centennial celebration in 1967: "It's inconceivable I think that in a given society, one section of the society have a treaty with the other section of the society. We must all be equal under the laws and we must not sign treaties amongst ourselves. . . . We can't recognize aboriginal rights because no society can be built on historical 'might-have-beens.'" This from the man who brought us the Canadian Charter of Rights and Freedoms. There is no shortage of contradictions when it comes to the history of natives and newcomers.

A year or so later Trudeau was forced to change his mind, persuaded by a few landmark cases: a Supreme Court decision involving the Nisga'a people of the west coast, which went against them but included a landmark recognition of Aboriginal title as a legitimate concept in Canadian law; an injunction handed down in the Mackenzie Valley by Justice William Morrow of the Northwest Territories on behalf of the Dene inhabitants, effectively putting a cloud of prior Aboriginal interest on the title of land over which a natural gas pipeline was proposed (which bothered the New York financiers who were going to bankroll the venture); and by an eloquent land claim put forward by the Council of Yukon Indians, the first formal claim involving an entire territory since the nineteenth- and early-twentieth-century treaties. It was titled *Together Today for Our Children Tomorrow*, which could have been the motto for the Blackfoot and the newcomers in the foothills—not for all of them, perhaps, but for most of them in that period between 1885 and 1905.

It was an unsettling time of change for everybody, so it produced some uneasy relationships that occasionally appeared quite wildy contradictory but allowed a path forward for a lot of

people. For example, the missionaries, who were competing for
the souls and minds of the Blackfoot, had to seek the alliance of
the chiefs for permission to establish churches and schools on
the reserves; the chiefs in turn listened courteously to them, and
analyzed the vagaries of both Catholic and Protestant fortunes
in the territory—strategically, and comfortably, meshing
together several spiritual regimes as they did the secular counterparts in law and medicine and politics. The men of the North-
West Mounted Police, for their part, while supposed to be
maintaining law and order quite often engaged in their own dis-
orderly conduct, especially with Indian women—which of
course caused bursts of convenient outrage from the missionaries (and others). And at the same time the police—the keepers of
law and order—generally refused to enforce the prohibitions
against Indian spiritual ceremonies that were intermittently
proposed by Ottawa and by some Indian agents—belligerent
"I-know-best" bullies with a lot of power and little sympathy for
what they considered primitive or pagan rituals.

The authoritarianism of the agents was one of the most
wretched legacies of the past for many First Nations peoples,
though not all those who served the Blackfoot were as inclined
to Babylonian practices as some agents elsewhere on the prairies. For example, agents determined to use the letter to fulfill
the spirit of the treaties were in office fairly consistently at the
Siksika agency in Gleichen, and cooperation was the result. The
Gooderhams, father and son, served as successive Indian agents,
mostly based there, for nearly seventy years, balancing habitual
paternalism with capable peacemaking, and facilitating moves
towards self-sufficiency that the tribe approved. Their style was
not by any means always welcomed; but they were respected,

and when George Gooderham retired he was made an honorary chief of the Blackfoot.

In a nice illustration of the continuities that occasionally exist, George Gooderham's daughter Elizabeth married Basil Robinson, who (along the way to becoming Canada's under-secretary of state for external affairs) was deputy minister of Indian affairs in the 1970s. He was responsible for the first comprehensive claims policy that followed Pierre Trudeau's change of heart, and I worked for him in 1972 and 1973, when he was dealing with the fallout (which he had inherited) from Trudeau's White Paper. In a quiet way he profoundly influenced the life and the language of Aboriginal peoples in country. He brought his diplomatic instincts to bear on Indian affairs, recruiting to the department a senior diplomat named Geoff Murray (who had worked in the United Nations) to help change the way people thought and talked about relations between Canada and its indigenous peoples. Robinson believed that the Department of Indian Affairs was in the business of inter-national relations, as surely as the Department of External Affairs; and that the bands defined in the Indian Act were Canada's "first nations." He used this term well before it had currency across the country—the Assembly of First Nations only took its name in 1982, and before that it had been called the National Indian Brotherhood. I am sure his approach was influenced by his wife's understanding (from growing up on the Siksika reserve in Gleichen) of how Blackfoot pride and sense of purpose flowed from their sense of national auton-omy and the authority of their chiefs in the confederacy. And Basil Robinson had some direct association with the Blackfoot earlier, for during the late 1950s, over a decade before he took over as deputy minister of Indian affairs, he had been seconded as foreign affairs advisor to Conservative prime minister John Diefenbaker when he extended citizenship to Aboriginal peoples in Canada and appointed James Gladstone, a Blackfoot from the Blood tribe, as Canada's first Aboriginal senator.

. . .

In 1911 my grandfather bid farewell to his friends in the foothills, where he had lived for the past twenty-five years, and moved to Vancouver. He had visited often over the preceding few years and knew folks there (including my godmother, Margaret Williams, her father, and her indomitable mother whose childhood journal held her memories of her visits to Louis Riel in prison); and his older children were also looking to the west coast. Gus had gone to school in Ontario, and then to the University of Toronto, where he dabbled in literature and history and took a couple of years of medicine, almost certainly inspired by his slightly older cousin Vincent. But he had inherited his father's impatience with school, and before much more time had passed he was back in Macleod, where he helped with the ranching and went hunting with the Peigan. He had learned some of the elements of trade and commerce from his father, and was hoping to go into the import-export business in Vancouver (with a sideline in the fledgling movie industry with a retired bronc rider who competed in the 1912 Calgary Stampede, named Arthur "Cowboy" Kean). And Mary was anxious to move there too. So my grandfather rented a house on Nelson Street, bought land in what is now Jericho Beach and West Point Grey, built a home for Mary (who had become engaged) and then for himself, and made plans to bring his family together.

So he called for my mother, who was twelve by this time, to come from Ingersoll and live with him. And Diddy too, if she would. He said he had found a young girl about my mother's age named Margaret, whose parents and grandparents he knew, and they could go to school together just down the street from where my mother and he would live. He hoped she would like school, but they both knew that wasn't a sure thing since she had never been to one; and truth be told, he hadn't been much of a fan himself.

I can't imagine what it must have been like for my mother to travel several thousand miles away from the only home and the only family she'd ever had, to live with a man who brought chocolates and smoked a pipe and told stories. But she did. Or what it must have been like for Diddy to follow the niece she had raised since birth from the only place they had both ever known to settle in a strange town called Vancouver on the other side of the world. But she did. Or for my grandfather to pick up where he had left off a dozen years earlier with Gussie, and make a new home with memories of marriages and births and deaths like the hinges on every door in the house. But he did.

Later, when my mother was thirty-one—her mother's age when she died—she opened a little shop on Howe Street in Vancouver. She called it The Jade Box; and in photographs from those days I can see she was still wearing her mother's tear-shaped jade pendant.

During those years, the early 1930s, my mother said she heard a song recorded by the Carter Family which she remembered overhearing her father sing when she came to live with him in

Vancouver. It had first been recorded by others in 1901, she found out later; but her father never sang it to her. Just to himself. The song was called "Hello, Central, Give Me Heaven."

Papa, I'm so sad and lonely,
Sobbed a tearful little child
Since dear mama's gone to heaven
Papa, darling, you've not smiled
I will speak to her and tell her
That we want her to come home
Just you listen and I'll call her
Through the telephone.

Hello, Central, give me heaven
For my mama's there
You can find her with the angels
On the golden stair
She'll be glad it's me who's speaking
Call her, won't you please
For I want to surely tell her
We're so lonely here.

. . .

The two young girls—my mother and her best friend Margaret Williams—were late for school. It was 1912, and they were teenagers. So was the school, which had been founded in 1898, housed in an old building at the corner of Jervis and Nelson Streets in Vancouver. Every afternoon the students, all girls, would gather for tea in a large upstairs room—an attic, really, with a high, sloping ceiling—where they were instructed in the fine art of ladylike behaviour. And first thing every morning the girls and their teachers would traipse up the narrow stairs to the tea room for assembly and prayers.

But on that particular June day, by the time my mother and Margaret had thumped their teenage way up the stairs to the door at the top, it was shut. The morning hymn had just begun, and they heard the words of the first verse.

New every morning is the love
Our wakening and uprising prove

Uprising? The two girls looked at each other. Without saying a word, they rose up and bolted the door. They heard another line—"Fit us for perfect rest above"—and they giggled at the thought of all the students and teachers sleeping together like dolls on the floor. They giggled through the announcements, which included a warning to the girls to be careful when they crossed the road because there were now over a thousand automobiles in the city; and through the roll call when they were the only ones who didn't say "Here, ma'am"; and they giggled when Margaret said the dilapidated boards on the staircase ceiling reminded her of her grandpa's missing teeth when he smiled. And they were still giggling when the headmistress led the school to the door at the top of the staircase and tried to open it.

My mother would never tell me what happened next. "Use your imagination," she'd say with a smile. "That's where real things happen." In my imagination, over a century later, Margaret and my mother are still there, two giggling girls sitting on the staircase at Crofton House School wondering what they have done, and what to do next. Their uprising may have lasted only a moment; but that moment—and the wonder that filled it—became mine. Stories offer us our first experience in uncertainties, which is why they are so important; and that story of my mother and Margaret, unfinished as it is, has become my touchstone for all stories, including the one I have just told, set in the years between 1885 and 1905 in the district of Alberta in the territory called North-West. Blackfoot territory. The story of the country called Canada is uncertain and unfinished too, reminding all of us to wonder what we have done, and what to do next.

. . .

In 1919, a year after the First World War, my grandfather took my mother on a boat through the new Panama Canal, almost certainly with Canal Flats and Chief Not-Bear somewhere in mind. He was never without an adventure in hand; and by that time he had bought a ten-ton yawl to sail up and down the coast, and would later purchase a sturdy west-coast motor launch on which he and my mother travelled the islands and channels and up the fjords that make up the northwest coast, navigating the gloriously beautiful passages studded with sovereign First Nations communities.

Later, when he was in his mid-seventies, my grandfather took his son Gus to Alaska—not on a cruise but riding on horseback from Garibaldi up through the Chilcotins to Anaheim Lake, making camp along the way until they reached Stuie in what is now Tweedsmuir Park, then down to Bella Coola and the ocean, where he borrowed a Tlingit canoe and they headed up the inside passage—or inland passage, as he always called it—to the

Alaskan Panhandle with its wonderful rainforests and glaciers, just the two of them most of the way, the boys from Fort Macleod.

He lost Gus to cancer two years later, and much of his investment in gold with the stock market crash; and then my mother lost the sight in one eye with a detached retina, and the sight in the other deteriorated over the next few years. But not her spirit. She married my father in 1939, and my grandfather came to live with my parents and my sister and me and Diddy; and when we were away wrote wonderful letters (including one to me—Master Teddy—in a firm and steady hand, written a week before he died and hoping I had recovered from a cold).

My grandfather's other grandson, Gus's son, was also named Jack Cowdry. For my grandfather he was a wonder. By the age of eighteen, he was over six feet tall and weighed over two hundred pounds, a gentle giant. And a cluster of contradictions. He was a heavy-equipment mechanic with a pianist's delicate hands—hands that had the kind of memory both musicians and mechanics need—and he eventually built up a successful moving and transport company in Vancouver. He also gave my grandfather lots of good stories. One of my favourites was about something that took place when young Jack was just beginning his trade, driving logging trucks down the dangerous slopes of the coastal mountains around Vancouver. It had to do with another set of contradictions, between momentous events and minor courtesies. One day, while still apprenticed to an old timer, Jack was on the passenger side of a big old logging rig, no doors on the cab and three enormous logs on the flatbed, strapped down and held steady with the butt ends just about three feet behind the cab. Jack's mentor was telling him what to watch for—the slide-outs where rain had washed the road the night before, the bends where you could sail into the valley, the air gauge for the brakes that would tell you if you needed to bail out. Jack said the man was warming to his tragic tale when he exclaimed, "Oh damn, no air. Time to go." With that, and not another word, he reached over to the glove compartment in front of Jack, opened it, took out his lunch in a paper bag, and then—and this was the moment Jack cherished—gently shut the glove compartment door, the only door in the truck, and stepped out without saying another word ... by which time the truck was hurtling down the road and Jack was following the driver out his side of the cab.

Jack said he remembered nothing more clearly than that small gesture of courtesy, closing the glove compartment door—courtesy not to the truck itself, nor to Jack, but to something else—the spirits of logging, or lunch, or life, or whatever ... But for the rest of his life Jack believed in a world of courtesies, and in moments of wonder that bring large and small things together.

. . .

When my grandfather left Macleod, he did so with all sorts of regrets. The town possessed, in the words of a local promotional brochure, "no less than 45 automobiles in a town of 2510." Its population had grown from 1,000 to 2,500 in five years, and it seemed all set to flourish in the decades ahead ... though the Canadian Pacific Railway was never friendly to the town, running a line in the 1890s from Calgary to a point just west of Macleod, across the Old Man's River; and then a narrow-gauge line through the Crowsnest which passed south of town. Eventually, they put a spur line into Macleod, with the prospect of developing a divisional point there ... but after creating great expectations, the railway turned to Lethbridge for the divisional operations, and Macleod lost a major opportunity for expansion as the prairie gateway to the Pacific for shipments though the Crowsnest to Vancouver . . . and thence through the not-quite-yet completed Panama Canal to Europe.

But Macleod was a town my grandfather loved; and whatever its circumstances, he always thought of it as the centre of a new kind of conversation between the old nations of the territory and the new nation of Canada. It would be too easy to say that provincial status came in 1905 and undermined the need for any conversation at all, but certainly it played its part by creating a new set of metropolitan ambitions in which the hinterland First Nations did not directly figure. My grandfather's sale of his little bank in Fort Macleod to the national Bank of Commerce certainly didn't bring down the curtain . . . but it did represent a shift from local control to provincial and national priorities, as did the change in authority from the North-West Mounted Police first to the Royal Northwest Mounted Police (in 1904, forcing the creation of a local police force in Macleod for by-law enforcement) and then (in 1920) to the Royal Canadian Mounted Police. Fred Haultain's proposal for constituting the western prairies into one province was never likely to survive after the Liberal Wilfrid Laurier came to power, for even though he had resolutely maintained a non-partisan legislature in the territory, Haultain was associated with the Conservatives; and his idea lost out to the creation of the two provinces of Alberta and Saskatchewan.

With that change came a federally sponsored influx—an agricultural gold rush—of settlers, not only from eastern Canada but also from the United States and parts of Europe.

And this resulted in the further loss of Indian lands, even with the dubious "protection" offered by the treaties, on a scale not quite comparable to the loss of lands following the 1887 Dawes Act in the United States—which alienated over ninety million acres of Indian lands and proved to be what President Theodore Roosevelt approvingly called "a mighty pulverizing engine to break up the tribal mass"—but still devastating to many prairie First Nations. And new draconian measures were instituted by the federal government to keep Indians on reserves, including that on-again, off-again pass system, a requirement to secure the local Indian agent's permission for the sale of agricultural goods as well as for many other commercial and civic activities, and regulations governing education and religion (brought together in the witch's brew known as residential schools) that fostered a culture of dependence and despair for many First Nations peoples. Only the most isolated First Nations communities (mostly in the north) and the strongest confederacies (such as the Blackfoot) were able to maintain a measure of traditional integrity; but for some it was at an enormous cost.

. . .

The Blackfoot, even when they resisted most fiercely and said no most firmly, were always looking for what John Henry Newman once called a "grammar of assent," a way of saying yes—their peacemakers and peacekeepers waiting for the warriors to finish their task so they could begin theirs. But woe to anyone, such as Agent Wilson, who tried to harass or humiliate them. One of the things that characterized the foothills during the time my grandfather was there was that, in most situations when there was a discussion, a disagreement or a showdown between the different attitudes and ambitions—and the often unpredictable personalities—of the Blackfoot and the Banker, the Mounted Police and the Department of Indian Affairs, the politician and the citizen, the warmonger and the peacemaker, everyone recognized that they needed to find common ground . . . even if it was on a bed of gravel like the town itself. But a town with a unique and beautiful prospect, and promises to keep.

It is the unique character of each First Nation that gets lost in many accounts of their past and much accounting of their histories and hopes, which are jumbled together into something called "the Indian question" and applied to every indigenous community in the Americas in countless reports and commissions and inquiries going back to the beginning of the sixteenth century. These litanies of lamentation, however righteous, effectively homogenize the situations of peoples from widely different cultures living in widely different geographies and communities and speaking different languages, peoples whose histories of dislocation and dispossession and disillusionment and despair are stunningly similar but whose hopes and dreams and possibilities and beliefs are specific to their situation. In many ways, the Indian question is like the "overwhelming question" that T.S. Eliot's sad sack J. Alfred Prufrock (in a poem ironically called a "Love Song") describes as the culmination of his attempt to "force the moment to its crisis . . . bit[e] off the matter with a smile . . . squeeze the universe into a ball." Meanwhile, he waits nervously for someone to say—as someone always will—"That is not what I meant at all. / That is not it, at all." Just so; there is no single answer to the Indian and Inuit and Métis question, because there is no single question.

Instead, like Prufrock, we should say, "Oh, do not ask, 'What is it?' / Let us go and make our visit."

. . .

One thing that encouraged my grandfather as he left Macleod in 1911 was the planning for the first Calgary Stampede the following year, bankrolled by Burns and Lane and Cross and Maclean to the tune of $25,000 each (which they recovered, because it was a great success). Ranching was changing with the closing down of the open range and the parcelling up of the foothills with settlement fences, and the 1912 Stampede was conceived by them as a "final celebration" of the ranching heritage they had helped nourish, and in which my grandfather's bank had played a significant part. But the reason my grandfather found this Stampede interesting wasn't the riding and roping and other events that brought the skills and storyline of ranching to the wider public, or the nostalgia of his friends among the ranchers, but the prospect of wide participation by the Indian horsemen and the tribal communities of the Alberta plains, whose courtesy and hospitality he had enjoyed for a quarter century. He knew that Guy Weadick, the promoter of the event, had approached Crop Eared Wolf about this; and that his friend was very keen, especially now that he had rid the reserve of that meddlesome Indian agent, and had come up with several ideas on how to highlight their participation in the event.

Banff Indian Days, an elaborate display of foothills First Nations traditions, had begun in 1894 and became a major attraction just after the turn of the century, continuing through the 1970s. Crop Eared Wolf, among other leaders, saw these occasions as offering an opportunity to educate as well as entertain; and he fiercely dismissed the attempts of some of the Indian agents to discourage participation, and of some up-to-date "friends of the Indians" to see it as exploitation. So with Crop Eared Wolf's encouragement, Weadick's energy and the support of the four ranchers of the range, Indians from the Blackfoot Confederacy along with the Stoney Indians led the parade at the opening of the Calgary Stampede on September 2, 1912, followed by the old-time traders, the North-West Mounted Police, some of the early stagecoaches and drivers and settlers, and the ranchers and cowboys with their chuckwagons and cavvy of horses. The Indians camped with their traditional tipis on the rodeo grounds to signal their presence at the heart of this life on the prairies, and the celebration of its ranching heritage, with over eighteen hundred Indians there for the occasion and for genial conversation between them and other spectators and participants (along with considerable education for many of the citizens of Calgary who had never met an Indian).

Working on this book, something caught my eye in the Blood agency files: an item for the treaty payments in November 1900, identifying 261 persons in Crop Eared Wolf's Fish Eaters band. After payments to him and his family, there is one to "Tom Three Persons," listed simply as "boy." Five years later, he is listed again, this time "aged 15." I think Crop Eared Wolf's determination to encourage the involvement of the Bloods in fairs and parades and pageants—and in rodeos—may have nourished a dream he had of this young Indian becoming the king of the cowboys. And sure enough, he dreamed into reality the success of this twenty-two-year-old Blood tribesman, the very same Tom Three Persons, riding a notorious unconquered outlaw called Cyclone, who had thrown off all 129 cowboys who tried to ride him in rodeos throughout the west, twelve of them that very week. Tom almost didn't make it to the Stampede. He was being held in the police cells in Macleod for some minor offence and not due to be discharged until after the rodeo. But Ned Maunsell heard about the situation, went to the sympathetic inspector of Indian agencies and secured his early release for the competition where he rode Cyclone to a standstill, winning the premier event—the bareback bronco competition—at that first Calgary Stampede. The star cowboy that year, the only "Canadian" in the final round, was an Indian; and Tom would soon become one of the most famous rodeo riders of his generation.

Crop Eared Wolf declared himself very proud; though sadly he missed the Stampede because he was also very ill. But his dream came to pass in more ways than even he might have imagined, for Tom Three Persons incurred the wrath of the Blood Indian agent later in 1917 when he voted against a land surrender. The agent, W.J. Dilworth, was so angry that he somehow forced Tom Three Persons off the reserve; but Dilworth was gone by 1919, and when Tom Three Persons returned he became one of the wealthiest, as well as one of the most generous, men on the Blood reserve.

The judge for the bareback bronc-riding at that Calgary Stampede was Johnny Franklin, who had tied with Billy Stewart in that famous rodeo in Fort Macleod in 1891. Over the next few years, he had earned a reputation as the very best in the business, a bronc rider who had ridden every horse he ever got on. Asked how he would judge the winner if two men should tie, he said, "I'll just ride both them horses myself. That's the only way to find out which bucks hardest."

. . .

My grandfather had gone back to the foothills from Vancouver for the Stampede, and he said to my mother that he also had some ranch business to attend to. I'm sure he did, though he had already sold most of his interest to Ned Maunsell. But his real reason for the trip was to see Crop Eared Wolf.

From 1900, when he succeeded his father Red Crow as head chief of the Bloods, until his death in 1913 at the age of sixty-eight, Crop Eared Wolf had led his people with a sternness of purpose that has inspired the tribe for over a century since, maintaining their reserve as the largest in the country, and almost certainly the loveliest. He lived his life bravely. Though crippled at an early age in that war raid against the Cree, he was one of the most renowned "custodians" of horses on the northern plains, and one of the best storytellers. In his younger days he could ride like the wind, was renowned as a scout, and throughout his life he understood horses and dogs and people so well that he could be in and out of an enemy camp gathering horses—or interfere with an Indian agent's belligerent scheming—without interrupting their dreams. He gave Blackfoot imagination new direction and Blackfoot intelligence new meaning with his uncanny gift for knowing what was happening before it happened, and for seeing new possibilities in the old ways. Like his horses, he hardly slept; he was a fighter, and a dangerous one; he was a peacemaker, and a good one; and he was proud, a saving grace for the Blackfoot then and now.

At the beginning of this book, I said that it seemed my grandfather was looking for something when he came to the foothills and Fort Macleod; and I suggested later that it may have been himself, and a home. I think it was also a friend. He found more friends than he expected, perhaps; but the most unlikely one was also one of the most important. And he wanted to say goodbye to him. Crop Eared Wolf died the following year. They never met again. Until now. And anytime that quirt is brought out, especially in Blackfoot territory.

. . .

"The only way we can kill you, Cowdry, is with an axe," said one of his doctor friends when he turned eighty. It didn't come to that, though he watched all his own children except my mother die before he did.

Sorreltop Jack died in Vancouver at the age of ninety, after taking friends to the Yacht Club for tea and returning to the nursing home for a whisky.

18

GOING FORWARD

"I have lived in important places, times
When great events were decided."
PATRICK KAVANAGH, "EPIC"

...

THERE IS A POEM WRITTEN IN 1938 by the Irish writer
Patrick Kavanagh that reminds us how local happenings are at
the heart of all storytelling. Kavanagh called it, with crafty irony,
"Epic"; and while I am not pretending that the story I have told
belongs in that category, the stories it draws upon—about relations between unlikely friends, between settling newcomers and
unsettled natives, and between human, natural, and supernatural happenings—might remind us of something else: the fundamental importance of these local relationships in the country
called Canada. Here is Kavanagh's poem:

I have lived in important places, times
When great events were decided: who owned
That half a rood of rock, a no-man's land
Surrounded by our pitchfork-armed claims.
I heard the Duffys shouting "Damn your soul!"

And old McCabe stripped to the waist, seen
Step the plot defying blue cast-steel—
"Here is the march along these iron stones."
That was the year of the Munich bother. Which
Was most important? I inclined
To lose my faith in Ballyrush and Gortin
Till Homer's ghost came whispering to my mind.
He said: I made the Iliad from such
A local row. Gods make their own importance.

We hear the news every day about how local rows precipitate national and international arguments, arguments that occasionally spin out into conflicts like the European and Middle Eastern wars that Kavanagh refers to. My story is more modest, but perhaps a more useful model too, recalling a place of promise and a time when good people, including Sorreltop Jack and Crop Eared Wolf, believed in keeping promises. It begins with a treaty binding Indians and non-Indians alike into a new dispensation that would only work if they were *all* treaty people, but each as distinct as two sides always are when they enter into a deal. For treaties and covenants are first of all deals between peoples, and sometimes between people and higher powers. Covenants have strong biblical associations for many of us, distinct in the Old and the New Testaments—"testament" itself being a translation of the Greek word for covenant; and for the Blackfoot, the covenant called Treaty Seven was entered into under the watch of the Great Spirit. Whatever their sanction, such covenants often have legal as well as religious authority; and the prairie treaties had both, binding the new country of Canada together as surely as the railway, becoming part of its formal as well as its informal constitution, and representing the spirit that inspired its creation and its first (and rather limited) constitution, in 1867.

A constitution is an interesting concept, moving (in its European coinage) from being a point in classical rhetoric—framing a question or argument—to describing the nature of the human body, and finally to regulation ... which is the sense in which it was used by Henry II in England in the middle of the twelfth century to describe his early attempt to turn unwritten custom into statute. Nowadays, constitutions often refer to the whole structure of a society—akin to a human body—and to the rights and duties of individuals in relation to the power of the state or the church; and when Canada adopted a formal constitution in 1982 it incorporated much of that spirit. Still, like covenants, constitutions have an elusive character, nicely illustrated by the way in which England was described in the eighteenth century as the only monarchy in the world with a constitution, and in the nineteenth century as the only democracy without one; and by the continual re-interpretation of national constitutions by the courts.

Stories and songs that define a community are often said to provide its constitution, and it is this connection that gives literature its edge. But the same stories and songs also give a covenantal stamp to collective solidarity, sealing a deal the way a word and a handshake do, and at the same time allowing for surprises and sudden rightnesses that are specific to that particular community. Literature is a fancy name for stories and songs; and being by definition testimonial it is also covenantal, and is one of the ways in which we define our difference from others. It is also one of the things that binds us together. We are easily convinced that a community doesn't amount to much if it doesn't have a literature; and we can see this conviction at work in the ambition of groups within society to have their own—women's literature, or queer literature, or black literature. In this scenario, a literary tradition is the covenant—you are either in or out of the deal—and its critical criteria, its unique ways of reading and listening, become the constitution. That is why stories, including those told in writings without words and requiring different modes of interpretation, are such an important part of Blackfoot identity, past and present and future. It is why I have spent so much time talking about storytelling in this book. And it is why I keep returning to those ceremonies of belief—rather than any particular beliefs—that we share as humans. Our children and grandchildren remind us of this every evening at storytime.

The treaties that led up to the 1880s are still the covenantal and constitutional heart and soul of this country—east and west and north and south. Even for those parts of the country not under treaty they establish some ground rules for respecting the sovereignties of First Nations within the nation of Canada . . . and they remind us that not only the gods make their own importance. So do we.

. . .

I remember a prayer I used to say when I was growing up, and my grandfather still alive. It went like this:

God bless
Mummy, Daddy,
Diddy, Grampy,
Elizabeth, Roguey,
And all the royal family.

Most of this was predictable: my mother and my father, my great-aunt Diddy (who was more like my grandmother) and my grandfather; my sister and the family dog. But the *royal family?* Indeed, *all* the royal family? That seems to me a rather dramatic flourish, especially since I certainly wasn't raised to sing their praises. It may have had something to do with Diddy, who would stand up with righteous urgency in the middle of dinner if she heard "God Save the King" (and after 1952, the Queen) on the radio. Or maybe it was because the bank my father worked for was the old Imperial Bank of Canada, a name I teased him about mercilessly for he was a republican of the old Irish sort, and would respond quickly that whatever its unfortunate name, its motto was "the bank that service built."

But my little prayer must also have been shaped by the stories my grandfather told about the Blackfoot and the deal they had made not long before his time with Her Majesty the Queen, Victoria. My grandfather had explained that she wasn't there personally to treat with the Blackfoot but had sent representatives, who told them that the promises they were making were *her* promises, and the Blackfoot believed she would be as good as her word. Maybe this bedtime liturgy was my way of underwriting those promises with a prayer.

Later, much later, I came upon a poem that caught the covenantal character of these promises—Robert Frost's haunting meditation "Stopping by Woods on a Snowy Evening." Its curiously phrased opening line—"Whose woods these are I think I know"—echoes the dreamy identification of Crown title (to all of Canada as well as Blackfoot territory) and the Great Mother, her "house" not in the village but over the seas; the mystified horse in the poem adds wonder and surprise to the scene, which no Blackfoot story would be without; and its sudden turn into the language of deal-making, the quintessential signal of a covenant, reminds us all of our covenantal responsibilities to the land and its first peoples. "I have promises to keep." That phrase also reminds us that we need to look backward to those promises and the unfinished story they represent, in order to go forward to build a better country, one whose story we can be proud to tell. The Blackfoot and other First Nations kept their promises. Canada did not. We do indeed have miles to go before we sleep.

Ironically, we are better at coming together around our promises to the land than to its people—not necessarily keeping them, but at least acknowledging them. Most of us recognize that we have obligations to the natural world, and these days we are learning all over again that nature will enforce them even if nations will not. The word "environment" was first used in its now familiar ecological sense only half a century ago, but it was given the broader meaning of "everything around us" by Thomas Carlyle a century earlier, just before Confederation. Carlyle said a lot of questionable things, but one of his wise coinages came in the form of the phrase "natural supernaturalism," a phrase that appealed to revolutionaries and reactionaries alike, and helped give credit to the idea that the imagined world is the only world that matters because it is the only world we know. We need to respect the imaginings as well as remember the realities of the first peoples of this land.

. . .

My grandfather's stories shaped my own life in ways that I didn't recognize until recently. But recollecting them may offer some insight into what the Saskatchewan civic leader Lloyd Barber, the first Indian claims commissioner, described just after Canada's centennial in 1967 as "a significant piece of unfinished business that lies at the foundations of this country."

With my grandfather's stories somewhere in the muddle that was my teenage mind, I applied for and was granted a homestead in the Peace River district, to take up as soon as I finished school. My parents didn't seem dismayed, but they may have been relieved when life took me in other directions and I turned instead to teaching literature. Perhaps I sensed that this would also bring me into the company of my grandfather's storytelling days, as the folk songs of the 1950s and '60s did when they brought cowboys songs back into currency.

Early in my career, and picking up some of the pieces of my grandfather's life, I wrote a couple of books, both of them about what used to be called the history of ideas. The first was titled *The Harrowing of Eden: White Attitudes Towards Native Americans*, and it traced some differences between Canada and the United States in their historical relationships with Aboriginal peoples. Its most contentious argument—a heritage of my grandfather, I recognize now, but surprisingly controversial when I wrote it in 1975—was that we need to take treaties seriously. In practice, they were sometimes colonial scams; but in principle, they were sacred agreements certified and sanctified by spiritual leaders on both sides, and they did indeed represent one thing that the signatories and governing groups on both sides believed in, even if some of them didn't much like it: that Aboriginal peoples constituted national communities and that the incoming settler societies must deal with them as such.

My second book, a couple of years later, was *Ripe Was the Drowsy Hour: The Age of Oscar Wilde*. It took the tellers of tales as seriously as my first had taken the makers and breakers of treaties. Wilde was one of the first modern writers to outline a theory of how the imagination creates reality—in his signature phrase, how "life imitates art"—and through him I began a long, slow return to the wisdom of my childhood when, like every other child, I had taken stories to heart.

By then I had spent a good amount of time in the east Kootenays, where I got to know many of the Kootenai and Shuswap Indians living near the headwaters of the Columbia River; and then in the Spatsizi region of northern British Columbia, with the Sekani and Tahltan peoples—and my writing on the history of their relationships with settler society brought me to work with Thomas Berger on the Mackenzie Valley Pipeline Inquiry in the mid-1970s, and then again with him on the Alaska Native Claims Commission, sponsored not by settler governments but by the Inuit Circumpolar Conference to look into the effect of the 1981 Alaska Native Claims Settlement Act on native Alaskans, who had become the most powerful economic force in the state with control of the newly established native corporations . . . but were finding that corporate responsibility often conflicted with tribal interests. During that time I also worked with First Nations on land claims and Aboriginal rights, and along the way brought together ideas that would become a book about horses, and how they have shaped civilizations around the world for thousands of years.

Then I went to Australia to find out what was happening with Aboriginal rights there. I found anger and frustration, but also hope and possibility. An Aboriginal Arts Board had just been established, as part of the Australian equivalent of the Canada Council; and its first director was an Aboriginal actor and political activist named Gary Foley, who had led the famous "tent embassy" when Aboriginal communities settled down for months on the lawns of Government House in Canberra. Foley was determined to demonstrate how the Aboriginal imagination might shape a new Aboriginal reality through the stories and songs and bark and sand paintings and dancing and drumming and all the other forms of imaginative expression that grace and define their communities . . . and he spent most of the first year's budget funding young Aboriginal artists to create murals in their communities, imagining the world they want to live in and deciding what kind of home they want to build. Later, in South Africa, I spent time with the Khoisan (Bushmen) people in the Kalahari who had put forward a land claim (at the encouragement of the new African National Congress government). There, I found an indomitable spirit in the persons of three sisters and their cousin, women of great courage who both literally and figuratively sang in the land to which they were returning.

Which brought me to writing a book I called *If This Is Your Land, Where Are Your Stories?*—its title taken from a question posed by a Gitxsan elder from the northwest of British Columbia to government foresters arguing about jurisdiction in a part of the country without treaties—and its subtitle, *Finding Common Ground*, referring to neither a spot of land nor a set of stories but to a state of mind in which wonder holds us close. I had come to realize that teaching English and Comparative Literature at the University of Toronto, on the one hand, and on the other spending time as a consultant to Aboriginal communities and governments around the world on land claim settlements, were two sides of the same coin, and that the currency was stories. Stories that tell us who we are and where we belong. Stories that keep us together and others apart. Stories about the past, the present and the future. National literatures are collections of such stories, as are the literatures we organize along lines of race, gender and religion. When Aboriginal communities go to court to claim jurisdiction over land and livelihood, or to recover the promises of treaties, they tell stories and sing songs that are ceremonies of belief as well as chronicles of events. And even though such beliefs often differ and other people's ceremonies often seem strange, it is by understanding the character of these ceremonies—these "customs that are the reality," in the words of William Stanner—that we find some continuity and common ground in a world preoccupied with differences, and realize that the imagination and reality are fellow travellers.

Certainly different languages and different cultures experience reality differently, and different places shape that experience in distinct ways. How to make this apparent, other than by mutual incomprehension and disbelief, is a continuing challenge, and it is one we have continually shied away from. During the Royal Commission on Aboriginal Peoples in the 1990s, I was asked to design an Aboriginal History project that would bring different kinds of First Nations stories together, along with an Aboriginal Atlas that would illuminate different classifications of land and water, for example, and of flora and fauna, the natural and the man-made, the spiritual and the material.

Over a period of eighteen months I gathered with Aboriginal and non-Aboriginal elders, tribal and academic historians, anthropologists, geographers, mapmakers, filmmakers, tribal leaders, lawyers and artists, many of them deeply involved over a very long period in the development of strategies for nourishing Aboriginal traditions, and of finding ways of putting performances on the page, and writing without words into words. Discussions took place in large and small settings, and were often extremely awkward—the awkwardness playing itself out, not surprisingly, across Aboriginal cultures (and sometimes along gender and class and generational lines) as well as between Aboriginal and non-Aboriginal participants.

The project began as a request to rewrite history—to put it right in writing, to tell the true story, to affirm the position of Aboriginal peoples in the country. But with our hearing sharpened by tribal historians and storytellers, this increasingly sounded like trying to answer that old "Indian question"; and it became clear that there must be *Histories*, not a single History, and that these histories must reflect not only the different experiences of the many First Nations, Métis and Inuit communities in the country but also the unique forms of chronicle and ceremony in which these histories are revealed, undistorted by the kind of colonial *or* anti-colonial polemic that essentializes and exoticizes and homogenizes Aboriginal voices. And so we came up with a plan for a series of books that would be conceived, designed and produced by Aboriginal communities and would present their histories, often going back thousands of years (in which white folks like me make a very, very late appearance), in a way that reflected their traditional storytelling and tribal historical practices. We had a couple of volumes well along in development, drawing on material that had been put forward in land claims and Aboriginal rights cases; and there was much discussion of subsequent volumes taking up different historical traditions across the country. We had a generous and flexible publishing contract in hand for the whole open-ended series, from one of the country's major publishers, including development funds and the offer of resources towards further fundraising for the (very expensive) Atlas project; and a firm guarantee that each volume would be autonomous and Aboriginal centred—with different editorial boards for every volume, each having a majority of members from the particular Aboriginal community.

The commissioners had put substantial funds into our work . . . but then we ran into an old problem. The problem wasn't about money. It was that the royal commissioners wanted to be in control of the message—an old story, sadly—while we insisted that for the project to succeed, control must be vested in each Aboriginal community (or clusters of communities, whether they be hard-won confederacies like those of the Blackfoot and the Iroquois, or regional alliances like the Coastal First Nations in British Columbia, or gatherings along lines of language or livelihood or legacies of collaboration). Otherwise, even though a revisionary history might revise the record, it might do little more than replace one orthodoxy with another and maintain the role of an imperial (rather than the local) tradition as the certifier of historical standards, the empire in this case being the commission. Instead, we proposed a project that would bring the Aboriginal makers of this country now called Canada into the foreground as actors in the long, long history of this land, stretching back far before Confederation, rather than as victims acted upon in the short hundred years of Canada's constitutional existence. We suggested that *this* was a central part of the unfinished business of Canada; and indeed a generation later, with knowledge of particular Aboriginal histories, such a project might give the government's and industry's consultations with First Nations on the encroachment on territory and the exploitation of resources, which have been mandated by the Supreme Court, a much better chance of finding common ground, and affirming the power and the pride of Aboriginal peoples.

But the commissioners decided not to proceed. In fairness, several of them argued passionately for the project—one of the most eloquent was the Métis elder Paul Chartrand, undoubtedly with Louis Riel's local uprising on his mind—but to no avail. Some of it has taken on a life of its own anyway, and parts are moving ahead in their own way, at their own pace, inspired by books such as *Mapping My Way Home: A Gitxsan History*, written after a lifetime of listening to his people's stories by Neil Sterritt, the Gitxsan leader who brought *Delgamuukw* to trial. So there is hope. There is always hope. And possibility.

. . .

It was stories—boasting and toasting, civil and ceremonial— that sustained Blackfoot pride and nourished Blackfoot prosperity during the dangerous years after the destruction of the buffalo. In these no less dangerous times today they could do so again, for young and old across the country. Our Aboriginal peoples are under new threats from both within and without; and some of their reserves are refugee camps in everything but name. They are struggling with scarce resources, damaged lives and seemingly hopeless prospects. And without water, which almost defies credibility in a country like Canada, in the twenty-first century. The crisis in Macleod in the late nineteenth century over water supply and the sewage system might remind us that all of what I have just said in this book is like waste water if Aboriginal communities do not have clean water . . . and many, many do not. Clean water in Canada should have a place as a constitutional or charter right. Without spending more time assigning blame, and given that decades have passed without much improvement, we need to put some legal instruments in place that would require governments to ensure a clean water supply for all citizens, Aboriginal or otherwise, and would give governments not just the mandate but the obligation to intervene in community business, if required, to provide the technology and expertise and funding. This is contentious territory, I realize, and goes against some of the principles I have been advocating; but surely we can come together to agree that the promise of clean water is a basic human right in Canada. For all I have said about the ways in which the imagination creates reality, it is hard to imagine clean water if you haven't had any for years. Housing comes next; but housing requires care and attention to indigenous traditions. Water does not, or at least not in the same way (and I say this well aware of the cultural and spiritual importance of waterholes for the desert peoples of Australia and southern Africa). But think of water on reserves like rations back in the 1870s and 1880s, after the buffalo had gone and the plains Indians were starving, and how those rations were sometimes withheld as surely as clean water is being withheld to punish First Nations for not doing as they are told . . . like moving somewhere else. Think of it like Canadian citizenship for Aboriginal peoples nearly a century later, in the 1950s and '60s, but only after two world wars in which many Indians had fought and died for Canada. Think about it any way you want. But think about it.

. . .

Aboriginal people are at the heart of what this country is all about. And stories, their and ours, are at the heart of how we think about ourselves, and each other. I believe that if we were to encourage a set of stories—a series of Aboriginal histories— they would gather with other histories and become a new kind of national history—always unfinished, but always underway. If governments were to give to this even a small portion of the substantial support that they routinely offer to threatened industrial enterprises like the automobile industry or to struggling harvesting sectors such as agriculture or fishing or forestry, Canada would reap benefits beyond our imagining . . . and also set an example to the world.

Stories give us a way of navigating the world, both personal and public. I have made the association with seafaring already, suggesting that navigation offers a model for living with uncertainty; and since we still use the word when we talk about navigating the world wide web, we can see that it continues to be part of how we find our way in the world. That being the case, it is worth remembering that before GPS there were two fundamentally different conceptions of ocean navigation, nicely represented by European and Polynesian traditions. Both worked. For the Polynesian navigator, the boat was always imagined as fixed in place, while everything else—the sun and the moon and the stars as well as a matrix of islands—was in motion relative to the boat. For the European navigator, on the other hand, the boat was always moving, with everything else—the same sun and moon and stars—fixed at any given moment. Polynesian navigation identified "here" as where the boat was seen to be on the ocean. In European navigation, "here" was where the boat was determined to be on a map, with reference points established on that map according to scheduled observations, or "fixes." For the Polynesian navigator, even the ultimate point of reference—the island destination— moved through the stages of the voyage in relation to the boat, even though the navigator "knew" perfectly well that it did no such thing. It was a kind of navigational storytelling, a functional fiction. Likewise, a European navigator, using one of the various mapping projections that represented the curved surface of the earth on a plane surface, imagined that he was going in a straight line when he knew he wasn't. Both methods of navigation were remarkable; and together they tell the story of humankind. A distinguished scientist once said that an ocean traveller has a more vivid impression that the ocean is made up of waves than that it is made of water. We might keep both in mind as we work our way across the gulf between each other.

When Crop Eared Wolf hovered between dream and waking in his storytelling on the quirt, he was moving comfortably between the two ancient methods of navigation. We need to get used to the existence of more than one way of understanding the world, and of finding our way home.

. . .

Listening to others is the first courtesy, and a custom which my grandfather and Crop Eared Wolf both rendered and respected. They are the presiding spirits of this book. Each of them, in their own way, "rode both horses," to pick up Johnny Franklin's response at that first Calgary Stampede. They opened doors; and they also shut doors against the Gradgrinds of the world. They left us with a line of credit, to be used in building a world of customs and courtesies. And most of all they left us with some promises to keep, and a couple of questions. What have we done? And what do we do next?

ACKNOWLEDGEMENTS

I COULD NOT HAVE WRITTEN this book without my beloved wife, Lorna Goodison. She has been with me every step of the way, picked me up after each misstep, and put up with my whinging and whining with remarkable grace and generosity and good humour. And she has given me consistently wise advice, drawn from her lifetime's experience as a poet and from writing her celebrated memoir of her mother and her people.

I no longer have children, I have adults: Sarah, Geoff and Meg—no less precious but much more patient. They asked me all the right questions, and (bless them) never expected sensible answers; their good wishes have meant the world to me. Their great-grandfather would have been as proud of them as I am. Meanwhile Fin and Thomas giggled and called me Grampy, catching the spirit of this book.

My mother's stories—and some of my father's—are at the heart of this book; and my debt to them goes beyond words. The widespread Cowdry clan has also been indispensable: Jack Cowdry, like me a grandson of the banker; my sister Liz Food; the banker's other granddaughter Nancy Tinning, and her son Ret Tinning; Nat's granddaughter Margie Haun, and her son Howard Park; Ned Cowdry's granddaughters Mi Haas—and her grandson Adam Shoemaker—and Marnie Ovens—and her son Peter who, along with his father Frank, prepared and updated the Cowdry family genealogy. On Gussie Thompson's side of the family, Edith Crichton and her son Ted Boon. And my godmother Margaret Williams. I am also very grateful to Annabel Crop Eared Wolf for conversations about her great-grandfather. Her admiration for him made me more than ever conscious of my responsibility to portray him with corresponding respect, and I hope I have done justice to his legacy as well as to his friendship with my grandfather.

Some of my old friends from the foothills—such as John Burns—are mentioned in the text. Others, from elsewhere, belong right here. George and Dianne Laforme have been with me for most of my life; and George, a master storyteller, has helped me more than he knows and probably more than I realize. The friendship of John and Barb Murray has been both a rock and a touchstone, for which I am forever thankful. Neil Sterritt, a good friend for many years, brought blessings to our home, *Wilp Skimsim*, and has been a fellow traveller on the book-making trail. As has Dan Chamberlain, and time and again he and Monica have cheered me on and cheered me up. And the wit and wisdom of Gary Holthaus always keeps me company.

There are many other people who have played an important part in this book. Kate McAll from the BBC started me off with a radio program about my grandfather, produced on location in southern Alberta in 2002. Arni Brownstone has been very generous with his knowledge, and shown me something of what the venerable traditions of writing without words are all about. Jennifer Glossop's wise counsel sharpened my craft. The judgement of my old friend John Jennings has been invaluable and inspiring. Tina Loo opened many doors, Simon Evans gave me direction and support, and Meg Stanley offered suggestions. With unfailing enthusiasm, Don Smith has turned me to sources, scholars and snippets of information I would not have found otherwise. And like many others, I am immensely grateful to Hugh Dempsey for his work of a lifetime—indeed, it sometimes seems of many lifetimes—in this field. He also kindly made himself open to my questions, and always answered with uncommon courtesy. The Glenbow Museum is a treasure house for anyone interested in the history of the west. Doug Cass made working in the archives there a pleasure, he and his colleagues always prompt and professional in responding to my many requests. Jan Reeves took up my family's story with enthusiasm as curator of the Fort Museum in Fort Macleod; Gordon MacIvor gave early advice and assistance in his capacity as director of the Main Street project in town; and Elizabeth Matthews welcomed me at the United Church archives.

Along with these, a host of friends and fellow travellers have been with me and encouraged my work over the years, for this book has been a long time coming. Some have given me particular assistance, or opportunities to try out ideas; others have kept me going by the inspiration of their own lives and livelihoods; several of them are sadly gone; but all of them have shown me the importance of friendship, and of storytelling. They include George Anderson, Lloyd Barber, Marie Battiste, Tom Berger, Alan Bewell, John Borrows, Nick Bradley, Diana Brydon, Keith Carlson, Jane Clement Chamberlin, Bill Charlton, Barry Chevonnes, David Chrislip and Carol Wilson, Diana Crosbie, Brian Corman, Stan Cuthand, Regna Darnell, Wade Davis, Ramsay Derry, Vine Deloria, Martha Demientieff, Chris Douglas, Britt Ellis, Len Findlay, Rob Finley, Sander Gilman, Susan Gingell, Karl Goodison, Keith Goodison, Miles Goodison, Trevor Goward, Jan Guerth, Dick Harrison, Derek and Sue Hopkins, Linda Hutcheon, Roger Hutchinson, Janet Irving, Joerg Jaschinski, Teresa Jordan, Camille Joseph, Daniel Justice, Sean Kane, Bob Kahgee, Fanny Kiefer, Neil ten Kortenaar, Richard Landon, Diane Longboat, John Lutz, Ian MacRae, Mark McLean, Paul McLean, Dorik Mechau and Carolyn Servid, Joe Miskokomon, Victor Mitander,

Karen Mulhallen, Tak Nakajima, David Naylor, John O'Brian, Simon Ortiz, Art Pape, Ian Pitfield, Dave Porter, Maggie Redekop, Stephen Regan, Basil Robinson, Rick Salter, Richard Sanger, David Smith, Rowland Smith, Andrew Stewart, Paddy Stewart, Tim Stewart, John Stubbs, Jacob Thomas, Tommy Walker, Jeremy Webber, Graeme Wynn, Dan Yashinsky, Gaither Zinkan, Ted Zinkan and Bettie Vajda.

Louise Dennys, my publisher and editor, believed in me when I began thinking about this memoir, and worked with me on it from the start. She listened to my words, and made me make sense by the quality of her attention. Her friendship kept me company and her spirit kept me going, while her editing—deeply informed, unfailingly intelligent and refreshingly imaginative—made this book. She paid inspiring attention to the details, and often saw the storyline before I did. And she never let me take the easy way out.

Kate Icely managed this complicated project with extraordinary tact and sure instinct, coordinating the technical details and balancing a very wide range of demands with exceptional composure, giving me genial nudges exactly when I needed them, and seeing many things I missed. Jane McWhinney's copy editing is simply the best; Jennifer Griffiths took on the design with creative care; Deirdre Molina kept the book on track with quiet resolution, as she always does; Anne Collins was enthusiastic from the get-go; and Lynn Henry encouraging at every turn. I am fortunate once again to have an index by Barney Gilmore; and my publicist Shona Cook knows the territory I am talking about, and believes in the book—a lovely combination.

Which brings me back to my friend Lorna. Thank you, with all my heart.

SOURCES AND ENDNOTES

MANY OF MY GRANDFATHER'S personal notes and banking records are in the Glenbow Museum archives in Calgary, as well as in papers and letters and journals held by the Cowdry family. And in his stories, held in the memory of family and friends. I remember his storytelling; but I was very young and many of the stories I tell come from my mother, Edith Cowdry, who was born in 1899 and lived until 1986, and from family members such as his other grandson (also named Jack Cowdry) and his granddaughter (Nancy Tinning), both of whom knew him well, and from my sister, Liz Food, and other members of the Cowdry clan past and present. I have also relied on a genealogy prepared by Frank and his son Peter Ovens, Ned's great-grandson, along with material from Margie Park, Nat's granddaughter; and there are records relating generally to this period as well as specifically to my grandfather in Lethbridge and Fort Macleod, as well as in the Methodist (United Church) archives in Toronto. There are some excellent academic and popular histories to draw on, but many of the details in this story are to be found in reminiscences published locally, catching the voice and much of the spirit of those who lived in these remarkable years. It is storytelling, mine and theirs, that shapes this book, weaving together the personal and the political, the local and the literary, anchored in the realities and celebrating the imaginings of the newcomers living in this brief period and this particular place.

The stories of the Blackfoot, unique in both their forms and their functions, are also at the centre of my narrative. I have been careful, because they are Blackfoot stories, not mine; but I have tried to give a sense of how deeply a few of them are interwoven, or knotted up, with the settler stories of these years, even as they are sometimes at cross purposes with each other. And while my account of the *Niitsítapi* draws on a wide range of sources, it is worth mentioning the inspiration offered to us all by the permanent exhibition *Niitsitapiisinni: Our Way of Life,* developed collaboratively by the Blackfoot and the Glenbow Museum.

PREAMBLE. The name "Chinook" comes from an Indian tribe living along the lower reaches of the Columbia River, where winds from the Pacific rise up over the coastal mountains, bringing warm air as they fall down the other side, more moderate than in the foothills but always surprising. Chinook is also the name of a creole language that facilitated communication between Aboriginal and trader and settler communities on the west coast. It has wide currency in the late nineteenth and early twentieth centuries among peoples from over a dozen language families looking for common ground. As Terry Glain wrote about the Chinook language: "It opens up a history of collaboration, co-existence and practical traditions of the reconciliation to which we are now summoned.... Remembering [Chinook] might allow us to *mamook mesika youtl tumtum,* to make our heart glad again about who we were, and about what, if we could just find the words, we can be." (From "This Canada Day, remember Chinook—our shared, lost language." *National Post,* June 30, 2015.)

CHAPTER ONE. William Johnson's remarks are from a letter he wrote to the Earl of Shelburne in 1767, quoted by Duncan Campbell Scott in "Indian Affairs, 1763–1841," the first of his three essays on Indian administration in British North America and Canada, commissioned for *Canada and Its Provinces: A History of the Canadian People and Their Institutions*, eds. Adam Shortt and Arthur Doughty, published in 1913. (That was the year Scott became deputy superintendent general of Indian Affairs, a position he held until 1932.) I relied on Patricia W. Hart, *Pioneering in North York: A History of the Borough* for the description of York Mills; Chester B. Beaty's *The Landscapes of Southern Alberta* offered useful background information about Chinook country. The newspaper description of Fort Macleod is from the papers of the Methodist missionary John Maclean in the United Church of Canada Archives in Toronto; the first grumpy account of the town is from a letter written by Mary E. Inderwick to her sister (and published in the *Alberta Historical Review*, ed. Hugh Dempsey, in 1967), and the second is by John D. Higinbotham in his book *When the West Was Young*. The list of buildings in Fort Macleod is from both John Maclean's journal notes and from *Fort Macleod—Our Colourful Past: A History of the Town from 1874 to 1924*, published by the town's diligent History Book committee and a source for many other details; I have also learned from the monographs *Fort Macleod: The Story of the Mounted Police*, ed. H.G. Long, and *A Walking/Driving Tour of Fort Macleod's Historic Downtown and Residential Area*, put together by the Fort Macleod Provincial Historic Area Society. The account of the mail system is from Edward Brado, *Cattle Kingdom: Early Ranching in Alberta*, to which I have often turned in writing this book; and from North-West Mounted Police inspector Cecil Denny, quoted in a typescript by William Pearce, "The Early History of Western Canada," in the Thomas Fisher Rare Book Library at the University of Toronto. I am indebted for the line about flies walking to Gary Holthaus (in *Wide Skies: Finding a Home in the West*); for the description of the berries to Alex Johnson's *Plants and the Blackfoot*; and for the legend of Chief Mountain and the naming of Cowley to *A History of the Early Days of Pincher Creek*, prepared by members of the Women's Institute of Alberta. The Blackfoot place names are from Hugh Dempsey's *Indian Names for Alberta Communities*. Some details about Harry Taylor are from an obituary written by Fred Haultain and published in the *Lethbridge News* in March 1901; and about Francis Dickens, from Roderick C. Macleod's article in the *Dictionary of Canadian Biography*.

CHAPTER TWO. The phrase "to acknowledge the Indian title . . . as if with a sovereign power" is Duncan Campbell Scott's, from his essay "Indian Affairs, 1763–1841." Adams Archibald is quoted by Sidney L. Harring in his essay "'There Seemed to Be No Recognized Law': Canadian Law and the Prairie First Nations" in *Laws and Societies in the Canadian Prairie West, 1670–1940*, eds. Louis A. Knafla and Jonathan Swainger. George Stanley's memorable phrase is from his chapter "The 1870s" in *The Canadians*, eds. J.M.S. Careless and R. Craig Brown. The anecdote about the pace of railway construction is from Pierre Berton's *The Last Spike: The Great Railway 1881–1885*. The discussion of treaties throughout the book is drawn from a range of sources, in particular Michael Asch's eloquent *On Being Here to Stay: Treaties and Aboriginal Rights in Canada* and Hugh Dempsey's *The Great Blackfoot Treaties*. Others I will mention along the way, but I must pay special tribute to Dempsey's many historical accounts of Alberta and the Blackfoot; they are the basis for much of the work in this field, and an inspiration to all of us who are trying to clear some common ground. Also, Gerald Friesen's history of *The Canadian Prairies: A History* offers an excellent account of these times, and I am much indebted to him. Thoreau's sentence is from *Walden*. My commentary throughout the book on peacemakers and peacekeepers owes much to *Matsiyáítapapiiyssini: Káínai Peacekeeping and Peacemaking* by Annabel Crop Eared Wolf, great-granddaughter of Crop Eared Wolf. Red Crow's tribute to James Macleod is quoted in Hugh Dempsey's *Red Crow: Warrior Chief*; and my comments on the idea of a commonwealth does, to my welcome surprise, echo a much earlier meditation by Lewis G. Thomas in "The Umbrella and the Mosaic," written during Canada's centennial year and published in *Ranchers' Legacy: Alberta Essays by Lewis G. Thomas*, ed. Patrick A. Dunae. The quotation describing the "plains outpost" is from Edward Brado. For my description of Harry's Table and Fred Haultain I have drawn from Grant MacEwan's *Frederick Haultain: Frontier Statesman of the Canadian Northwest*, as well as *The Haultain Story*, a monograph compiled by Doris and Claud Stevens for the Fort Macleod Historical Association. Haultain's law office has been restored in the Fort Museum. The story of Jerry Potts is from several published accounts, most notably Hugh Dempsey's *Jerry Potts, Plainsman*, and from my grandfather's stories. The description of the remittance men and Lord Brook is from Bob Edwards in his Calgary tabloid the *Eye Opener*; from the collection of Pincher Creek reminiscences; and from Edward Brado, who also provided the anecdote about the cowboy wearing velvet slippers to the dance. The story of *Natawista* is recounted at the beginning of Hugh Dempsey's *Red Crow*, and the celebration of her triumph at the dance is by R. B. Nevitt in *A Winter at Fort Macleod*. The stories about Ned Maunsell throughout the book are drawn from accounts in the various histories of western ranching mentioned in these notes, as well as from two sources: "The West of Edward Maunsell," Parts 1 and 2, edited by Hugh Dempsey and published in *Alberta History* in 1986–87; and from the Maunsell papers in the Glenbow Museum in Calgary. Maclean's tribute to Red Crow is from his book *Canada's Savage Folk: The Native Tribes of Canada*, the irony of its title taking away from the well-informed ethnographic accounts he provides (with some fictional portraits, one of which is titled "Apokena: The Adventures of a Blackfoot Indian in the Land of the White Savages," praised by Hugh Dempsey in his essay "The Fearsome Fire Wagons" in *The CPR West: The Iron Road and the Making of a Nation*, ed. Hugh Dempsey). Annabel Crop Eared Wolf's tribute is from her monograph on *Káínai* peacekeeping and peacemaking. The broad sweep of Blackfoot history, the details of some of the events, and some of my descriptions of the life and livelihood and cultural traditions of the people in this and the following chapters are informed by the two-volume collection *Alberta Formed, Alberta Transformed*, eds. Michael Payne, Donald G. Wetherell and Catherine Cavanaugh, published to celebrate Alberta's centenary as a province, with essays by (among others): John W. Ives, "13,001 Years Ago: Human Beginnings in Alberta"; Alwynne B. Beaudoin and Gerald A. Otelaar, "The Day the Dry Snow Fell: The Record of a 7,267-year-old Disaster"; Trevor R. Peck and J. Rod Vickers, "Buffalo and Dogs: The Prehistoric Lifeways of Aboriginal People on the Alberta Plains, 1004–1005"; Fritz Pannekoek, "On the Edge of the Great Transformation: 1857–58"; the generously ubiquitous Hugh Dempsey, "1870: A Year of Violence and Change"; Sarah Carter and Walter Hildebrandt, "'A Better Life With Honour': Treaty 6 (1876) and Treaty 7 (1877) with Alberta First Nations"; Bill Waiser, "Too Many Scared People: Alberta and the 1885 North-West Rebellion"; Brian Calliou, "1899 and the Political Economy of Canada's

North-West: Treaty 8 as a Compact to Share and Peacefully Co-exist"; and David Hall, "1904–1905: Alberta Proclaimed." I rely on these essays again in chapter 5 and intermittently throughout. Mike Mountain Horse's *My People the Bloods* offers a testimony of tribal stories and personal recollections; and Hugh Dempsey's *Indian Tribes of Alberta* is an important sourcebook. The description of the tipi design is from Dempsey, *Red Crow*, and John Ewers's work on the "Painted Tipis of the Blackfeet Indians" for the Museum of the Rockies in Bozeman, Montana. Crop Eared Wolf's exploits gathering horses are described in Dempsey's *Crop Eared Wolf & Other Horse Thieves*, written as a curriculum resource for the Ontario Institute for Studies in Education. My use of phrases such as "bringing in" or "bringing home" horses instead of stealing them is influenced by Methodist missionary John McDougall's description of horse raiding, quoted by Sarah Carter in *Lost Harvests: Prairie Indian Reserve Farmers and Government Policy*. My mention of the long tradition of mischief in human societies draws from Lewis Hyde's *Trickster Makes This World: Mischief, Myth, and Art*. Thoreau's comments on *"extra vagance"* are from *Walden*.

CHAPTER THREE. The poncy ranching patron was Alexander Staveley Hill, one of the principal backers of the Oxley ranch near Willow Creek, and he is quoted in Brado, *Cattle Kingdom*, from John R. Craig's 1903 account of *Ranching with Lords and Commons; or, Twenty Years on the Range*. For the banking background and some details about Cowdry Brothers Bank, I have turned to Henry C. Klassen, author of *A Business History of Alberta*; but it is his article "Cowdry Brothers: Private Bankers in Southwestern Alberta, 1886–1905" in *Alberta History* (1989) that has been most helpful. The anecdote about "interest" is from George Gooderham's article "The Blackfoot Indians at Gleichen, Alberta," published in 1940 in *Canadian Cattlemen*. (Gooderham was Indian agent with the Siksika from 1920 to 1946.) Marshall McLuhan's phrase is from *The Gutenberg Galaxy: The Making of Typographic Man*. The brief discussion of medicine bundles is drawn from Clark Wissler's 1912 article "Ceremonial Bundles of the Blackfoot Indians," referred to by Hugh Dempsey in his essay "Blackfoot" in the Smithsonian's *Handbook of North American Indians, Plains*, Vol. 13. For my comments on the relationship between trade and culture, I drew on James Dempsey's essay "Effects on Aboriginal Cultures Due to Contact with Henry Kelsey" in *Three Hundred Prairie Years: Henry Kelsey's "Inland Country of Good Report,"* ed. Henry Epp. My comments on usury, and some of my later reflections on gift giving, are indebted to Lewis Hyde's *The Gift: Imagination and the Erotic Life of Property*, where Hyde also mentions Thomas Jefferson on "the merchant" (quoted in chapter 4 here). L.V. Kelly's book *The Range Men: The Story of the Ranchers and Indians of Alberta* is an invaluable resource, written so close to the time by someone who knew most of the characters and much about the business of ranching, and who can tell a good story. His putting my grandfather right at the beginning of the book says something about the perceived importance of the bank both to ranching and to the foothills community.

CHAPTER FOUR. The epigraph is quoted from the permanent Glenbow exhibition. The winter count is taken from Hugh Dempsey's monograph *A Blackfoot Winter Count*. William Pearce's comments are from his "Early History of Western Canada"; and background on Pearce is from Simon Evans's magisterial *The Bar U and Canadian Ranching*

History, which tells us about much more than a single ranch, however important it was. I am much indebted to his work, and his advice. The recipe for homemade refreshment is provided by Charles Aeneas Shaw in his *Tales of a Pioneer Surveyor*, ed. Raymond Hull. The border-marking pyramids are described (and pictured) in Tony Cashman's *An Illustrated History of Western Canada*, as well as in *An Illustrated History of Canada* by D.G.G. Kerr and R.I.K. Davidson. The letter from Snookum Jim is in the Pearce typescript; it is also quoted in, among other places, a genial collection of sayings titled *Sounds Like Alberta (1754–1905)*, eds. Colin A. Thomson and F. Lee Prindle. The story of the arrival of the North-West Mounted Police at Fort Whoop-Up has often been told; but all accounts of that time and place are indebted to Paul F. Sharp's *Whoop-Up Country: The Canadian-American West, 1865–1885*. The cost of policing is taken from A.O. MacRae's *History of the Province of Alberta*, published in 1912.

CHAPTER FIVE. William Hornaday's extraordinary assessment is from his report "On the Extermination of the American Bison," published as part of the annual report of the United States National Museum in 1887. Among other books that I consulted were Andrew C. Isenberg's *The Destruction of the Bison: An Environmental History, 1750–1920*; Harold P. Danz's *Of Bison and Man*; and the essay by Trevor R. Peck and J. Rod Vickers in *Alberta Formed, Alberta Transformed*. John Macoun's description of a grass fire is from *Manitoba and the Great North-West*. I am grateful to Sean Kane and his elegant writing on "wonder" for my quotation from *Sir Gawain and the Green Knight*. The Spanish observer on the pampas was Vásquez de Espinosa, and both his and the later traveller's report from the Rio Grande are quoted by Deb Bennett and Robert S. Hoffmann in "Ranching in the New World" from *Seeds of Change*, eds. Herman J. Viola and Carolyn Margolis. John C. Ewers's *The Horse in Blackfoot Indian Culture* is an indispensable resource on this subject, of such importance both to the Blackfoot and to the foothills at this time. The comment on buffalo horses is from John Maclean's notebooks; and it was John Cotton who said the Bloods had the fastest horses, quoted by Hugh Dempsey in "The Wise Old Ones," from *The Amazing Death of Calf Shirt and Other Blackfoot Stories*, in which Dempsey also makes the remark about Blackfoot stoicism in facing their "last days of freedom and the destruction of their old ways of life," and gives a description of the laughing dance told to him by his father-in-law, James Gladstone. Thomas Huxley is quoted in *The Resilient Outpost: Ecology, Economy and Society in Rural Newfoundland*, ed. Rosemary E. Ommer. Josiah Wright Mooar's buffalo count is mentioned in Tom McHugh's *The Time of the Buffalo*. Echoing Psalm 50, Red Crow said to North-West Mounted Police officer Percy Neale at a meeting in 1888, "God has taken all the game away." My comments on the Sun Dance here and later are drawn from Dempsey and others, including Walter McClintock in *The Old North Trail: Life, Legends and Religion of the Blackfeet Indians*, and from the essay "Sun Dance" by JoAllyn Archambault in *Handbook of North American Indians, Plains*, Vol. 13. I first heard the phrase "the sacredness of suffering" (which I use again in chapter 15) from the native American psychologist Eduardo Duran in 1996 at a gathering in Saskatoon attended by many who knew a great deal about both.

CHAPTER SIX. The descriptions by Frank Oliver and Cecil Denny are from John W. Chalmers's *Laird of the West*; and the speeches by Crowfoot and Red Crow and James

Macleod are from Dempsey's books *Crowfoot: Chief of the Blackfeet* and (his most recent) *The Great Blackfoot Treaties*. The deadly consequences of the government's actions and inactions are recounted in chilling detail in James Daschuk's *Clearing the Plains: Disease, Politics of Starvation and the Loss of Aboriginal Life*. My conversation with Adrian Stimson was recorded for a fifty-minute BBC radio program "Another Country, As a Tale That Is Told," broadcast on BBC Radio 3 on November 10, 2002, and again on September 1, 2003. It was produced by Kate McAll on location in southern Alberta. My discussions later in this book with Gerald Conaty and Frank Weasel Head about the quirt were also recorded for that program, and I have been careful to go no further than they took me in my interpretation of that gift. Big Swan's signing of the treaty is marked by some confusion, for in the treaty text he is mistakenly listed as *Akka-Makkoye*, or Many Swans, a reminder that written documents, no matter how they are sanctioned, offer no guarantee of truthtelling—a point made not only by First Nations historians but by many others, including Gerald Friesen. The lines from the judgement in *Badger* are quoted in Asch's book *On Being Here to Stay*, along with his compelling commentary on the prairie treaties and treatymaking, and on truthtelling. A fascinating insight into both native and non-native conceptions of territory is provided in Mark Warhus's *Another America: Native American Maps and the History of Our Land*. Aboriginal land claims, and the mappings that they represent, also offer valuable insights into the misconceptions and misunderstandings as well as the malice and mischief that have been part of the history of occupied countries. The Gitxsan leader Neil Sterritt's *Mapping My Way Home: A Gitxsan History* (which I mention in chapter 18) is a masterful weaving of traditions and of testimonies—oral and written, verbal and visual. Brian Friel's play *Translations* was first performed by the Field Day Theatre Company in Derry in 1980. Pete St. John wrote "The Fields of Athenry" in the 1970s. Daniel Kemmis's description of the Montana constitution is from his book *Community and the Politics of Place*. By coincidence, the son of the British physician Richard Bright, who first described Macleod's cluster of symptoms that were later brought together under the term "nephritis," had a ranch near Pincher Creek, where Macleod lived after he left the police force. The story of the move by the Bloods to the new reserve is well told by Dempsey in *Red Crow*.

CHAPTER SEVEN. My account of the round-up draws on Simon Evans and Lewis G. Thomas, as well as reminiscences in Frederick W. Ings's *Before the Fences: Tales from the Midway Ranch*, ed. Jim Davis, and *Leaves from the Medicine Tree*, compiled by the High River Pioneers' and Old Timers' Association; and there are valuable essays in *Cowboys, Ranchers and the Cattle Business: Cross-Border Perspectives on Ranching History*, eds. Simon Evans, Sarah Carter and Bill Yeo. This is also a good opportunity to credit some of the other western Canadian historians such as David H. Breen, Max Foran and John Jennings on the ranching side, and Don Smith closer to the towns and cities. And women come into the picture in a significant way in the writing of Sheilagh Jameson and Sarah Carter, though their work includes all aspects of prairie life; and it is from Jameson's essay "Women in the Southern Alberta Ranch Community, 1881–1914," in *The Canadian West: Social Change and Economic Development*, ed. Henry C. Klassen, that I take the quotation from Lewis G. Thomas below. Serious (and engagingly unserious) storytelling about the foothills is nourished by all these distinguished historians. The Stimson-

Nolan exchange is told by Brado; and stories about John Ware are included in almost every account of that time and place, most thoroughly in Grant MacEwan's *John Ware's Cow Country*. Richard Slatta's *Cowboys of the Americas* is a book I have turned to many times in writing this memoir, along with a dictionary of Spanish terms from the American west called *Cowboy Talk* by Robert N. Smead. The composition of the song "Riding Old Paint," as well as of the western cowboy community in the late nineteenth century has been recounted by Hal Cannon, founding director of the Western Folklife Center in Elko, Nevada, in a National Public Radio program titled "Who Were the Cowboys Behind 'Cowboy Songs,'" broadcast on December 4, 2010.

CHAPTER EIGHT. Frank Oliver's tirade is quoted by Grant MacEwan in his book on Haultain. For some unfamiliar details about the Riel rebellion I have turned to Desmond Morton's *The Last War Drum: The North-West Campaign of 1885*. Gordon E. Tolton gives a sense of the paranoia that was fostered following the uprising in *The Cowboy Cavalry: The Story of the Rocky Mountain Rangers*. The comments by Archbishop Taché and Father André are from newspaper clippings kept by John Maclean.

CHAPTER NINE. The description of the trading in town following treaty payment day is from the *MacLeod Gazette* in the fall of 1888, quoted in *Fort Macleod—Our Colourful Past*; and some details of benefits to the town are from John Maclean's notebooks. The economic historian is Henry Klassen. The stories about Dave Cochrane are from L.V. Kelly, Edward Brado and Robert E. Gard's *Johnny Chinook: Tall Tales and True from the Canadian West*. My portrait of Annie Saunders is drawn from a very fine essay "Assembling Auntie" by Cheryl Foggo in *Alberta Views* in 2009. The tradition of horse races is recalled in almost every account of the foothills during this time; some of the details here are from Fred Ings's *Before the Fences* and *Leaves from the Medicine Tree* as well as Lewis G. Thomas's essay "The Ranching Tradition and the Life of the Ranchers" in *Ranchers' Legacy* and, interestingly, Shelley A.M. Gavigan's *Hunger, Horses, and Government Men: Criminal Law on the Aboriginal Plains, 1870–1905*. J.W. Morrow's *Early History of the Medicine Hat Country* provides some entertaining anecdotes about horses and horse breeding, and much else. There is also a brief tribute to polo in *A History of the Early Days of Pincher Creek*. The difference between the Canadian and American frontier has received much attention from a number of historians, with some (such as Warren Elofson) extending the comparison to other jurisdictions such as Australia. For me, Simon Evans has been the touchstone with his study of the Bar U; and John Jennings has recently raised the bar and widened the path, bringing literature and history together in his splendid portrait *The Cowboy Legend: Owen Wister's Virginian and the Canadian-American Frontier*. I owe a great deal to him from many conversations over the past sixty years. The Alberta cowboy's comment about "barb wire" is quoted in Richard Slatta's *Cowboys of the Americas* from Florence B. Hughes's "Listening in at the Old-Timers Hut," published in *Canadian Cattlemen* in 1941. A detailed account of the invention and invasion of barbed wire can be found in Henry D. and Frances T. McCallum's *The Wire That Fenced the West*. My description of the Blackfoot trip east draws on Dempsey's *Red Crow*, where Dempsey also quotes Red Crow's acceptance speech to the Gros Ventres. The comment by Chief Joseph appeared at the time in the *North American Review*. And the story about Tennessee is recalled by Maunsell in his memoir "The West of Edward Maunsell."

CHAPTER TEN. The rancher who described his winter wear was Fred Godsal, quoted by Evans. Godsal also gave Cowley its name, sponsored many memories for the old timers of Pincher Creek, and described the I.G. Baker hospitality, mentioned later, while its common practice is observed by Brado. John Maclean's conversation draws some of its details from his journals and notebooks. The story about Mills's literal translation is from Dempsey's chapter "Black White Man" in *Calf Shirt*; Potts's rejoinder during the Treaty Seven exchanges is reported in *Laird of the West*. Some of the banking details are from Klassen's article "The Cowdry Brothers"; many are from the Cowdry papers in the Glenbow. Roman Jakobsen mentions the Majorca storytellers in his 1958 essay "Linguistics and Poetics"; T.S. Eliot's phrase provides the title of his collection *The Sacred Wood*, in which his essay "Tradition and the Individual Talent" appeared; and Jonathan Foer's anecdote is from his essay "Why a Haggadah?" published in the *New York Times Sunday Review*, in April 2012. James Dempsey has given a good account of Crop Eared Wolf's buffalo robe, along with many other forms of warrior pictographic representation, in his *Blackfoot War Art: Pictographs of the Reservation Period, 1880–2000*; and the robe is discussed by Dempsey as well as by Barbeau. The widely circulated story about "the music of what happens" is recalled by James Stephens in his 1908 collection of *Irish Fairy Tales*. Maclean's question about the food and implements left with surface burials is taken from his notebooks; the book was *Canada's Savage Folk*. I was first alerted to Maclean's warning about "the danger of educating [Indians] away from their real life" by its mention in the article "Reverend John Maclean and the Bloods," written by Arni Brownstone at the Royal Ontario Museum and published in 2008 in *American Indian Art Magazine*. A few years earlier, Brownstone had curated an important exhibition in Lethbridge of artifacts (many used in horse-mounted parades and dances) collected by the issuer of rations on the Blood reserve from 1884 to 1901, Frederick Deane-Freeman and his wife, Maude. Brownstone's catalogue for the exhibition, which appeared in *American Indian Art Magazine* in 2002, is titled "Ancestors: The Deane-Freeman Collections from the Bloods"; and his books *War Paint: Blackfoot and Sarcee Painted Buffalo Robes in the Royal Ontario Museum* and *War Paintings of the Tsuu T'ina Nation* provide crucial insight into this tradition. He has been very helpful to me with his knowledge and advice about the Aboriginal communities with whom he works, and their traditions of belief and interpretation. Momaday's injunction is from his essay "The Man Made of Words"; Stanner's comment about custom is from "The Dreaming" in *The Dreaming & Other Essays*. The calculation of the start-up cost of a ranch is from Alexander Begg's accounting in John Macoun's *Manitoba and the Great North-West*, included in David Breen's section, "The Ranching Frontier in Canada, 1875–1905," in *The Prairie West to 1905: A Canadian Sourcebook*, ed. Lewis G. Thomas.

CHAPTER ELEVEN. Nat's son Vincent went on to a distinguished medical career, spending time in Africa, where he discovered the cause of heartwater disease in cattle and sheep and new connections between malaria in animals and humans. Later, he undertook important cancer research at Washington University, St. Louis, Missouri; and he is credited with establishing the medical field of gerontology. Etta Haultain's story about the police officer who felt "very sorry for Cowdry" is from her memoir *With the Mounties in Boot and Saddle Days*. Jordan's family story about *The Virginian* is from *Stories That Shape Us*, eds. Teresa Jordan and James R. Hepworth. Much of my commentary about

The Virginian and the characters (such as the Sundance Kid) who came north along the trail from Montana and Wyoming is indebted to John Jennings's *The Cowboy Legend*. Some of my comments and quotations about the frontier are from the lively account by Richard White and Patricia Nelson Limerick in *The Frontier in American Culture*, ed. James R. Grossman; and the dynamics and details of western American history are well told in Limerick's *The Legacy of Conquest: The Unbroken Past of the American West* and White's *"It's Your Misfortune and None of My Own": A New History of the American West*. The story about the tie between bronc riders Franklin and Stewart is told in Hugh Dempsey's *The Golden Age of the Canadian Cowboy: An Illustrated History*, where I also found his comparison of the Canadian and American frontiers; the account of the bar-room "gun fight" between Murray and Leeper has wide currency, beginning with my grandfather and L.V. Kelly. More details of Harry Longabaugh's arrest for cruelty to a horse he was breaking are in Simon Evans's book on the Bar U, while the horse-taming methods of the *vaquero* are described by Fred Ings, quoted in Richard Slatta's *Cowboys of the Americas*.

CHAPTER TWELVE. The railway contract to the Montana border is mentioned by Henry Klasssen in *Eye on the Future: Business People in Calgary and the Bow Valley, 1870–1900*; and many of the details about the Blackfoot turn to farming are from Dempsey's books as well as contemporary accounts. John Lubbock's meditation on "savage nations" is from his chapter "The Beauties of Nature" in his book *The Pleasures of Life*; the "same as 'taturs" story is from Horace G. Hutchinson's *Life of Sir John Lubbock*. Haultain's biographer is Grant MacEwan. The marriage of D.W. Davis and Revenge Walker is recounted in Brado; and the description of her outfit at Fort Whoop-Up is by Donald Graham, quoted in Dempsey's *Red Crow*. Sarah Carter's observations are from her essay "Creating 'Semi-Widows' and 'Supernumerary Wives': Prohibiting Polygamy in Prairie Canada's Aboriginal Communities to 1900" in *Contact Zones: Aboriginal and Settler Women in Canada's Colonial Past*, eds. Katie Pickles and Myra Rutherdale. The anthropologist, quoted by Carter, was Esther Goldfrank in *Changing Configurations in the Social Organization of a Blackfoot Tribe during the Reserve Period*. Carter provides further insight into the condition of women in her essay "Categories and Terrains of Exclusion: Constructing the 'Indian Woman' in the Early Settlement Era in Western Canada" in *Great Plains Quarterly*, 1993. Red Crow's dream, mentioned in association with the quirt, is recalled in Dempsey; and Mose Teneese's dreaming is celebrated in Dix Anderson's memoir *Trails I Have Travelled*, ed. Bill Dubois.

CHAPTER THIRTEEN. A full run of *The Outlaw* is in the United Church of Canada archives in Toronto, a partial run in the Glenbow, and a few issues here and there in other libraries. The ideologies around settlement of the west are nicely analyzed by Doug Owram in *Promise of Eden: The Canadian Expansionist Movement and the Idea of the West, 1856–1900*. Edmund Morris's account of the robe can be found in *The Diaries of Edmund Montague Morris: Western Journeys 1907–1910*, transcribed by Mary Fitz-Gibbon. His father, Alexander Morris, is quoted by Michael Asch in *On Being Here to Stay*. The legal system on the prairies is described in well-informed detail in Knafla and Swainger's collection of essays *Laws and Societies in the Canadian Prairie West*, and in *Law and Justice in a New Land: Essays in Western Canadian Legal History*, ed. Louis Knafla, where Sir John Davies is quoted at length in Knafla's essay "From Oral to Written Memory: The

Common Law Tradition in Western Canada." Shelley Gavigan is also a valuable resource on this subject; and Hugh Dempsey's *Charcoal's World* illuminates what Dempsey describes as a clash both between the secular and the sacred and between two cultures, "neither completely understanding what was motivating the other." The scholarly writing about Thucydides is Paul Veyne, in *Did the Greeks Believe in Their Myths? An Essay on the Constitutive Imagination*, trans. Paula Wissing. Coleridge's affirmation is from his essay in his periodical *The Friend*. My comments on covenants and codes and "chosen people" here and in chapter 18 are much influenced by historian Donald H. Akenson's *God's Peoples: Covenant and Land in South Africa, Israel and Ulster*. Red Crow's statement is quoted by Dempsey, and by Hana Samek in *The Blackfoot Confederacy 1880–1920: A Comparative Study of Canadian and U.S. Indian Policy*. Yeats's words are from "The Second Coming"; Wallace Stevens's lines are from his poem "Notes Towards a Supreme Fiction," and the phrase "essential gaudiness," which I use on the following page, is his as well.

CHAPTER FOURTEEN. John Maclean's account of White Calf's denunciation is from his notebooks. Alfred Andrews's comment was published in the *Globe* in March 1886. John McDougall's description of the "despotic power of the ration house" is quoted in K.D. Smith, *Liberalism, Surveillance, and Resistance: Indigenous Communities in Western Canada, 1877–1927*. The stories told in local and national newspapers of the time are surveyed in *Seeing Red: A History of Natives in Canadian Newspapers*, by Mark Cronlund Anderson and Carmen L. Robertson.

CHAPTER FIFTEEN. The movement of the bands to the gathering place for the Sun Dance is described in more detail in John C. Ewers's *The Horse in Blackfoot Indian Culture*. The agent mentioned on this occasion was James Wilson (not Robert); he was the one who ordered the beef tongues cut in two, and his belligerent actions were recorded in the winter count as the time "Indian Agent James Wilson stopped the Sun Lodge." Mortimo Planno (also known as Ras Kumi) wrote a history of Rastafari titled *The Earth Most Strangest Man*, from which this quotation is taken. It was transcribed from the handwritten original by Lambros Comitas (at the time with the Research Institute for the Study of Man in New York) and given back to Ras Kumi in a ceremony at the University of the West Indies in Jamaica in 1997. The full text has circulated in the Rastafarian community, but not far beyond. In 1999 I published excerpts (with Ras Kumi's permission) in an issue of *Index on Censorship* titled "Tribes: Battle for Land and Language." William Stanner's description of "a kind of vertigo in living" is from his monograph *After the Dreaming*, the text of a lecture he gave on the Australian Broadcasting Corporation. Looking-glass mirrors had come into Blackfoot use some time earlier, and (along with the telescope) into their language (as John Maclean confirms in his notes when he was learning Blackfoot). My account of Hettie Edwards relies on an essay by Patricia A. Roome, "'From One Whose Home Is Among the Indians': Henrietta Muir Edwards and Aboriginal Peoples" in *Unsettled Pasts: Reconceiving the West Through Women's History*, eds. Sarah Carter, Lesley Erickson, Patricia Roome and Char Smith. Harold McGill's comments on the residential schools and the inadequate medical services on reserves are from letters he wrote to Judith Robertson, editor of the Toronto tabloid *NEWS* in December 1945. McGill's personal papers are in the Glenbow, as well as official records that he brought with him into retirement (to ensure they survived as a record of that fraudulent surrender of the Dunne-za lands, I believe). Record

Group 10 (Indian Affairs) in Library and Archives Canada and Record Group 18 (for the North-West Mounted Police) are still major sources for documentary evidence in this field, but they always need to be complemented, and sometimes corrected, by historical accounts in the highly disciplined oral traditions of indigenous peoples.

CHAPTER SIXTEEN. Edward Brado has a good account of the circumstances leading up to the purchase of the Cochrane cattle. Maunsell's opinions about Oliver are available in resounding and polysyllabic detail in his papers in the Glenbow, along with his reaction to my grandfather's refusal to sign the leases over to him. The story of Pat Burns himself offers an interesting perspective on foothills history during this period. Born Patrick O'Byrne (a year before my grandfather, and just down the road in Oshawa) to a family fleeing brutally hard times in Ireland, he came to the west in stages after being given two oxen in wages for a summer's work chopping wood; he slaughtered them to bankroll a homestead west of Winnipeg, moving to Calgary in 1890. His success as a cattleman and meat packer is well known in the west; but what is not so well known is his environmental work, fencing groves of apsen and poplar in the coulees to protect them from his cattle, and his generosity. Among many other contributions to the community, when the Great Depression hit the prairies he celebrated his seventy-fifth birthday in 1931 by giving a five-pound roast to every family in Calgary in which the head of the household was unemployed, and a ticket for a meal at any restaurant in the city to the unmarried unemployed. Two thousand families received the roasts, and four thousand single men and women dined out on Pat Burns.

Some of the material about Wilson in the following pages is from his own accounts in the Glenbow; some from selected Blood agency files, also there. The description of the Big Die-Up draws from the ranching historians mentioned earlier in these Notes. The desciption of John Collier's "two loves" is from William H. Kelly, "Indian Adjustment and the History of Indian Affairs," in the *Arizona Law Review* in 1968. Reesman Fryer, who was Indian agent with the Navajo at the time and a close associate of Collier, said later in an unpublished monograph (kindly made available to me by his daughter, Ann Van Fossen) that he thought that single phrase—"sheep units"—inflicted a deeper wound on the Navajo than almost anything else in those times of suffering and sacrifice. Leslie Hall Pinder's phrase forms the title of a monograph published as *The Carrier of No: After the Land Claims Trial*; the trial referred to was *Delgamuukw*. The struggle over surrender of both land and culture is well documented by Dempsey, and well remembered by the Blood tribe. Big Swan's turn to a lawyer over a fraudulent surrender is mentioned by Claudia Notzke in "The Past in the Present: Spatial and Landuse Change on Two Indian Reserves" in *Essays on the Historical Geography of the Canadian West: Regional Perspectives on the Settlement Process*, eds. L.A. Rosenvall and Simon M. Evans. Other surrenders sought from the Blackfoot receive attention in Samek, *The Blackfoot Confederacy 1880–1920*, and Smith, *Liberalism, Surveillance, and Resistance*.

CHAPTER SEVENTEEN. The song "Hello, Central, Give Me Heaven" was written by Charles K. Harris and first recorded by Byron G. Harlan. Harris also wrote the immensely popular "After the Ball," which sold over two million copies of sheet music in the early 1890s. The description of the Calgary Stampede draws on a wide range of accounts, among them Morgan Baillargeon and Leslie Tupper's *Legends of Our Times: Native Cowboy Life*. Edward Brado tells the story of Ned Maunsell securing Tom Three

Person's release from the police cells in Fort Macleod. Johnny Franklin's remark is widely quoted, from Kelly onwards. Agent Dilworth's vindictive action against the rodeo hero is recorded in Mary-Ellen Kelm's *A Wilder West: Rodeo in Western Canada*. The first of the reports on "the Indian question" was by the Spanish priest Bartolomé de las Casas in 1515, proposing remedies to prevent the harm being done to the Indians, one element of which was the recognition of self-governing Indian communities; another, tragically, was to replace their forced labour with that of African slaves—a recommendation he later recanted. "Natural Supernaturalism" is a chapter title in Thomas Carlyle's novel *Sartor Resartus*. And my reference to the cultural dimensions of housing reminds me of the motto for a research report on *Patterns of Housekeeping in Two Eskimo Settlements*, published in 1969 and describing some of the mistakes made in housing projects in the north. The motto was in the form of a fable from Asia:

> Once upon a time a monkey and a fish were caught up in a great flood. The monkey, agile and experienced, had the good fortune to scramble up a tree for safety. As he looked down into the raging waters, he saw a fish struggling against the swift current. Filled with a humanitarian desire to help his less fortunate fellow, he reached down and scooped the fish from the water. To the monkey's surprise, the fish was not very grateful for this aid.

CHAPTER EIGHTEEN. The scientist talking about waves and water is Arthur Eddington, in *The Nature of the Physical World*.

PHOTO CREDITS

Glenbow Archives. Macleod Hotel, Fort Macleod, Alberta NB-9-15; Main street, Fort Macleod, Alberta, 1880s NA-3321-9; Lieutenant Colonel James F. Macleod, North-West Mounted Police NA-354-1; Bloods at Fort Whoop-Up, Alberta NB-9-7; Red Crow, head chief of Bloods NA-668-53; Buffalo bones gathered for shipment by Gull Lake, Saskatchewan NA-250-15; Tipi of Red Crow, head chief of the Bloods NA-668-6; North-West Mounted Police scouts at Fort Macleod, Alberta NA-556-1; Crop Eared Wolf, Head Chief of Bloods, Blood Reserve, Alberta NB-3-9; Leading chiefs of the Blood NA-201-1; Blackfoot on visit to Ottawa, Ontario NA-13-2; Main street of Fort Macleod, Alberta, ca. 1896-1899 NA-622-4; John Ware ranch at Millarville, Alberta NA-266-1; Group outside John Black store, main street, Fort Macleod, Alberta NA-3251-18; *The Outlaw*-May19-1896-no 1; Blood Sun Dance lodge, pole in place NA-668-34; Big Swan Peigan NA-4133-13; Reverend John Maclean, Methodist missionary and author NA-1297-1; Tom Three Persons with Calgary boy NA-3164-170; Tom Three Persons, Blood cowboy, at Calgary Exhibition and Stampede grounds, Alberta NA-335-79; Blood tipis at Calgary Stampede 1912 NA-446-91; Indian parade at Calgary Stampede 1912 NA-335-5; Early touring car, Fort Macleod, Alberta NA-495-2

Cowdry Family Collection. John Cowdry on a Red River cart; John Cowdry with Gus and Mary; Cowdry Brothers Bank 1900; Gussie Thompson; Edith Cowdry

The images of the quirt courtesy of Arni Brownstone.

INDEX

The identification of First Nations as bands or tribes or peoples, as well as the term Indian, follows common usage in the foothills during the period 1885–1905, and in the contemporary historical and cultural accounts on which I have relied. (In some cases this terminology is still current in Canada, as well as in the United States.)

Note: italic references at the end of a line denote the two photographic inserts, *A* and *B* respectively.

J. EDWARD CHAMBERLIN's renowned book *If This Is Your Land, Where Are Your Stories? Finding Common Ground* was a finalist for the Charles Taylor Prize and a finalist for the Pearson Writers' Trust Award. He worked on the Mackenzie Valley Pipeline Inquiry; was Senior Research Associate with the Royal Commission on Aboriginal Peoples; has worked extensively on Aboriginal land claims in Canada, the United States, South Africa and Australia; and has lectured widely on literary, historical and cultural issues. His other books include *The Harrowing of Eden: White Attitudes Towards Native Americans*; *Come Back to Me My Language: Poetry and the West Indies*; and *Horse: How the Horse Has Shaped Civilizations*. He is University Professor Emeritus of English and Comparative Literature at the University of Toronto, an Officer of the Order of Canada, and lives with his wife, Lorna Goodison, in Halfmoon Bay, British Columbia.